THE AMERICAN NATION
A HISTORY

FROM ORIGINAL SOURCES BY ASSOCIATED SCHOLARS

EDITED BY

ALBERT BUSHNELL HART, LL.D.
PROFESSOR OF HISTORY IN HARVARD UNIVERSITY

ADVISED BY
VARIOUS HISTORICAL SOCIETIES

DANIEL WEBSTER

[By courtesy of Little, Brown & Co.]

THE RISE OF
AMERICAN NATIONALITY

1811–1819

BY
KENDRIC CHARLES BABCOCK, Ph.D.
PRESIDENT OF THE UNIVERSITY OF ARIZONA

GREENWOOD PRESS, PUBLISHERS
NEW YORK

Originally published in 1906
by Harper & Brothers Publishers

First Greenwood Reprinting, 1969

Library of Congress Catalogue Card Number 69-13805

SBN 8371-1346-6

PRINTED IN UNITED STATES OF AMERICA

TO
G. P. B. AND A. E. H.

CONTENTS

EDITOR'S INTRODUCTION

TO attempt a volume on the War of 1812 after Henry Adams and Captain Mahan is a daring task; yet there is room for a brief treatment which shall show the causes of that struggle, its main events, and the effect upon the nation. Taking up the controversy over neutral rights where Channing's *Jeffersonian System* (chapter xx.) leaves it, President Babcock in two introductory chapters (i. and ii.) sketches the party situation, including the expiration of the United States Bank; then describes frontier conditions and relations with the Indians; then the devious French and English diplomacy of 1811 and 1812, preliminary to the war.

Chapters iv. and v. discuss the actual outbreak and the play of party and passion in Congress and in the states. Three chapters (vi.–viii.) describe in succession the northern, the naval, and the southern and central campaigns. In this space it is possible only to sketch the actual military movements; but room has been found for characterization of the armies, navies, and officers contending against each other.

Chapter ix. goes into the internal struggle between the supporters and opponents of the war, culminating in the Hartford Convention of 1814; and the book brings out clearly how dangerous the crisis really was. The peace negotiations at Ghent occupy chapter x.; and chapter xi. is a brief but lucid summary of the immediate results of the war upon national feeling.

The remainder of the book justifies the title of *Rise of American Nationality*, for in four chapters (xii.–xv.) the evidence of a new national spirit is shown in the status of parties, in the foundation of a new national finance, including the second bank and the tariff of 1816, and in the progress of internal improvements. Chapters xvi. and xvii. include the diplomatic relations with England down to the fisheries treaty of 1818, and the relations with Spain through the treaty of 1819. The attitude of the supreme court to the rise of American nationality is studied in chapter xviii., which follows the subject from the point where it was left by Channing's *Jeffersonian System*, chapter ix.

The author does not shrink from laying bare the mistakes of our fathers in the War of 1812: the ineptitude of the military administration; the violence of party opposition; the disgraceful defeats in most of the conflicts on land; but the helplessness of the war period is strongly contrasted, first, with the brilliance of the naval operations; second, with the growth of national pride and national consciousness when the war was over; and, third, with the new point of view of European nations towards the great American republic.

AUTHOR'S PREFACE

IN the pages of this volume I have striven to show how the United States achieved its real emancipation from European domination and became a nation—how, in a word, like the ship in Kipling's story, the nation found itself. Certainly not until after the Napoleonic period and the War of 1812 did the United States come really to the knowledge of what was meant by the fine words, "free, sovereign, and independent." How the United States wrestled against principalities and powers, through good fortune and ill; how it struggled with warring forces and factions within its borders, even within its own government; how in the flush of victory and the shame of defeat there was born a sense of unity and the possibility of a new and really national life; how old party lines and old party cries were abandoned; how the west loomed large in national councils for the first time; and, finally, how the potent force of several great personalities worked on and through the other factors —all these things I have tried to bring out clearly.

I have not hesitated to elaborate accounts like that of the struggle for the recharter of the first

Bank of the United States, where by so doing I could illustrate concretely conditions or forces of primary importance. The final chapter is given to "The Great Decisions of the Supreme Court," because the work of the court was the cementing of the otherwise loosely laid wall on which vigorous, expansive nationality was to rise.

The injunction to rely chiefly upon original materials has been cordially observed, even when it has necessitated reference to rare and obscure books. On the other hand, certain secondary works, such as Henry Adams's *United States* and Mahan's *War of 1812* have such peculiar elements of strength that it would be folly for a writer of a more general work to neglect them.

My obligations to the editor of this series for his generous and wise suggestions and helpful criticisms may be expressed here only in general; they are but one more group of entries in an already long account extending over ten years. For valuable assistance I desire to express my obligations to Professor Clyde A. Duniway, of Leland Stanford Junior University; Professor Samuel B. Harding, of Indiana University; and Professor Sidney C. Newsom, of the University of Arizona, who read critically a good part of the manuscript of the volume; to the librarians of Harvard University, University of California, and Leland Stanford Junior University, and to Mr. David M. Matteson for assistance in preparing the maps.

KENDRIC CHARLES BABCOCK.

THE RISE OF
AMERICAN NATIONALITY

THE RISE OF AMERICAN NATIONALITY

CHAPTER I

THE REIGN OF FACTION

(1809–1811)

WHEN James Madison became president, in 1809, the United States had been nominally a "free, sovereign, and independent" nation for a quarter-century, but no one knew better than the president himself, who had served eight years as secretary of state, how far from the full reality of independence the nation was. Between the millstones of English orders and French decrees he had seen the freedom of American commerce, the honor of the nation, and the safety of its citizens ground to dust. The problem before the young nation in the decade following the inauguration of Madison was how to attain to a freedom that was real, an independence which was not merely recognized but respected, a sovereignty which was at once dynamic and efficient. In this period the nation, by wrestling with "principalities and powers" abroad and at home, was able to find itself, to escape from a half-colonial position towards the Old World, and to turn its energies, after 1815, to the necessary social, economic, political, and international readjustments incident to the new national status. The history of this time of transition and re-creation, its forces, its men, and its important measures, constitutes the theme of this volume.

The first two years of Madison's administration, from 1809 to 1811, brought him the bitter fruits of Jefferson's foreign and domestic policies—the non-intercourse acts; deeper and more inextricably tangled relations with England and France; the trouble with Erskine; the ambiguous and inconsistent replies of the French; more deep-seated and venomous hatred of the commercial classes, especially of New England Federalists; and, lastly, a factional fight within the Republican party which has rarely been equalled for unscrupulous methods and use of power. In the face of such factionalism, the mild and uninspiring Madison made but a poor figure, with no weapons save patience and concession, and with few trustworthy advisers save Gallatin and Jefferson. By 1811 both the executive and legislative departments were reduced to the lowest terms compatible with the continuance of the federal Union.[1]

---

[1] On the first two years of Madison's administration, see Channing, *Jeffersonian System* (*Am. Nation*, XII.), chaps. xvii.-xix.

In the personnel of his cabinet from 1809 to 1811 Madison must have been conscious that he had at once some of the weakest as well as some of the strongest, some of the most disloyal as well as some of the most loyal, of all the men who had ever been called to cabinet office. At the outset he had felt compelled, for political considerations, to refuse to transfer Gallatin from the treasury to the state department, a promotion to which, by all the unwritten laws of succession and eminent fitness, he was really entitled. Instead, Madison appointed the dull, incapable, half-loyal Robert Smith to the first place in his cabinet, quite as much to the surprise of Smith's friends as of his foes, since the president knew the man thoroughly, from eight years' service with him in Jefferson's cabinet.[1]

Robert Smith, secretary of state, and his brother, Samuel Smith, senator from Maryland and leader of a faction in the Senate, hated Gallatin, secretary of the treasury, with a cordial and sleepless hatred which lost no opportunity to defeat his plans and to humiliate him personally. For two years they thwarted the wisest policies of the administration, particularly the financial measures, and in speeches and in the newspapers of allied editors, like Duane of the Philadelphia *Aurora*, they aired their malignity. It is not greatly to Madison's credit that he endured these humiliations for two years.

[1] *Federal Republican* (Baltimore), April 4, 1811; Adams, *United States*, V., 5-11.

By far the most important measure which suffered from the attacks of these malcontents was the bill for renewing the charter of the Bank of the United States upon the expiration of its original term of twenty years, March 4, 1811. The American stockholders of this great financial institution, as provident business men, presented to the Senate as early as April, 1808, a memorial for renewal, so that if Congress should decide to refuse extension of the charter, the business of the bank might be closed up without shock. There was good ground to doubt whether the undeniable success of the bank would appeal to the political leaders of a party which for twenty years had denounced it as an unconstitutional Federalist invention. Albert Gallatin, as secretary of the treasury, presented a report on this memorial in March, 1809, just before the expiration of the tenth Congress. His judgment was highly favorable; he stated the advantages of the bank to the United States, and suggested the outlines of an amended charter. He showed that in round numbers, with a capital of $10,000,000, it had paid annual dividends of eight and one-fourth per cent., had notes in circulation amounting to $5,000,000, liabilities of $13,000,000, and resources of $33,000,000. He approved the bank's management as sound and conservative.[1]

Not until the following year, however, did Con-

---

[1] *Am. State Paps., Finance*, II., 301; *Annals of Cong.*, 10 Cong., 2 Sess., 456.

gress give serious consideration to the petition of the stockholders; but even then it was so much absorbed in the non-intercourse measure that postponement again resulted. The previous petition remaining unanswered, a new one was presented, dated December 10, 1810, setting forth the reasons why renewal should be granted. At the request of Senator William H. Crawford, of Georgia, a man in financial matters after Gallatin's own heart, the secretary of the treasury presented once more the reasons favoring renewal of the bank's charter. He indorsed substantially the arguments of the petitioners, declaring that banks were necessary for the business of the government, that a responsible, well-capitalized, wide-reaching, government-controlled bank had inestimable advantages over state banks. "It is not perceived," he said, ". . . that a single advantage will accrue to the public from the change. . . . In the critical situation of the country, new evils ought not to be superadded and a perilous experiment be attempted, unless required by imperious necessity."[1]

While the constitutionality of the bank was not a matter for the secretary of the treasury to decide, he was willing to give his opinion "that the bank's charter having for a number of years been acted upon or acquiesced in as if constitutional by all the constituted authorities of the nation, and thinking myself the use of banks to be at present necessary for the exercise of legitimate powers of government,

---

[1] *Annals of Cong.*, 11 Cong., 3 Sess., 112, 123.

the continuation of the bank of the United States has not . . . appeared to me to be unconstitutional." That the Republicans should revamp the constitutional argument against the bank might have been foreseen, although Jefferson himself had signed a bill for establishing branches in the territories; and the United States by the sale of its original stock had made a net profit of about $670,000.

Weighty as were the arguments of the petitioners, the secretary of the treasury, and Senator Crawford, they availed little against Congressional ignorance of finance, strong partisan prejudices, and, whenever Gallatin was concerned, the unremitting vindictiveness of Smith, Giles, and Leib, backed by Duane's *Aurora* in Philadelphia and by the Richmond *Inquirer*. Arrayed against the arguments just stated were these: the unforgivable circumstance that the bank was a Federalist device denounced by all good Republicans when out of power; that eighteen thousand of the twenty-five thousand shares of the bank were owned in Europe, chiefly in England—a state of things really "equivalent to a score of British frigates or regiments lent to the United States to use against England in war";[1] that convenient doubt existed as to the constitutionality of the original act; and that the bank in making loans had committed the awful crime of too closely investigating would-be borrowers. Last, but not least, of the forces opposing the recharter were those per-

[1] Adams, *United States*, V., 328.

sons and states interested in the multiplication of state banks. The bank had been like a system of Roman roads and fortresses for the treasury department, offering easy transport and safety. Out of the ruins of this bank, local banks, financiers, politicians, and speculators would hastily build chalky and insecure structures which the United States would be compelled to use, paying always a high rental.

Bills for renewal were introduced independently in the Senate and in the House, and the speech-making on an elaborate scale began. The legislatures of Virginia and Pennsylvania, states which held stock in their own banks, "instructed" their senators and "requested" their representatives to prevent the renewal of the charter of the bank.[1] In the course of the debate in the Senate, the palm for clear understanding and logical, judicial presentation of the merits of the question belonged to Crawford. Giles, of Virginia, spoke in favor of the doctrine of implied powers and against the binding force of instructions, but voted against the bill. One man of the opposition spoke words which rose up day and night for a generation to trouble him. "The power to charter companies," said Henry Clay, of Kentucky, "is not specified in the grant, and I contend is of a nature not transferable by mere implication. . . . Is it to be imagined that a power so vast would have been left by the wisdom of the constitution to doubtful

[1] *Annals of Cong.*, 11 Cong., 3 Sess., 201, 706.

inference?" Five years later, and thenceforward throughout his lifetime, these sentiments were the shibboleth by which Clay's opponents were tested.[1]

The recharter bill, in January, was postponed indefinitely by the House by a vote of 65 to 64; in the Senate, after another month of suspense for Gallatin and the bank, the corresponding bill was killed by Vice-President Clinton, who broke the tie of 17 to 17 by casting his vote against recharter. The bank applied to the legislature of Pennsylvania for a new charter, offering the generous bonus of forty thousand dollars a year. But even a Pennsylvania legislature, after instructing its senators against the recharter of this bank, or the chartering of any new bank, was not willing to change its principles for this shining price. The bank, therefore, put its effects in the hands of trustees to wind up its business.[2]

Thus, by an act of political vandalism, the United States was deprived of a most efficient financial agent at a time, of all times between 1789 and 1860, when there was the greatest need for the resourcefulness and steadying power of a solid bank. Revenues declined with the revival of non-intercourse with England. War, with its inevitable loans, was imminent. There was strong pressure to multiply weak and unsafe state banks. All these things

---

[1] *Annals of Cong.*, 11 Cong., 3 Sess., 211.
[2] *Ibid.*, 346, 826; *Niles' Register*, I., 336; cf. Dewey, *Financial Hist. of the U.S.*, § 58.

should have helped to open the eyes even of wayfarers in the fields of finance. It took five years of the most dismal and disheartening experiences, with a handicapped and sometimes bankrupt treasury, to bring the Republicans to favor a national bank. When at last the time did come to revive the institution, even Senator Smith, of Maryland, and Henry Clay voted for the bill; and President Madison, who had seemingly done nothing to help Gallatin in 1811, signed the act creating a new bank with three and a half times the capital of the first bank of the United States.[1]

The full meaning of the defeat of the bank bill was probably clearer to Gallatin than to any other man. It was, in fact, a turning-point in the history of Madison's first administration, for it proved that faction was triumphant. The simple, obvious fact was that a bill which Gallatin deemed vitally important to the success of his department had been deliberately defeated. Yet this was only one, though perhaps the culminating, instance of the refusal of the Republicans in Congress to recognize the president and cabinet as their real leaders. Other measures of scarcely less importance than the bank bill, measures recommended by the administration, had been mutilated beyond usefulness, or had been stifled by the "invisibles" in the Senate and cabinet. The administration had been humiliated by repeated rejections of nominations sent to the Senate, not-

[1] See below, chap. xiii.

ably that of Alexander Wolcott as successor to Justice Cushing of the supreme court.[1]   Well might John Randolph declare in a private letter in 1811: "The truth seems to be that he [Madison] is president *de jure* only.   Who exercises the office *de facto*, I know not, but it seems agreed on all hands that 'there is something behind the throne greater than the throne itself.'"[2]

Gallatin properly concluded that under existing conditions, after ten years of continuous and most devoted service as head of the treasury department under Jefferson and Madison, his usefulness as a cabinet officer was at an end.   In March, 1811, just after the adjournment of Congress, he wrote frankly to the president: "I am convinced that . . . I can [not] be any longer useful under existing circumstances. . . . New subdivisions and personal factions equally hostile to yourself and to the general welfare, daily acquire additional strength.   Measures of vital importance have been and are defeated. . . . Public confidence in public councils and in the executive is impaired, and every day seems to increase every one of these evils.   Such state of things cannot last; a radical and speedy remedy has become absolutely necessary.   Under these impressions . . . I beg leave to tender you my resignation."[3]

Madison refused to accept this resignation, and at

---

[1] Fish, *Civil Service and Patronage*, 52–54.
[2] Quoted in Adams, *Gallatin*, 430.
[3] Gallatin, *Writings*, I., 495.

last screwed his courage to the sticking-point of re-
constructing his cabinet with a view to something
like the harmony and efficiency which for two years
had been so noticeably lacking. Having made up
his mind, he proceeded with characteristic caution
to seek a successor, not for Gallatin, but for Robert
Smith. James Monroe, who had been Madison's
rival for the presidency in 1808, retired from national politics after his defeat, to bide his time
in Virginia, where he became governor. Without
openly opposing the administration, he let it be
known that he would not accept any minor appointment.

President Madison first ascertained indirectly
through Senator Brent, of Virginia, that Monroe
would accept the offer of appointment as secretary
of state if it came to him without obligation to follow
an already determined policy in foreign affairs. The
president gave the desired assurance, and Monroe
accepted his frank offer, thus deliberately removing
himself from the list of Madison's opponents and
rivals, and giving himself generously and loyally to
the support of the administration. His diplomatic
experiences in Paris and London, and his executive
ability, combined with his energy and patience, made
him a most desirable addition to the president's
official family.[1]

Madison has left an elaborate memorandum of his
painful final interview with Robert Smith, to whom

[1] Monroe, *Writings* (Hamilton's ed.), V., 110, 178, 183, 185.

he pointed out the want of harmony and unity in the cabinet and charged him with representations on the outside calculated to diminish confidence in the administration; he told Smith "that whatever talents he might possess, he did not, as he must have found by experience, possess those adapted to his station," and that he was unsystematic and unpunctual in his business, compelling Madison to write many of the state papers himself, thus adding to the already heavy duties of the president. He ended by offering Smith the mission to St. Petersburg, which he expected John Quincy Adams soon to vacate to accept a seat on the bench of the supreme court.[1]

The secretary avowed a preference for the justiceship or for the mission to London, but Madison gave no ear to such suggestions. Smith's resentment at these "shameful intrigues" waxed hot with meditation and with consultation with his friends. He declined the mission and resigned from the cabinet with the threat, which he afterwards carried out, of appealing to the people, as his successor, Monroe, had done in 1797. "He took his leave," wrote Madison, "with a cold formality, and I did not see him afterward."[2] The passing of Secretary Smith is unique in the history of the cabinet. For eight

[1] Madison, *Works* (Congress ed.), II., 494.
[2] *U. S. Gazette* (Phila.), June 27, July 1, 1811; Monroe, *View of the Conduct of the Executive* (1797); Madison, *Works* (Congress ed.), II., 506; cf. Channing, *Jeffersonian System* (*Am. Nation*, XII.), chaps. xvii.–xix.

years he had served with Madison as secretary of the
navy, and for two more, by the appointment from
his eight-years associate, he had been secretary of
state. After ten years of continuous cabinet service
and the attainment of the highest appointive office
in the gift of the president, he was dropped with
scanty warning—"a shabby Genevan trick," declared
the *Aurora*. From the seat nearest the throne he
was thrust outside the gate, a querulous, soon-for-
gotten political nonentity.

Another measure passed at this session, scarcely
less significant than the bank bill, was the act providing for the admission of part of the Louisiana
purchase as a state in the Union. This statehood
bill raised one of the most famous and acrimonious
debates in this notorious eleventh Congress. The
Federalists, under the leadership of Josiah Quincy in
the House, assumed high ground against the admission as a state of this or any other territory outside the original cession of 1783, under the existing
Constitution. If new states could be carved at will
out of territory already acquired or which might
come to the United States by future cession, the
influence and prestige of New England must suffer
eclipse. There was no Federalism in the west, nor
was there a good atmosphere in which to produce it.
The radical Federalists, therefore, declared that the
admission of new states could be valid only with the
consent of the parties which originally agreed to the
Constitution. Any attempt to bring in such states

as the one proposed, without the consent of Massachusetts, for example, would be a violation of the Constitution sufficiently great to warrant extreme measures.

Quincy voiced these sentiments on January 14, in a speech in the House, and under pressure from that body put in writing this famous sentence: "If this bill passes, it is my deliberate opinion that it is virtually a dissolution of this Union; that it will free the states from their moral obligation; and, as it will be the right of all, so it will be the duty of some, definitely to prepare for a separation,—amicably if they can, violently if they must." [1]   A mild uproar followed this remarkable statement, so deliberately made.   The speaker declared the language disorderly, but the House, on appeal, overruled the speaker by a vote of 56 to 53, and Quincy continued his argument.

Of course, the arguments of such Federalists as Quincy and Pickering, no matter how strong and logical they might be, moved the Republicans not a hair's-breadth.   The party in power had purchased Louisiana, and in the treaty with France solemnly promised that "the inhabitants of the ceded territory shall be incorporated in the Union of the United States, and admitted as soon as possible, according to the principles of the Federal Constitution, to the enjoyment of all the rights, advantages, and im-

[1] *Annals of Cong.*, 11 Cong., 2 Sess., 524; abridged in Johnston, *Am. Orations*, I., 180.

munities of citizens of the United States."[1] For seven years that article had been a part of the law of the land, and, to Republicans, it seemed a mere partisan quibble, disguised as a high constitutional objection, for their opponents to say that the United States had no power to execute the law embodied in the treaty. The House accordingly passed the bill promptly by the decisive vote of 76 to 36, and it became a law February 20, 1811.[2]

The boundaries of the state of Louisiana as defined by this statute were, on the east, the Iberville River and the lakes; on the west, the Sabine River. West Florida was not included, for this territory, which was merely in sequestration pending further negotiation, could not claim admission under the third article of the Louisiana treaty. But this virtue of self-restraint did not long trouble Congress after all: by the act of April 8, 1812, Louisiana was declared a state, having complied with the requirements of the enabling act of the preceding year; and to it, within a week, was added so much of West Florida as lay south of thirty-one degrees and west of the Pearl River. All claims, however, were still subject to "friendly negotiation" and "adjustment" with Spain.[3]

Factionalism and bitter partisan differences were

---

[1] *U. S. Treaties and Conventions*, 332; cf. Channing, *Jeffersonian System* (*Am. Nation*, XII.), chap. v.
[2] *U. S. Statutes at Large*, II., 641.
[3] *Ibid.*, 701, 708.

not confined to Washington. The spring elections of 1811 in Massachusetts and Connecticut showed unusually violent feeling on the part of both Republicans and Federalists. The latter fully realized the crisis to which recent events had brought them. Madison's "acceptance" of Napoleon's ambiguous repeal of his Berlin and Milan decrees, together with the knowledge that Great Britain would refuse withdrawal of the orders in council, thus reviving nonintercourse with her, meant renewed attacks upon the commerce of New England. The expiration of the Bank of the United States and the premium thus set upon loose state banking threatened the foundations of New England credit. The admission of Louisiana and the probability of carving other new states out of the vast northwest and the trans-Mississippi region must lessen the relative importance and prestige of the New England states. Newspapers like the Boston *Columbian Centinel* teemed with flaming appeals and resolutions. Pickering, Otis, and Quincy renewed the attacks so characteristic of 1796 and 1798. The most extreme expressions of this rampant Federalism were to be found in the "Boston Resolutions" adopted March 31, 1811, "at an immense meeting of the Citizens of Boston, assembled in Faneuil Hall (the Cradle and Sanctuary of Liberty)." [1] These directly attacked the president and Congress for subserviency to the French emperor, and declared that Napoleon merely pretended

[1] *Columbian Centinel* (Boston), April 3, 1811.

to relax his decrees without meaning ever to fulfil his promise. They declared that the recent statute was unjust, oppressive, and tyrannical to a degree which demanded the election of such state officers as would oppose by peaceable but firm measures the execution of laws which if persisted in must and will be resisted. By violent and vituperative denunciation of Gerry, who was a candidate for re-election as governor against Christopher Gore, the Federalists defeated their own ends: the voters of Massachusetts re-elected Gerry and for the first time gave control of both Houses of the legislature to the Republicans, enabling them to elect a successor to their Federalist arch-enemy, Senator Pickering.

It was in the flush of this victory and with the passion of the recent struggle upon them that the Massachusetts Republicans entered upon a series of measures which in some degree justified the fears and predictions of their opponents. They replaced two solid Boston banks by a state institution with Republican incorporators and the unusually great capital of three million dollars; they reorganized the state courts of inferior grades; they made an open attack upon the support of the Congregational clergy by town taxes, which since colonial times had been levied for such support; they redistricted the state for the election of state senators in such a way as to secure a Republican majority—a process which has ever since borne the name of "Gerrymandering," from the name of the local political chieftain by whose connivance or direction the scheme was first evolved.[1] This "rasping" of his "herd of traitors" won for Gerry the approval of so high an authority as Jefferson himself, who must have felt that Nemesis had at last overtaken his ancient enemies in their own stronghold.[2] Even in Connecticut there was a break among the Federalists; and by the fusion between Republicans and Federalists, and by strong objections to restrictions on commerce, Roger Griswold, who represented the younger and more aggressive elements in both parties, was elected governor.

With the adjournment of the eleventh Congress on March 3, 1811, an era in the history of the United States came to an end, all unconsciously to those most prominent in national affairs. The stage was cleared for the appearance of a new play, a tragedy perchance, by a new set of actors, moved by new forces and youthful energies. As the drama developed it would become clear that the sceptre of power had passed from the hands of the Revolutionary fathers, for even the president hardly belonged to that class; the political centre of interest was about to shift from the White House, where the familiar figures were still coming and going, to the other end of Pennsylvania Avenue, where a new Congress, already elected in 1810, would enter upon the scene. Faction, too long dominant, would decline. The

---

[1] *Laws of Mass.* (1809–1812), V., 387, 424, 501, 517.
[2] Jefferson to Dearborn, August 14, 1811, Jefferson, *Writings* (Washington's ed.), V., 607.

coming leaders, like Gallio, who "cared for none of these things," would have done with "peaceful wars," commercial weapons, interminable discussions of national rights and national honor, and meek endurance of multiplied affronts by European belligerents.

CHAPTER II

PROBLEMS OF THE SOUTHWEST AND NORTH-WEST

(1810–1812)

THE persistent desire of the United States to possess the Floridas, between 1801 and 1819, amounted almost to a disease, corrupting the moral sense of each succeeding administration. Jefferson's instructions to Monroe and Livingston in 1803, when they were sent to purchase control of the mouth of the Mississippi, explicitly stated that "a cession of the Floridas is particularly desired as obviating serious controversies." Under the terms of the Louisiana treaty the United States, without any real right, chose to assume that West Florida was a part of Louisiana as ceded by Spain to France and by France to the United States. Spain knew well and asserted vehemently that the United States was wrong, and the repeated attempt of Jefferson to quiet the issue by bribing or coercing Spain into yielding at least West Florida, added to her sense of outrage. The weak Spanish government in the Floridas, the presence of a mixed and turbulent population including many Americans in West Florida, and the spread of

revolutionary spirit in Spanish America, combined to
produce a crisis in 1810, when an insurrection against
Spanish authority took place in West Florida. During the summer a convention was held for the purpose of securing a settled government. A quarrel
with the governor, an assault on Baton Rouge, and
the killing of the young commandant of that post,
which followed, were mere incidents in that larger
revolutionary struggle which was going on in Buenos
Ayres, Caracas, and Mexico, for liberty and separation from Spain. The United States and Great
Britain were alike interested politically and com-
mercially in the outcome of these insurrections, the
former in the Floridas and in Mexico, the latter in
South America.[1]

After the capture of Baton Rouge the revolution-
ists, whose leaders were chiefly English and Irish,
in convention assembled declared themselves the
representatives of the people of West Florida and
proclaimed that territory a free and independent
state. Hardly was this done when the convention
urged upon the secretary of state at Washington the
annexation of the province to the United States.
Madison knew all the ins and outs of the scheming,
haggling, and negotiating of the previous seven years,
looking to the acquisition of the territory; he knew
the increasing importance of controlling the Gulf
outlets of the rivers of the Alabama and Mississippi
country; he saw also the numerous and seemingly

[1] *Am. State Paps., Foreign*, II., 511, 541, 636; III., 394.

insuperable obstacles in the way of recognition of the independence of West Florida. In a letter to Jefferson, in October, 1810, he revealed his mind: "The crisis of West Florida, as you will see, has come home to our feelings and our interests. . . . There is great weight in the considerations that the country to the Perdido, being our own, may be fairly taken possession of, if it can be done without violence: above all if there be danger of it passing to a third and dangerous party." Here was the whole thing in a nutshell—a desirable province, a convenient claim under the ambiguous Louisiana treaty, a weak and troubled opponent, and a shadowy "third party" eager to snatch the prize away.[1]

The solution was Madison's remarkable proclamation of October 27, 1810, which declares that the United States has acquiesced in the temporary continuance of Spanish authority over West Florida; that complete adjustment of conflicting claims has been too long delayed, through no fault of the United States; that further failure to possess themselves of the territory might be construed to the detriment of the claim of the United States; "that in the hands of the United States it will not cease to be a subject of fair and friendly negotiation and adjustment"; and, finally, that Governor W. C. C. Claiborne, of the Orleans territory, has been directed to take possession of all the territory from the Mississippi to the

---

[1] *Am. State Paps., Foreign*, III., 396; Madison, *Works* (Congress ed.), II., 484.

Perdido, and to govern it as an integral part of his own territory. The chief restriction upon Claiborne was that he should not proceed to employ force in the seizure of territory belonging to a just and friendly power. Jefferson had acquired Louisiana by regular and proper negotiation, swallowing his doubts as to the unconstitutionality of his proceedings. His successor in the Republican presidency, without the formality of negotiation, with scarcely a compunction at the disregard of international usages, with a speciousness bordering on recklessness, asserted jurisdiction over the province of West Florida, still the subject of fair and friendly negotiations.[1]

Small wonder that Morier, Great Britain's *chargé d'affaires*, wrote a vigorous protest to the secretary of state.[2] But under the circumstances the good or ill opinion of a British diplomatic officer mattered little to the administration. Congress promptly took up the question of organizing the new territory, and there was much reference back to the acts of 1803–1804, authorizing the occupation, and directing the organization of the Louisiana cession. Senator Giles went so far as to propose a bill for the extension of the territory of Orleans to the Perdido River, but even the wisest men were not ready to assert quite so dogmatically that West Florida belonged to Louisiana. In the end, part of the district

[1] Richardson, *Messages and Papers*, I., 480; *Am. State Paps., Foreign*, III., 397.

[2] *Am. State Paps., Foreign*, III., 399 (Morier to Smith).

was added to the new state of Louisiana, as already described; and the remainder was annexed to the territory of Mississippi by the act of May 14, 1812, thus giving the desired outlet for all the country tributary to Mobile Bay.[1]

The success of the president in securing possession of West Florida, together with the continuance of unsatisfactory conditions in East Florida, led to a movement for the annexation of the latter province also, although not one of the reasons, principles, or articles relating to West Florida was applicable to the sister province. Yet the president requested Congress, in a secret message in January, 1811, to give him authority to take "temporary possession of any part or parts of the said territory [of East Florida], in pursuance of arrangements which may be desired by the Spanish authorities, and for making provision for the government of the same during such possession." The old bugbear of the possible occupation of the territory by some foreign power was also again raised: "The peculiar interests they may otherwise have in its destiny" made seasonable "a declaration that the United States could not see without serious inquietude any part of a neighboring territory in which they have so just a concern, pass from the hands of Spain into those of any other foreign Power."[2]

These Florida incidents furnish the first instances

---

[1] *U. S. Statutes at Large*, II., 734.
[2] Richardson, *Messages and Papers*, I., 488.

of the enunciation of certain peculiar arguments to justify the United States in possessing itself of choice bits of territory here and there, arguments which have been used with great and continued effect in relation to Texas, Hawaii, Mexico, and Cuba. There has always been enough reasonableness in the contention to make it somewhat more than merely plausible. The argument of natural boundaries, the control of the Gulf, and an adequate outlet for the interior states, broadly justified the United States in its declaration that its interest was primary and determinative in Florida. Improved communications by land and sea ultimately made the Hawaiian Islands as near to the United States and as important to proper protection of its coasts and its commerce as was Florida in 1811. Hence they were at last removed from possible foreign domination or possession.

Congress debated the confidential message in secret session; for the House as well as the Senate frequently held executive or secret sessions during the year 1811–1812. By the secret act of January 15, 1811, the president was authorized to take possession of Florida, either with local consent or in case of attempt of a foreign power to occupy it; and he appointed as commissioners to execute the statute George Matthews and John McKee.[1] As

---

[1] *U. S. Statutes at Large*, III., 471. The statute was not published until 1818, and appears out of chronological order in the *Statutes at Large*.

their written instructions were more or less vague and loose, leaving them to regulate their conduct "by the dictates of their own judgments on a close view and accurate knowledge of the precise state of things and of the real disposition of the Spanish government," they proceeded to govern their acts more by the president's spirit, and perhaps by his verbal explanations, than by the letter of their orders. In a word, they assumed, as did Jackson at a later time, that they were sent to Florida for a definite purpose.[1]

Conditions in St. Mary's River upon Matthews's arrival seemed to warrant prompt action; the river was full of British smuggling vessels, while Amelia Island with the town of Fernandina had been for two years the centre of a large smuggling trade carried on at least by connivance of Spanish authority.[2]

With the Baton Rouge precedent fresh in mind, here was pretext sufficient for occupation, since that seemed to be the desire of the United States. Matthews ascertained, however, that East Florida could not be obtained by amicable negotiations, but that the inhabitants of the province were ripe for revolt. In an official report to the secretary of state in August, 1811, he even declared: "They are, however, incompetent to effect a thorough revolu-

---

[1] *Annals of Cong.*, 11 Cong., 3 Sess., 1117 et seq.; 12 Cong., 1 Sess., 1518 et seq.; *Am. State Paps., Foreign*, III., 571.

[2] *U. S. Gazette*, January 22, 1810.

tion without external aid. If two hundred stand of arms, and fifty horsemen's swords were in their possession, I am confident they would commence the business, and with a fair prospect of success. These could be put into their hands by consigning them to the commanding officer at this post, subject to my order. I shall use the most discreet management to prevent the United States being committed; and although I cannot vouch for the event, I think there will be but little danger."[1]

The president, cognizant of all this chicanery, maintained a discreet silence, and listened for sounds of revolution in the direction of Florida. The two hundred insurgents made their appearance before the garrison at Fernandina, received its surrender, declared independence, and permitted General Matthews to cross over with a company of regulars of the army of the United States and take possession of Amelia Island, March 19, 1812. To his surprise, in the following month the envoy received notice of a disavowal of his act by the United States, on the ground that a legalized contingency had not arisen; which, being interpreted, meant that the so-called revolution on Amelia Island was not quite large enough. Of course, Matthews was angry, and could not understand why he had been thus disavowed. The truth was that the occurrence in Florida was somewhat inopportune, and placed the

[1] Quoted in Adams, *United States*, VI., 239.

administration, as Madison said, in "the most distressing dilemma," which consisted in the need to reconcile the desire to keep possession of the island with the difficulty of so doing.[1]

With his usual inconsistency, the president decided, so Monroe told the French minister, "that nevertheless now that things had reached their present condition there would be more danger in retreating than in advancing; and so while disavowing the general's too precipitate conduct, they would maintain the occupation."[2] Probably not a little of the pressure producing this determination came from the state of Georgia, which was dissatisfied with the president's disavowal of the acts of his agent. The Georgia legislature even went so far as to resolve that whether Congress authorized it or not, the possession of Florida was so essential to their safety that they would proceed to raise a state army and carry on an invasion of Florida even in defiance of the federal authority. Matthews was succeeded by the governor of Georgia, but the occupation of Amelia Island continued. An attempt to secure congressional authorization for the particular occupation failed, and the president continued to act under authority of the act of 1811, until May, 1813, when the troops of the United States were finally withdrawn, leaving the soil of East Florida

---

[1] Madison, *Works* (Congress ed.), II., 534; *Am. State Paps., Foreign*, III., 572 (Monroe to Madison).

[2] Adams, *United States*, VI., 242, quoting from French archives.

free from occupation by United States troops for the long space of four years.[1]

These events in themselves seem of trifling significance, and it is only when they are considered in their influence upon the final cession of the whole of Florida to the United States that they become suggestive. If the president could thus possess himself of a portion of Spanish territory for a period of a year, Spain might well ask herself whether any of her possessions bordering on the United States could be considered safe from the graceless ambition of the presidents of the great republic.

In the mean time, in the spring and summer of 1811, renewed trouble broke out with the Indians of the northwest, particularly in Indiana, which had its bearing upon the foreign relations of the United States as well as upon the domestic policy. In its causes and in its progress the campaign of this year did not differ materially from those of earlier years, when the western and southern Indians made spasmodic attempts to stem the on-coming tide of white settlers. The same old causes operated to produce friction, trouble, bloodshed. The land cessions which the white men, commonly agents of the United States, had secured from the Indians during the preceding twenty years were usually on terms disadvantageous to the Indians. The Indian's idea

---

[1] *Am. State Paps., Foreign*, III., 572; *Annals of Cong.*, 11 Cong., 3 Sess., 324; *Niles' Register*, III., 259, 311; Lodge, *Cabot*, 522.

of the cession of land differed radically from that of the white parties to the transaction; he could never quite understand that the occupation by the white settlers forbade his continued utilization of the land as a temporary abiding-place and hunting-ground.[1] The story of persistent trespassing by the whites beyond the limits within which they had solemnly promised to stay, is as old as the first settlement on the continent and as new as the latest report of Indian discontent on the most favored reservation. The whites with whom the Indians on the frontier came in contact were of necessity strong - fibred, coarse - grained, independent, and unscrupulous of the means for obtaining their ends where inferior peoples were concerned. In fact, no other class could expect to survive the trials of the wilderness journey and the long strain of redeeming the wilderness. The struggle of the Indians against these conditions naturally produced degeneracy and the development of the most undesirable traits of Indian character.

The discontent of the Indians with the government and people of the United States had been fostered for a generation by British commercial interests, as one of the means by which the fur-trade could be kept in the hands of the British traders. The packs of furs went north across the portages from the upper Mississippi to Canada. British arms

[1] See map in Channing, *Jeffersonian System* (*Am. Nation*, XII.), chap. vii.

and British goods were found in the hands of the Indians, and the belief was wide-spread in the United States in 1811 and 1812 that the British government was more or less directly inciting the Indians to revolt and that its agents were supplying them with guns and ammunition. Governor William Henry Harrison, of Indiana territory, in a letter published in December, 1811, explicitly states that "within the last three months the whole of the Indians on this frontier have been completely armed and equipped out of the king's stores at Malden. . . . The Indians had, moreover, an ample supply of the best British glazed powder—some of their guns had been sent to them so short a time before the action, that they were not divested of the list covering in which they are imported."[1]

While the popular conviction was that the British in Canada were responsible in large degree for Indian disturbances in the northwest, and though it found voice in the press, in speeches in Congress, and even in presidential utterances, the British minister and the governor of Upper Canada made the most emphatic denials of the charge. They even went further, and declared that they had used their influence to restrain the Indians who strove to stir up trouble. Governor Brock, of Upper Canada, who must have known, expressly stated in 1812 that Tecumseh and the Prophet had for two years carried on active war against the United States "contrary

[1] *Niles' Register*, I., 311; II., 342-344.

to our remonstrances." That the unscrupulous British traders sold guns and ammunition to the Indians in Indiana and Michigan, just as the local American traders did, in competition for the same business, is probably true; that this was by direction or connivance of the British or Canadian governments, is entirely unproved.[1]

The centre of the agitation in the northwest was on the headwaters of the Wabash at the mouth of a small creek called Tippecanoe. It was in this region that the opposition to the treaty of Fort Wayne, made in 1809, between the United States and the four tribes possessing land on the Upper Wabash, made itself manifest. The treaty ceded about three million acres to the United States and meant complete extinguishment of the Indian title to some of the best land in the territory of Indiana. Tecumseh and his twin brother, the Prophet, who belonged to the Shawnee tribe, which was not one of those interested in the cession, undertook to overthrow the treaty, vowing death to the chiefs who participated in it, because the Indian lands, as they declared, belonged to Indian tribes taken together and not to any one tribe. These two men carried on their active and eloquent agitation from 1809 down to the great defeat in 1811, visiting different tribes in the

---

[1] *Am. State Paps., Indian*, I., 797–804 (reports and letters of governors, citizens, etc., to the war department); *Am. State Paps., Foreign*, III., 462 (Foster to Monroe, June, 1812); Tupper, *Brock*, 253.

northwest and the southwest, reaching the Creeks and Choctaws as well as the tribes of Indiana territory; they endeavored by every art and craft known to the Indian chieftain to unite all the Indians into an actively hostile league against the United States. In ambition, wide-spread influence, and persistent agitation, Tecumseh was no mean successor to the great Pontiac of the preceding century. General Brock wrote of him, "a more sagacious or a more gallant warrior does not, I believe, exist."[1]

Governor Harrison's efforts at calming the tribes in several conferences with the chiefs all came to naught; and when the marauding began again in the spring of 1811, he gave final warning to Tecumseh that violence must cease or he would march into the Indian country to chastise the offenders. In pursuance of this policy, Harrison finally gathered a considerable force of militia and a regiment of regulars at Vincennes in September, 1811, and proceeded quickly to the Indian village known as the Prophet's town on the Tippecanoe. Here several parleys took place, after which the Indians, being convinced that Harrison, with his thousand men, meant to give battle in any case, attacked him on the morning of November 7, and the battle of Tippecanoe was fought. Harrison lost sixty-one killed or fatally wounded, and one hundred and twenty-seven wound-

[1] Tupper, *Brock*, 253; *Am. State Paps., Indian*, I., 761, 763, 800; Richardson, *War of 1812* (1902), 154, gives an appreciative estimate of Tecumseh; cf. Drake, *Tecumseh*, chaps. v., vi.

ed less severely; thirty-eight dead Indians were counted. The next morning the troops found the Prophet's town deserted; they took certain supplies from it and burned the village, after which they rapidly marched back to Vincennes.[1]

The effect of this victory was far-reaching; it greatly diminished the influence of the two Indian leaders, though it did not prevent a renewal of trouble in the following spring. While the Indians were probably waiting to see if war between the United States and Great Britain would break out, there was evidence that they meant to make war in any case. Captain Rhea wrote in March, 1812, from Fort Wayne: "I have every reason to believe we shall have an Indian war this spring, whether we have a British war or not." In the end, hundreds of them crossed into Canada where they were found fighting under the leadership of Tecumseh in the British armies. The people of the west looked upon the defeat of the Indians as decisive, and gave great praise to Harrison, whose prestige as a leader in frontier warfare, as a result of the campaign, was of just the advantageous sort which a rising and ambitious politician in the west would desire.[2]

---

[1] Dawson, *Harrison*, 196, 206, 233, 244; *Am. State Paps., Indian*, I., 776 (Harrison's report); *Niles' Register*, I., 255; cf. Channing, *Jeffersonian System* (*Am. Nation*, XII.), chap. xx.
[2] *Am. State Paps., Indian*, I., 806; Dawson, *Harrison*, 219.

CHAPTER III

FRENCH DUPLICITY AND ENGLISH STUBBORNNESS

(1810–1812)

THE question of the Floridas and of the Indians of the frontiers concerned chiefly certain new and remote sections; they were merely perplexities of an administration which was at the same time wrestling as for its life with matters pertaining to the relations of the United States to Great Britain and France, which vitally affected markets, persons, and policies of the nation.[1] These relations reached another acute stage in February, 1811. By the act of May 1, 1810,[2] non-intercourse with the two belligerents was given up as a policy, but it was provided that if either France or England would revoke its decrees or orders, and the other should fail to do likewise after three months' notice by the United States, then the president, by proclamation, should re-establish non-intercourse with such other nation. Napoleon succeeded, by Cadore's wily and

---

[1] On the general subject of this chapter, cf. Channing, *Jeffersonian System* (*Am. Nation*, XII.), chap. xix.

[2] *U. S. Statutes at Large*, II., 543.

ingenious note of August 5, 1810, in trapping Madison into the declaration that France had revoked the offensive Berlin and Milan decrees so far as they affected America; and the president gave the prescribed notice to Great Britain, in November, 1810.[1]

Not since 1807 had the commercial and shipping interests been so contented as in the "open season" of 1810; only the French attacked American commerce, and even this danger was minimized by the comfortable custom of asking and receiving protection from the British navy in the Baltic or West Indies. Customs revenue reached $12,757,000 for the year ending December 31, 1810; the registered tonnage amounted to 1,424,000, and the exports of domestic products, $42,366,000, for the year ending December 31, 1810.[2] Athwart the pathway of this busy, prosperous, satisfying traffic were thrust Cadore's note and Madison's proclamation of November 2, by which he gave notice that unless Great Britain also repealed the orders in council by February 2, 1811, non-intercourse with that country would revive. February came, but no concession from the British ministry, and the halcyon days of open trading ended. Great Britain stood firmly on the ground that France had not in good faith repealed the Berlin and Milan decrees, and the ministry reiterated the statement that the British government was entirely ready

---

[1] *Am. State Paps., Foreign*, III., 386.
[2] *Am. State Paps., Commerce*, I., 866, 873; *ibid., Finance*, II., 552.

to relinquish the system which the policy of France had imposed, whenever neutral commerce should be restored by France to its original status.[1]

On the other side, the president learned in February, 1811, that Napoleon had decreed that all American vessels arriving in French ports after November 2, 1810, should be, not seized under the Berlin and Milan decrees, but "sequestered" until February, when it might be clear what course the United States would pursue if England failed to yield. In this difficult situation, in spite of the deterrent evidence, Congress came to the rescue of the president, and in the act of March 2, 1811, gave full legal sanction to his course, authorizing him to suspend non-intercourse with Great Britain if that country would revoke the orders in council. Otherwise he was to enforce the revived act of 1809, but all shipments made from England before February 2, 1811, were to be exempt from seizure. One more chance England had to modify or revoke the offending orders.[2]

Of course, the opposition did not lose the opportunity to tell the administration some unpleasant truths about its conduct of foreign relations. The Federalists, led by Quincy, insisted that France was deliberately deceiving the United States with the purpose of drawing us into a war against Great Britain, either directly or indirectly, through an

[1] Richardson, *Messages and Papers*, I., 481, 483; *Am. State Paps., Foreign*, III., 408.   [2] *U. S. Statutes at Large*, II., 651.

alliance with France. Randolph also appeared with a new plan for settling the difficulty, and was able to muster 40 out of 107 votes for repeal of the act of May, 1810. When Congress adjourned, non-intercourse with England was in full operation, with no prospect of its removal by any concessions from the ministry. The "peaceful war" was to go on indefinitely, so far as any suggestions of policy on the part of the administrations were concerned. Signs, however, were accumulating that the people were ready for more positive action, and would welcome war with Great Britain, as the party against whom the United States had the oldest, most immediate, and most varied grievances.[1]

During the greater part of 1810 Great Britain was represented at Washington by a diplomatic person of no higher rank than a *chargé* or secretary, and Madison suspected that it was the deliberate policy to humiliate the United States by leaving the mission thus vacant. William Pinkney, United States minister to England, was discouraged and despairing at the opening of 1811; he had been unable to secure any concessions or arrangements of difficulties, either from the brilliant, irritable, and condescending Canning, or from his more suave successor in the foreign office, the Marquis Wellesley. Neither had he secured the sending of a minister to Washington to settle questions at that capital. Accordingly, he decided on his own re-

[1] *Annals of Cong.*, 11 Cong., 3 Sess., 863, 895.

sponsibility, but in accord with the spirit of his instructions of 1810, to express in most emphatic manner the high dissatisfaction of his government and himself with England's stubborn persistence in her policy of blockades, search, prize-taking, and assaults on neutral trade, by returning to America, leaving only a secretary in charge of the legation in London. So he took "inamicable leave," and came back to the United States in February, 1811, an act almost equivalent to a severance of relations preparatory to open hostilities.[1]

One immediate result of Pinkney's request for an audience to take leave was the sudden determination of Wellesley to send to the United States a regular minister. The person selected was Augustus J. Foster, who had been *chargé d'affaires* in Sweden, a person entirely acceptable to Madison and Monroe. He arrived in June, 1811, and shortly took up negotiations, or rather discussions, with the secretary of state. One matter he did adjust — in the autumn he made offer of atonement for the *Chesapeake* affair,[2] in the way of disavowing for his government the act of the captain of the *Leopard*, restoring the survivors to the deck of the *Chesapeake* in Boston Harbor, and paying proper sums to the wounded and to the families of the slain. The offer was accepted by the United States. Tardy

---

[1] *Am. State Paps., Foreign,* III., 373, 412 et seq.
[2] Cf. Channing, *Jeffersonian System (Am. Nation,* XII.), chap. xx.

as was the reparation, it undoubtedly served a distinctly good purpose in the removal of at least one cause of friction between the two countries.[1] Nevertheless, the old animosities sprang up when Monroe and Foster began to thresh over once more the old straw of commercial blockades, non-intercourse, and the orders in council. Foster distinctly threatened retaliation upon the United States if the non-intercourse act were continued, a threat which was soon followed by new attacks upon American commerce by British cruisers and the condemnation of vessels worth about a million dollars simply because they were bound for France without having touched at a British port. In the course of the exchange of elaborate notes in the summer and autumn of 1811, Monroe and Foster fully and officially defined the positions of the two countries on the eve of war.[2]

Officially stated, Great Britain refused to repeal her orders in council because of the necessity of offsetting Napoleon's warlike decrees, which were unauthorized by any legitimate doctrine of international law. The Berlin decree established no real blockade, and seizures under it were contrary to the law of nations. The orders, then, were "founded on a just principle of defensive retaliation against the violation of the law of nations committed by France, in the decree of Berlin," and such injuries as came to the commerce of neutrals should be

---

[1] *Am. State Paps., Foreign*, III., 499.
[2] *Ibid.*, 435 et seq.

charged to France and not to England, which, in the final analysis, was countering, not creating, attacks on neutral trade. Great Britain, he continued, was ready to return to the former condition whenever the French revoked their decrees. His government did not consider that this revocation had been made, for "the studied ambiguity of that note [Cadore's note of August 5, 1810] has since been amply explained by the conduct and language of the Government of France, . . . thus pronouncing as plainly as language will admit, that the system of violence and injustice, of which he (Napoleon) is the founder, will be maintained by him until the defensive measures of retaliation to which they gave rise on the part of Great Britain shall be abandoned." [1]

To these arguments Monroe replied with patient and diplomatic verbosity, reiterating the points that had been made so many times before in London and in Washington. He maintained that the fact of war between France and England could not by any interpretation of international law warrant such intolerable infractions of the rights of neutrals as those by which the commerce of the United States was in danger of annihilation unless most humiliating regulations were submitted to. "Heretofore it has been the usage of belligerent nations to carry on their trade through the intervention of neutrals, and this had the beneficial effect of extending to the

---

[1] *Am. State Paps., Foreign,* III., 436.

former the advantages of peace while suffering under the calamities of war. To reverse the rule, and to extend to nations at peace the calamities of war, is a change as novel and extraordinary as it is at variance with justice and public law." As to blockades, Monroe contended that for the most part the British closures of ports had been paper blockades which no neutral was in the nature of the case bound to observe. As before, Monroe solemnly asserted that Napoleon's repeal of the Berlin and Milan decrees was complete and unrestricted.[1]

No matter how often or how loudly the president and his secretary might assert the repeal, and parade their commitment to this view and its consequent policy, they knew, and Congress knew, and· all Europe knew, that Napoleon was capturing American ships just as he had done before. The reports of Minister Serrurier to the French foreign office, of his interviews with Monroe, as revealed by the researches of Mr. Adams in the French archives, are perfect evidence that the administration felt keenly the hypocritical position which it was obliged to assume. Monroe's part in the play was quite worthy of Napoleon himself: to assume with calm assurance to Foster, in the morning, that the decrees were completely repealed by France; and later in the day to berate Serrurier in angry sincerity because France gave no satisfactory evidence of the repeal. Consistency of utterance towards England became

[1] Monroe, *Writings* (Hamilton's ed.), V., 354.

imperative on the administration. "The revocation of the Decrees of Milan and Berlin," wrote Serrurier to Maret (Bassano) in July, "has become a personal affair with Mr. Madison. He announced it by proclamation and has constantly maintained it since. Tho English party never stops worrying him on this point, and saying that he has been made a tool of by France,—that the decrees have not been repealed." [1]

While these negotiations were in progress there occurred off the coast of New Jersey one of those exceedingly unfortunate episodes which operate, when international relations are severely strained, like the explosion of a percussion-cap in the midst of powder. In continuance of the policy which Great Britain had so insolently maintained for more than four years, the British cruiser *Guerrière*, one of the ships of war patrolling American waters, overhauled an American ship within eighteen miles of New York City and took off a citizen of the United States, a native of Maine. The United States frigate *President*, Captain Rodgers, was cruising in the same waters, determined to overhaul the *Guerrière* or any vessel bound upon the same mission. While thus engaged, Captain Rodgers was followed by the British sloop of war *Little Belt*, which took the *President* for her consort, the *Guerrière*. Rodgers was unable to make out the stranger, and so

[1] Adams, *United States*, VI., 51, 62, 65, 121, quoting from French archives.

turned the tables and gave chase. After sunset on May 13, an exchange of shots and broadsides occurred in which the *Little Belt* was badly riddled. The account of the fighting leaves one in doubt as to the responsibility for the firing of the first shot, for each captain disclaimed ordering it. An official investigation by the United States exonerated Captain Rodgers, and Great Britain found it convenient to adopt this conclusion.[1]

In spite of the great inferiority of the *Little Belt* to the *President*, the Americans generally exulted in the affair, looking upon it in some measure as a fair retribution for the outrages which had been inflicted upon American vessels, especially in the case of the *Chesapeake*. The action of the two governments, even though they did not agree in fixing the responsibility, soon removed the episode from the field of discussion.

While negotiations with Great Britain were taking place, during the spring and summer of 1811, Napoleon was renewing vigorous measures for excluding English goods from European markets. One difficulty which he had encountered was the illegal use of the American flag, as the flag of a neutral nation, by those who were forbidden to trade with ports of the continent—for example, by British merchants and the allies of Great Britain in the Baltic waters. As a war measure, Napoleon's attack upon the commerce of his enemy was entirely

[1] *Niles' Register*, I., 33 et seq. (official documents).

legitimate, and his enforcement of his own decree against ships really English could not be complained of by the Americans so long as their own commerce was left undisturbed. But the use of neutral flags by British ships made it difficult to maintain fair discrimination in favor of neutrals, and Napoleon was never scrupulously careful in his regard for neutral rights, nor did he withhold his hand from sweeping and inconsistent measures. "As for England, commercial relations with her must cease," Napoleon declared to a deputation from the French Council of Commerce in March, 1811. "I am armed cap-a-pie to enforce my orders and frustrate her intentions in the Baltic." "The decrees of Berlin and Milan are the fundamental laws of my empire. As for neutral navigation, I regard the flag as an extension of territory; the Power which lets it be violated cannot be considered neutral. The lot of American commerce will soon be decided. I will favor it if the United States conform to those decrees. In the contrary case their ships will be excluded from the ports of my empire."[1]

When the emperor received a copy of the act of March 2, 1811, indorsing the procedure of the president in executing the act of May, 1810, he appeared to be satisfied that affairs were moving in the right direction in America, and condescended to signify his pleasure. But no satisfaction would he give

[1] Napoleon, *Correspondence*, XXI., 484; Thiers, *Consulat et l'Empire*, XIII., 26–33; Adams, *United States*, V., 398, 399.

Madison on the one point which most needed specific statement—viz., a formal and categorical declaration that the decrees were revoked. The nearest to this desideratum which Madison ever got was the brief note of May 4, 1811, which by its silence on critical questions added to the contention, and left the principles of the decrees still in force. "I hasten to announce to you," wrote Bassano to Jonathan Russell who was then in charge of the legation in Paris, "that his Majesty the Emperor has ordered his Minister of Finance to authorize the admission of American cargoes which had been provisionally placed in deposit on their arrival in France. I have the honor to send you a list of the vessels to which these cargoes belong; they will have to export their value in national merchandise, of which two-thirds must be in silks." The Americans thus received back their goods, but this message was very poor proof to offer to Great Britain as evidence that the French decrees were actually repealed as Madison asserted.[1]

The year 1811 ended without progress in the negotiations with France and Great Britain beyond the point just mentioned. The only new note in the discussion seems to be the revival of interest on the part of the United States in the matter of impressments, and even in this the newspapers rather than the administration took the lead. If any remedy was to be found, warlike or peaceful, it

[1] *Am. State Paps., Foreign*, III., 505; Adams, *United States*, V., 404-407.

would be through Congress; Madison was incurably committed to "peaceful warfare." Niles wrote in the *Weekly Register* for November 2, 1811, a vigorous editorial in which he set forth his views on impressments and the public indifference to this national insult. "We are so accustomed to hear of British impressment that the acuteness of feeling so natural on account of it, has become blunted, and our sailors have begun to make a kind of calculation upon it. How base and degrading! How inconsistent with our pretensions to sovereignty and independence! But there are thousands in the United States who justify or palliate the practice; and to this turpitude must be attributed, in some degree, the want of energy in the government on behalf of injured society. . . . I do not believe there is a single British vessel of war upon the ocean that is not partly manned with impressed Americans, many of whom have been detained for eight or ten or twelve years. . . . I am not disposed to imitate the conduct of the 10th or 11th Congress. I hope the 12th will *act*."[1]

[1] *Niles' Register*, I., 147.

CHAPTER IV

NEW ELEMENTS IN CONTROL
(1811–1812)

THE twelfth Congress met in extra session, November 4, 1811. In the elections for this Congress in 1810, constituencies in several states impulsively chose young men of fresh courage and high quality, whose possibilities were not yet perceived, though one of these men, Henry Clay, had been sent to the United States Senate even before he was of legal age for election to that body. An on-looker familiar with the public men of previous Congresses would have been struck by the change of personnel in the Congress meeting now for the first time. Several of the well-known Federalist figures were gone, and in the Senate this party could muster only six out of thirty-four members, while in the House the number was thirty-seven out of one hundred and forty-two.

The new Congress soon developed a new spirit as well as new members and new leaders. Far more than the old faces had been put away, and the contrast between the old and the new grew daily more striking. In the very beginning, the House, by a vote of 75 to 38, chose for speaker Henry Clay of Kentucky, who embodied the energy and uncalculating enthusiasm of the rising west. As he marshalled into committees the older radicals who had been re-elected, Peter B. Porter of New York, Wright of Maryland, the energetic and defiant Troup of Georgia, and the grim old frontiersman, Sevier of Tennessee, and infused into them such new blood as Grundy of Tennessee, who had been elected with the express purpose of urging war, and the brilliant trio from South Carolina, Calhoun, Cheves, and Lowndes, no one doubted that the twelfth Congress would be as active and efficient in carrying out the chief features of its programme as the eleventh had been querulous and incapable. The new Congress and the new leaders might make mistakes, but they were certain to do something.[1]

This group of active, audacious, and ardently patriotic Republicans is interesting from many points of view. They were the first ripened product of the generation which had grown up since the Revolutionary War. They were patriotic by inheritance, optimistic and self-reliant by force of their surroundings; they had seen the nation grow at a marvellous rate, and they had the most uncompromising faith in the republic's strength and future. Their patriotism was untroubled by fear of war and its horrors, and untrammelled by any traditional

[1] *Annals of Cong.*, 12 Cong., 1 Sess., 329, 343; Adams, *United States*, VI., 137; Follett, *Speaker of the House*, §§ 41–46.

obligations or sentiments regarding foreign relations, unless it were a chronic suspicion of England, bordering on unreason. The insults heaped upon the United States by both France and England they felt keenly, and with the fine and ready resentment of youth, they scorned the vacillations and delays of Madison and led him and his administration speedily out of the devious labyrinth into which Jefferson had first guided the Republican party. Once upon the main high-road, there was no turning back.

The first striking evidence that the ardent younger element meant to take advanced ground came November 29, in the report of Porter, from the committee on foreign affairs, to whom had been referred part of Madison's message. After reciting in vigorous sentences the evils which the United States had so long suffered, the report concluded with six resolutions in support of the judgment of the committee that "the period has arrived when in the opinion of your committee it is a sacred duty of Congress to call forth the patriotism and resources of the country." Immediate choice must be made between total submission to England, or war against her—not a peaceful commercial war, but an aggressive war against her land and naval power. The resolutions called for filling up the ranks of the army, for ten thousand additional regular troops, for the acceptance by the president of fifty thousand volunteers, for the calling out of the militia, for the refitting of the navy, and for the arming of merchant vessels.[1]

The debate which followed this striking report was pitched in a high key. Porter and Grundy of the committee frankly declared that the adoption of the report meant nothing else than war; still the House promptly and enthusiastically adopted it by majorities running as high as 120 to 8, and 113 to 16. Special committees were immediately appointed to formulate the proposed measures, and their reports were in turn productive of strong speeches, not the least interesting of which was that of John Randolph. For two and a half hours he heaped sarcasm and invective, scorn and ridicule, upon the newly risen "war-hawks." He made savage thrusts at gentlemen calling themselves Republicans and at the same time advocating war, at those other Republicans who were "as infatuated with standing armies, loans, taxes, navies, and war, as ever were the Essex Junto." He paid his compliments to those who cast wistful and determined eyes towards Canada as an easy prey, and to those who so readily forgot the close ties which bound America to England in the bonds of language, religion, and law. Whether wholly sane or at times seriously unbalanced, his keenness, his volcanic temper, his daring use of the rapier in debate, and his readiness to join the minority on occasion, make John Randolph of Roanoke

[1] *Annals of Cong.*, 12 Cong., 1 Sess., 373; *Niles' Register*, I., 252.

without doubt the most unique and the most picturesque partisan in the history of Congress.[1]

John C. Calhoun's first great speech in Congress was a reply to this effort of Randolph's. In almost every characteristic Calhoun was the opposite of Randolph—a grave, handsome young man, just past thirty, polished and logical in utterance, persuasive and courteous in dealing with his opponents, subtle and ingenious in presenting his own arguments. His speech on this occasion carried a weight which could not be diminished by the youth and inexperience of the speaker. "The question, even in the opinion and admission of our opponents, is reduced to this single point: which shall we do, abandon or defend our own commercial and maritime rights, and the personal liberties of our citizens employed in exercising them? These rights are essentially attacked and war is the only means of redress. ... Which alternative this House ought to embrace, it is not for me to say. I hope the decision is made already by a higher authority than the voice of any man." [2]

Even the speaker descended from the chair and took part in the discussion of the measures introduced to carry out the policy enunciated in the report of the committee, strongly supporting in a speech, on the last day of December, the proposal

---

[1] *Niles' Register*, I., 269, 293, 294; *Annals of Cong.*, 12 Cong., 1 Sess., 441; Adams, *Randolph*, 183–185, 253–264.

[2] *Annals of Cong.*, 12 Cong., 1 Sess., 476.

to increase the regular army and to make liberal appropriations for the navy. It mattered not to men of the stamp of Clay whether Madison was right in forgiving French depredations and taking Napoleon at his word, or whether the Federalists were right in saying that the British were no worse than the French in their aggressions upon American commerce and upon the honor of the United States. Clay was not for waiting till a more convenient season, till the United States might be better prepared. To his mind war already existed. "Gentlemen say that this Government," he declared to the House, "is unfit for any war, but a war of invasion. What, is it not equivalent to invasion, if the mouths of our harbors and outlets are blocked up, and we are denied egress from our own waters? Or when a burglar is at our door shall we bravely sally forth and repel his felonious entrance, or meanly skulk within the cells of the castle?" [1]

That Calhoun, Clay, and the other speakers in this momentous debate voiced the sentiments of a large majority of the people throughout the country, save in New England, there cannot be much doubt. Beginning late in November, 1811, resolutions from state legislatures came pouring in upon Congress from all parts of the country—Georgia, Pennsylvania, Virginia, Ohio, Kentucky, and the House of Representatives of Massachusetts united in approving warlike measures. The Virginia resolution of De-

[1] Clay, *Works* (Colton's ed., 1863), V., 278, 283.

cember 17 declared in unmistakable terms for immediate war: "This assembly, speaking as they believe they do, the voice of the people of this commonwealth, have viewed with approbation the uniform zeal and just remonstrances pursued and adopted by the general government. . . . The period has now arrived when peace, as we now have it, is disgraceful, and war is honorable." The governors almost without exception pledged support to the administration and proceeded to put their militia on a war footing. The war was to be a national war, "a war of the *people of America* against the *government of England*," a war to "purify the political atmosphere."[1]

The first attempt of the war party to secure the legislation needed to carry out the policy adopted in the resolutions of the committee on foreign relations showed how difficult it was to transform the old partisan inertia into warlike energy. A bill introduced into the Senate by Giles raised the number of men to be added to the regular army from ten thousand, proposed by the House committee, to twenty-five thousand. The motive of the leaders of the Senate was the ill-concealed purpose to embarrass the administration, and particularly the treasury, by this large and expensive force, if, indeed, Randolph was mistaken in his fling that "it had not been demonstrated that these men could be raised; it would be an army on paper only." After some sparring between the Houses, the Senate bill finally

[1] *Niles' Register*, I., 297, 298, 337, 352, 361, 362.

became a law June 26, 1812, partly by the aid of Federalists who voted with the extreme Republicans to make it inconvenient for their enemies.[1] The next measure, for a volunteer force of fifty thousand men, presumably to come from the state militia, but to be put under the control of the United States and thus to be available for service outside the United States, as in Canada or in Florida, revealed the progress the Republicans were making towards the exercise of the broadest sovereign powers by the United States. This measure became a law February 6, but when the third plan, the naval programme, was presented, the Republicans held back. Cheves's request for seven million five hundred thousand dollars for the construction of twelve seventy-fours and twenty frigates staggered the House, which had a traditional, almost innate, prejudice against the navy; though his argument was strong, it was not strong enough to convert the House, and the scheme for new vessels was defeated by a majority of only three votes. Aggressive action at sea must thenceforth be confined to the little navy then in service, and to the volunteer, or privateer, navy which would spring up after the declaration of war.[2]

Gallatin presented, in November, 1811, a report

---

[1] *Annals of Cong.*, 12 Cong., 1 Sess., 35, 66, 707; *U. S. Statutes at Large*, II., 671.

[2] *Annals of Cong.*, 12 Cong., 1 Sess., 803 et seq., especially 811; *U. S. Statutes at Large*, III., 676, 699.

which showed that, without spending any money on war preparations, the treasury would have a surplus of several millions at the end of the year. As the war spirit developed during the session, the estimates of the secretary of the treasury were no longer valid for the new situation, and he accordingly submitted revised estimates, showing that if the war was undertaken there would be a deficit of at least four million dollars. Gallatin had so often of late years been disregarded in his recommendations that he did not in this case enter into any detailed specification as to the means by which the deficit could be provided for. If Congress would have war, it must devise its own means for the luxury.[1]

Congress, however, instead of meeting the issue squarely, made Gallatin's report a basis for a new attack on him. His bitter and relentless enemies, the Giles and Smith faction, asked why this great financier did not show his superior genius by devising original and adequate means for meeting the deficit. They declared that the report was a deliberate attempt to put "a damper" upon the new army, and that it was artfully drawn up for the express purpose of alarming the people and checking the decision of Congress. One of the severest criticisms made upon Gallatin's recommendation was that he could point to no other means of raising revenue for war purposes than those which had been resorted to by his Federalist predecessors, Hamilton and

[1] *Niles' Register*, I., 229, 382; Gallatin, *Writings*, I., 501.

Walcott—direct taxes, excises, stamp duties, and the doubling of import duties.[1]

War was upon the country, and millions must be supplied; the doubling of duties on imports would avail little, since importations would necessarily fall to a minimum when war really began. Yet Congress was not willing to resort to radical measures for increasing the revenue by taxation, and spent much time in the spring of 1812 discussing the weighty question whether the tax on distilled liquors in a pending bill should be laid on stills or should take the form of a gallon-tax. The outcome of the matter was not a tax act, but in June a postponement of the whole matter by a vote of 72 to 46.

This unwillingness of Congress, during the early years of the war, to draw liberally and directly upon the resources of the people, not only greatly hampered the administration by keeping down the revenues and impairing the credit of the United States, but really considerably increased the cost of the war to the people, since the later loans were subjected to heavy discounts. Even the resource of borrowing was used grudgingly at this first session of the twelfth Congress, which finally authorized a loan of only eleven million dollars at six per cent. Without the aid of a Bank of the United States such a loan was with much difficulty placed at par as provided in the authorizing act; hence, even before the

---

[1] *Niles' Register*, I., 368, 394, 408 (Giles's speech of December 17, 1811).

war began, the perplexities of war finance were experienced. In June, another act directed the issue of treasury notes up to five million dollars bearing interest at five and two-fifths per cent., such notes to be transferable by delivery and indorsement. The unusual rate of interest was chosen to facilitate such transfers, for the value of a note at any time, principal and interest, could easily be computed, the interest being one and one-half cents per day on every hundred dollars of the principal, each month computed as containing thirty days.[1]

War was not to be begun, however, without one more resort to the old and familiar weapon of an embargo, which might almost be called a proper measure in anticipation of war. No matter how dull its edge, no matter how resentfully it would be received by the commercial interests, to whom the very idea of another embargo was odious, Madison recommended on April 1 an immediate embargo, to last sixty days. The leaders of the House welcomed the significant suggestion, passed the bill in a single day, and sent it to the Senate, which secured its amendment so as to hold good for ninety days. The extension of time was merely a concession to the moderate Republicans, who still hoped that negotiations might bring adjustment.[2]

It was Madison's first step along the difficult and thorny road into which the War Republicans had

---

[1] *U. S. Statutes at Large*, I., 694, 766.
[2] *Ibid.*, II., 700; *Annals of Cong.*, 12 Cong., 1 Sess., 1597, 1602,

compelled him to enter. It is quite impossible to say how much longer the president, if left to himself, would have gone on with his reiterative negotiations, special envoys to London, and the old expedients of meaningless ultimatums. Madison himself had no liking for war, and of all the presidents of the United States, except Buchanan, none was less fitted for rallying the people to the support of a war or for carrying on the government during the stressful months and years of actual combat. A story has been frequently repeated and even set down in text-books, that Clay and other leaders presented to Madison in a formal manner the alternative of a pledge to recommend war, or the loss of the re-nomination for the presidency in 1812. Good historical evidence in proof of the story is lacking, and Clay and his confrères explicitly denied it. Madison knew that war was probably inevitable; he believed that the war party in Congress had the people behind them, and that if he were to continue president he must be re-elected through the aid of the war-makers. So all through the winter and spring of 1812, he made no effort to check the new patriots. Each side understood the other and tacitly accepted the situation; Madison secured his renomination, but with it the direction of a distasteful war; the war-hawks got their war, but with a most unwarlike commander-in-chief of the army and navy.[1]

[1] Williams, *Statesman's Manual*, I., 348; Adams, *Gallatin*, 456; Schouler, *United States*, II., 388 *n.*

President Madison was renominated in May by a congressional caucus at which eighty-two members were present. John Langdon of New Hampshire was tendered the nomination for the vice-presidency, but declined it, whereupon the second place on the ticket was given to Elbridge Gerry, lately defeated for re-election to the governorship of Massachusetts. Madison's chief rival in this campaign was De Witt Clinton of New York, a Republican strongly opposed to the Virginia dynasty. Young, able, ambitious of position, experienced and adroit in political management, he magnified the commercial and political importance of New York, and took advantage of the fact that that state had gone Federalist in the last election. Being the "boss" of the state and desiring the presidential nomination, he received it from the hands of the New York legislature ten days after Madison was named at Washington.[1]

The Federalists were much at sea as to their nomination, and a convention of men from the states north of the Potomac and from South Carolina, met in a sort of private session in New York in September to determine their course in regard to Clinton. Rufus King denounced Clinton as a second Burr, but Massachusetts urged the imperative need of defeating Madison as a means of peace, now that the orders in council were repealed. Hopes of success in New York were raised by the existence of the usual bitter factional fight in that state, and by the

[1] *Niles' Register*, II., 192, 235.

triumph of the Burr, or anti-Clinton, faction in securing a New York federal judgeship. By a strange combination of circumstances, the Federalists were finally brought to indorse Clinton's nomination, and then to place Jared Ingersoll, the attorney-general of Pennsylvania, a man of New England birth, upon the ticket with him.[1]

In this first war-time election Madison was chosen by an electoral vote of 128 against Clinton's 89. The president carried Vermont and Pennsylvania, but Clinton succeeded in carrying New York, largely through the efficient aid of Martin Van Buren, who thus made his appearance as a political figure in that long line of remarkably astute and skilful New York politicians which began with Aaron Burr. The Federalists also carried Massachusetts by a majority of twenty-four thousand, in spite of the fact that the state had but recently chosen Gerry as a Republican governor. It was hardly a good augury for carrying on a vigorous, liberally supported war against Great Britain, that such great, rich states as Massachusetts and New York, with their resources of men and money, should cast their votes against the administration.[2]

---

[1] King, *Life and Corresp. of King*, V., 276 et seq.
[2] Stanwood, *Hist. of the Presidency*, chap. viii.; *Niles' Register*, III., 368.

CHAPTER V

THE DECLARATION OF WAR

(1812)

WHILE Congress was hesitating to pass warlike measures, and while the determined leaders of the war party, by force of intellect and dogmatism, were bringing a reluctant body of conservative Republicans into line to support such measures, the president lost no opportunity, as soon as his political alliance was settled, to add impetus to the war movement. So eager was he that on March 9, 1812, he sent to Congress a collection of documents for which he had recently been duped into paying to John Henry fifty thousand dollars out of the contingent fund for foreign intercourse. These papers, Madison declared, proved that Great Britain in time of peace, and while professing friendship, had employed a secret agent to stir up disaffection in certain states, especially Massachusetts, with the purpose of producing resistance to the laws of the Union, and ultimately of destroying the integrity of the nation and bringing the eastern part into political connection with Great Britain.[1]

[1] Richardson, *Messages and Papers*, I., 498; *Niles' Register*, II., 19–27, reprints the documents thus submitted.

The facts were bad enough, but not so bad as the
president tried to make them out. ⟨John Henry,
an Irishman, had been employed in 1809 by Sir
James Craig, governor-general of Canada, to visit
New England and find out the sentiment of the
Federalists regarding separation, and connection of
some sort with Great Britain.⟩ Henry spent three
months in Boston and wrote numerous reports to
one of Craig's subordinates; which were in turn
transmitted to the home government in London.
He tried to secure from the British ministry the
sum of thirty-two thousand pounds for his services
as a political spy, and, failing in this, he had undertaken to get revenge and to fill his spendthrift
pockets with American gold. On his way to New
York he fell in with a French impostor, "Count"
Edward de Crillon, and this pair of precious scoun-
drels, with the countenance of Serrurier, the French
minister at Washington, finally persuaded Monroe
and Madison to buy the documents and thus to
bring discomfiture upon the administration's im-
placable Federalist opponents. The price paid to
Henry was speedily transferred to Crillon in exchange for French "estates" which that Napoleonic
spy never possessed.[1]

⟨ Henry's reports set forth the view that Massachusetts would probably lead in organizing resistance
to a war against Great Britain, but that even the

---

[1] Henry Adams, "Count Edward de Crillon," in *Am. Hist.
Rev.*, I., 51-69.

most rampant of the Federalists realized that secession must be resorted to only as an extreme measure. No names appeared in the copies which he sold to Madison, and to the great relief of the Federalist leaders the papers summarized his impressions without going into details. The disclosures were so inconsequential that their real effect was little more than the establishment of the fact of a semi-official intrigue against the United States, and consequently a deepening of popular antagonism to the British.

The investigation of Mr. Henry Adams in the British archives has revealed another side to this British-Federalist diplomacy. The British minister at Washington, Mr. Foster, without his suggestion, was visited by leading Federalists early in 1812, and received from them advice as to "a thorough amalgamation of interests between Great Britain and America": no concession by Great Britain in favor of revocation or modification of the orders, but a steady pressure upon the United States until it should give up its restrictive system. "They [the Federalists] seemed to think that Great Britain could by management bring the United States into any connection with her that she pleased." If war comes, said the Federalists, it will be a short war, the administration will be overthrown, and a solid peace with Great Britain will be established.[1]

The military spirit certainly rose fast, for hope and courage were stronger than fear and submission.

[1] Adams, *United States*, VI., 172–175.

The New York militia were prepared for duty along the northern frontiers; the New Jersey, Pennsylvania, Virginia, Georgia, Ohio, Kentucky, and Tennessee militia were put on a war footing. The men of the trans-Alleghany states and territories were waiting eagerly for marching orders to Canada. In the House of Representatives, Randolph, the insuppressible, was at length silenced. His attempt to debate the war in open House on an informal motion led the speaker to rule that he must reduce to writing his motion that it was "inexpedient to resort to war with Great Britain." The issue being thus made perfectly clear, the House, by a vote of 72 to 37, refused to consider the motion.[1]

Only here and there did the revolt against the war and war measures make itself noticeable. In New York City and in Boston there was strong feeling against the loans, the embargo, the Virginia cabal to maintain the presidential succession, and against the "madmen of Kentucky and Tennessee." In New York and New England the spring elections showed distinct Federalist gains; but for the rest of the country the youthful exultation in untried strength, and eagerness to exercise it against an underestimated enemy, showed no signs of abatement.

The message of the president, on June 1, definitely suggesting to the legislative department provisions

---

[1] *Niles' Register*, II., 134; *Annals of Cong.*, 12 Cong., 1 Sess., 1462, 1467, 1470; Tompkins, *Military Papers*, I., 318.

for "opposing force to force in defence of their national rights," was the sign of Madison's complete surrender to the war party. He recited, as the grievances of the United States, the violation of the American flag on the high seas; the blockading of our ports; impressment of seamen; the refusal of Great Britain to repeal the orders in council; the Indian disturbances in the northwest; and all the painfully familiar, reiterated arguments of the war Republicans.[1]

Further delay was obviously useless. The message was referred to a committee, whose report, presented June 3 by Calhoun, strongly favored resort to arms to defend the sovereignty and independence of the United States.

The declaration of war consisted of a single sentence draughted by William Pinkney, the attorney-general, "that war be and the same is hereby declared to exist" between the United States and Great Britain; and the president was authorized to use the whole land and naval force of the United States to make the declaration effective. Strong opposition developed, but it passed the House by a vote of 79 to 49. For twelve days the Senate held up the measure while the Federalists and the Giles-Smith faction proposed such alternatives as the granting of letters of marque and reprisal, and the arming of merchant vessels. All attempts to make radical amendment failed, and after a fortnight of

[1] Richardson, *Messages and Papers*, I., 499.

secret discussion the declaration passed the Senate, 19 to 13, the majority finally including the three senators most hostile to the administration—Giles, Smith, and Leib./ The president immediately signed the bill and issued a proclamation that war existed between the United States and Great Britain. \ The same day "he visited in person — a thing never known before—all the offices of the departments of war and navy, stimulating everything in a manner worthy of a little commander in chief with his little round hat and huge cockade." ¹∕

The remaining three weeks of the session were taken up with war measures. Letters of marque and reprisal were authorized, penalties were imposed upon all who should trade with the enemy, and a few of the most necessary acts for carrying on war were passed. But bills for war taxes, prepared by Secretary Gallatin, were gently postponed to the next session; to the credit of Calhoun and Cheves be it said that they voted against postponement.

Calhoun, perhaps better than any one else of his party, illustrated the complete break which had been made between the old and the new Republicanism. In a speech on June 24, he declared audaciously against commercial restrictions, and cut loose from the traditions not merely of Madison, but of his

---

¹ Richardson, *Messages and Papers*, I., 512; *Annals of Cong.*, 12 Cong., 1 Sess., 1632, 1637, 266, 268, 287 et seq.; *Am. State Paps., Foreign*, III., 567; MacDonald, *Select Documents*, 191; *Rush MSS.*, quoted in Adams, *United States*, VI., 229.

greater master, Jefferson. With fine courtesy and respect for the rights of those who had upheld the restrictive system he distinctly separated himself from them: "The restrictive system as a mode of resistance . . . has never been a favorite one with me. . . . It does not suit the genius of our people, or that of our government, or the geographical character of our country. . . . We have had a peace like a war: in the name of Heaven let us not have the only thing that is worse—a war like a peace." With this high note ringing in the ears of its members, Congress adjourned July 6.[1]

Whatever its shortcomings—its failure to make sufficient provision for supporting the war which it had declared, its failure to recognize the disparity in size and resources of the two powers—Congress had shown a most refreshing energy and optimism. For a time the west was in command, "rushing headlong into difficulties with little calculation of the needs, and little concern for the consequences,"[2] so long as the lodestar of patriotic zeal and just resentment of national insult led them on. The session of 1812 stands out as one of the momentous sessions of the first half-century of the republic.

The minority, checked in debate and silenced by secret sessions, found voice in a vigorous protest scattered broadcast over the land. It was signed by thirty-four members of the House, and set forth

---

[1] *Annals of Cong.*, 12 Cong., 1 Sess., 1539–1541.
[2] Minority Address, *Niles' Register*, II., 315.

at great length and in vigorous phrase the grounds of their opposition to the war. More distinctly than elsewhere in the speeches and papers of the Federalists, and if possible with more force, it denounced the anomaly of waging war to redress the wrongs of a section which opposed the war; of warring against the least offending party of the two; of entering upon a costly and indefinite war without the backing of the financiers of the nation; and, last of all, of waging a war of conquest upon the colonies of a nation in full command of the sea.[1]

New England denounced the war in strong terms in June and July, while the governors of several states quietly but effectively refused to call out their militia at the request of General Dearborn; and for these acts they were indorsed and supported by the legislatures and people of their states. Those who opposed the war in Baltimore experienced the odium and persecution meted out to peace-lovers in time of war. In that prosperous commercial city of fifty thousand inhabitants was a sturdy, conservative element which had for its organ the *Federal Republican*, edited by Jacob Wagner and Alexander C. Hanson, the former a common, slanderous writer, who had been chief clerk of the state department under Secretary Pickering, and under Madison until 1807; the latter a son of the chancellor of

---

[1] *Annals of Cong.*, 12 Cong., 1 Sess., 2196; *Niles' Register*, II., 309; cf. "Rockingham Memorial to James Madison," August, 1812, in Webster, *Writings* (National ed.), XV., 599.

Maryland, and a grandson of a president of the Continental Congress. There was also a large ruffian element, such as gathers in rapidly growing seaports, half pirate, half roustabout, and wholly brutal and unrestrained.[1]

The *Federal Republican*, after the declaration, spoke vigorously against the war about to begin, and announced its intention to continue this open criticism. Two days later its office was sacked and the types, presses, and furniture demolished, and Wagner compelled to flee for his life while the mob searched private houses to find him. Next day the mob continued the pastime of searching houses, burned the house of a negro who was accused of speaking well of the British, and dismantled several vessels alleged to be about to sail under British permits. Evidently Baltimore, and perhaps the whole south and west, believed that opposition to a war legally declared bordered on treason and should be punished by the prompt and unceremonious measures of "lynch law."

On July 27, the *Federal Republican*, with undiminished bitterness and vigor of utterance, was again received by its subscribers, issuing nominally from a house in Charles Street. This house was attacked by a new mob, and in the mêlée which followed, and in the later assault on the jail, whither Hanson and his friends allowed themselves to be taken, many men were killed, wounded, or terribly

[1] *Niles' Register*, II., 373, 405, gives full accounts of the riots in its home city.

beaten. Among these were two veteran officers of the Revolutionary War, General Lingan, who was killed, and General Henry Lee, who was made a cripple for life. It seemed as though a scene from the red drama of the French Revolution were being re-enacted in the city nearest the capital of the nation whose boast was freedom. The whole Baltimore episode created a profound impression unfavorable to the government and to the war. In the election which followed in October, the Federalists gained control of the Maryland Assembly, electing Hanson as a representative in Congress and sending a Federalist to the United States Senate.[1]

At the very time that the Americans were moving rapidly towards a declaration of war, and while the Federalists were advising the British minister to continue the orders in council, conditions in England were making imperative upon the ministry the revocation of these orders which constituted the chief cause of the war. The movement for repeal began as early as 1808, when Lord Brougham in the Commons and Lord Lansdowne in the Lords led the agitation for such a method of settling the difficulties with America. But the time was not ripe. Further bitter experience and hardship must be suffered by the manufacturers of England before they would put the needed pressure on the ministry. At length, in the spring of 1812, a parliamentary inquiry was authorized and long hearings against the orders were

[1] *Niles' Register*, III., 96, 112, 176.

conducted. Even the assassination of Spencer Perceval, chancellor of the exchequer, in the lobby of the House of Commons, May 11, was not permitted to interrupt the hearings. The evidence, which fills a ponderous volume, shows how seriously, even vitally, the industries of England had been hit by the orders, and how necessary was immediate revocation.[1]

Not merely was the loss of American trade already great, but there was danger of war with the United States, and still more permanent danger from possible American rivalry in manufacturing. The presentation of the alleged decree of Napoleon, bearing date of April 28, 1811, declaring the Berlin and Milan decrees fully repealed, also had weight with a government which had so often expressed its willingness to withdraw its orders when the French decrees were withdrawn. In spite of the elaborate arguments of Sir James Stephen and other supporters of the ministry in justifying the policy of the orders, there were many who held that these odious measures had no foundation either in law or expediency. The later sober thought of British jurists has generally conceded "that they were contrary to the law of nations and to our [England's] own municipal law."[2]

Two days before the Congress of the United States

---

[1] *Parl. Papers*, 1812, one vol., given to "Minutes of Evidence . . . Respecting the Orders in Council"; Hansard, *Parl. Debates*, XXIV., 630.

[2] Campbell, *Lord Chancellors* (4th ed.), IX., 285.

voted to declare war, Lord Brougham moved in the
House of Commons for the unconditional repeal of
the orders in council. The ministry, pressed upon
by the evidence before the House, troubled by its
own weakness, involved more deeply than ever in
the European struggle against Napoleon, and op-
pressed with fear of war with the United States at
a most inopportune time, grudgingly acquiesced in
Brougham's motion, and on June 23, four days
after President Madison's proclamation of war, the
repeal of the orders was accomplished, so far as they
regarded American vessels, with the reservation
that they should be revived if America persisted
in hostile acts. The British undoubtedly believed
that the concession was the utmost price they could
pay for the peace which they desired to have continued. Of course the plan had its advantages, for
it would open again to the British manufacturers
and merchants the American markets, closed to
them since February, 1811; and these markets just
then would be peculiarly important since those of
the Continent were still closed to English ships.[1]

It is not difficult to believe that the war would,
after all, have been averted had the present ocean
telegraphic - cable been available for sending to
Washington the news of this "surrender" of Great

---

[1] Cf. Mahan, "The War of 1812," in *Scribner's Mag.*, XXXV.,
470–474; Lord Liverpool's official statement in Hansard, *Parl.
Debates*, XXIII., 733; Brougham's claim to the credit of repeal
is in his *Autobiography*, II., 7.

Britain in such an important particular. But the news reached Washington too late to be effective with the Americans, even if the reservation in the repeal had not been offensive to them. Accordingly, they simply dropped one more of the valid causes for waging war, and accepted the defence of sailors' rights as sufficient in itself. In this there was no inconsistency, for wholesale impressment of Americans who were citizens by birth and not by naturalization, was not denied by the British. Lord Castlereagh admitted that there were in 1811, out of one hundred and forty-five thousand seamen actually employed in the British service, probably sixteen hundred native-born Americans serving by impressment on British ships, and nearly two thousand more who claimed to be American citizens. The noble lord declared that these cases were incidental and irritating errors which could not be prevented in the rigid enforcement of a proper and necessary policy decided upon by the British government. He further announced that all who were thus impressed would be discharged upon proving satisfactorily their American birth. How this proof was to be furnished while they were in semi-slavery in British fleets was not made clear.[1]

The number of complaints registered with the secretary of state of the United States before the war was not less than 6257, with strong probability of several thousand cases that were never filed.

---

[1] Hansard, *Parl. Debates*, XXIV., 601–602.

Waiving the validity and honesty of American naturalization as evidenced by the "papers" presented by seamen — and Great Britain did not formally recognize the right of expatriation until 1869—there were probably many more than sixteen hundred Americans impressed without any shadow of right whatever. When hostilities began, about twenty-five hundred of these impressed Americans refused to fight against their countrymen, and were sent to English prisons, particularly Dartmoor, and there remained until the end of the war, unable, of course, to satisfy Great Britain of their American origin. It was one of those curious anomalies of the war, that the very states which had suffered most from impressments as well as from assaults on neutral commerce, opposed the war most bitterly.[1]

The lack of foresightful preparation for war on the part of the United States in 1812 borders on the ridiculous. She declared war upon the mistress of the seas, upon the arch enemy of Napoleon and the great barrier to the realization of his ambitions, upon the mother of great and rich colonies to the north and south of the United States. England, furthermore, was a nation with a strong military tradition, with officers of great ability and experience, and with an army at the height of its efficiency

---

[1] Estimates of number of impressments in Roosevelt, *Naval War* (3d ed.); 42 *n*; Lossing, *Field-book of the War of 1812*, 1068; Admiralty return of prisoners in *Parl. Papers*, 1814–1815, XI.

in the midst of a great campaign. Against all of these, what did the United States oppose? A regular army of some sixty-seven hundred men, officered by old men, or men of petty spirit and petty experience, of whom General Winfield Scott, speaking from personal knowledge, said they were sunk in sloth and ignorance, many of them being ruined by intemperate drinking.[1]

There was no military tradition in the United States and no respect for the military service, as was shown abundantly in the appointments made in 1812 under the army reorganization act. Dearborn, who became senior major-general, had been a deputy quartermaster-general in the Revolution, later a colonel in the New Hampshire militia, and secretary of war under Jefferson. He left the collectorship of the port of Boston, at the age of sixty-one, to take command of the army. Thomas Pinckney, the junior major-general, who had seen his only service thirty years before in the guerilla companies of Marion and Sumter, was sixty-three; James Wilkinson, who was about all that an officer should not be—insubordinate, obstinate, negligent, and corrupt, if not positively traitorous — was the senior brigadier-general. Another brigadier was Governor William Hull, of Michigan territory, also an old Revolutionary soldier of about sixty years. Scott describes the group of new officers appointed after 1808 as either indifferent or positively bad, swagger-

---

[1] Winfield Scott, *Memoirs*, I., 31.

ers, political dependants (like Winder), poor gentlemen who were fit for naught else.[1]

The main reliance for both offensive and defensive operations was to be the militia and volunteers, the army of the free people, according to Jeffersonian dogma, rising to defend their rights. These militia and voluntoor soldiers were very raw material out of which to make an army, though they knew how to shoot and could shift fairly well for themselves. But with pompous, political incapables for officers before them and behind them, to command them and supply them, they never made a respectable army; not until the very last of the war, when capable, vigorous, and experienced officers drilled them into real soldiers, did they become formidable. Those men whom Amos Kendall saw in the spring and summer of 1814 in Pennsylvania and Kentucky were probably no exceptions to the general rule of recruits: "About three hundred militia from Adams County, Pennsylvania, entered the place [McConnellstown] on their way to Erie. They were without order, and apparently without officers—mean, dirty, ugly, and in every respect contemptible." In August he witnessed a temporary muster in Kentucky, and wrote in the flippant disgust of a fastidious young man from the east: "The soldiers arc under no more restraint than a herd of swine. Reasoning, remonstrating, threatening, and ridiculing their officers, they show their sense of equality

[1] Winfield Scott, *Memoirs*, I., 35.

and their total want of subordination." On the other hand, Jackson described his Tennessee militia of 1813 to Monroe in words of highest praise: "They are the choicest of our citizens. . . . They go at their country's call to do the will of the Government. No constitutional scruples [in comparison with Massachusetts militia] trouble them. Nay, they will rejoice at the opportunity of placing the American eagle on the ramparts of Mobile, Pensacola, and Fort St. Augustine." And Jackson saw to it that they had their opportunity.[1]

As for arms, ammunition, clothing, stores, and plans, the United States was guiltless of "goods laid by for many years." Fortifications were old and primitive, or designed chiefly for defence against the Indians. New York, Philadelphia, and Baltimore found out later that fortification was essentially a local issue.

The navy with which war was to be made on England with her eight hundred and more war vessels, two hundred and thirty of which were larger than any American craft, consisted of about a dozen vessels, the largest of which was a forty-four-gun frigate. The naval forces were five thousand Americans to one hundred and fifty thousand British. The navy had this advantage, however, over the army: there was a large body of the most expert sailors in the world in the merchant and fishing fleets of the United States, who could be relied on

---

[1] Kendall, *Autobiography*, 98, 124; Parton, *Jackson*, I., 372.

for service on the war vessels or on the privateers; and the regular naval officers had been trained in the Barbary wars. There was none of the spirit-lessness, none of the dead-wood, in the navy that there was in the army.[1]

The federal treasury was empty, or would be by the end of the year, for the revenues were derived chiefly from duties on imports, and the non-intercourse act cut off this source of supply. The country had been "embargoed and non-intercoursed almost into a consumption," as John Randolph passionately declared. In the distressed state of commerce and industry, no new taxes were laid to take the place of the lost duties. With a probable revenue of less than ten million dollars, with which to meet expenses of thirty million dollars, with a credit so poor that loans fell at once below par, necessitating resort to treasury notes, with the Bank of the United States gone and the sympathies of the financial classes of New England and the Middle States hopelessly alienated, the United States faced a government with an income from taxation reaching seventy million dollars, and with the machinery for producing even greater revenue if the need were great enough. Congress seemed to have reached its limit of preparation for war against the armies and navies of Great Britain, the wealthiest power of Europe, when it authorized a loan of eleven million dol-

[1] *Am. State Paps.*, *Naval*, I., 265; Roosevelt, *Naval War*, chap. ii.

lars and the issue of five million dollars of treasury notes.[1]

The chief advantage of America's eight millions of people against England's twenty millions, lay in geographical position. The great distance from England, over which she must transport, by the slow and uncertain means of sailing vessels, her men, arms, and supplies; and the vast extent of the interior of the United States, stretching back from the long coast-line running from the St. Croix to the St. Mary's, were prime factors in favor of the Americans. The attempts of England to penetrate into the great interior would be like the blows of a sledge-hammer struck into a bin of wheat: a few kernels would be bruised or destroyed, but the iron would soon bury itself harmlessly just under the surface of the mass. Against the united strength of Great Britain, the United States could oppose no strong national spirit in 1812; there was little or no appreciation of the tendency to unity. For twenty-five years there had been unrelenting emphasis on differences of opinions and interests, commercial against planting classes; Virginia, the Carolinas, and Kentucky against New England. Threats of secession in and out of season were calmly received.

The leaders of the new Republicans made themselves believe that war against England would unite the whole nation against its foes, no matter what

[1] *U. S. Statutes at Large*, II., 694, 766; Dunbar (ed.), *Laws*, 62, 63.

might have been the partisan prejudices and factional differences before the declaration. In this judgment they were profoundly mistaken, betraying once more their inability to comprehend the strength of New York party feuds, or the unique New England combination of conscience, relentlessness, and thrift in business. Madison's plan of throwing " forward the flag of the country, sure that the people would press onward to defend it," was therefore destined to failure from the very start. The English premier, Lord Liverpool, showed real penetration into American conditions when he asserted in February, 1813, "that the war on the part of America had been a war of passion, of party spirit, and not a war of policy, of interest, or of necessity."[1]

[1] *Niles' Register*, I., 252, quoting the *Federal Republican;* Adams, *United States*, VI., 210; Adams, *Gallatin*, 460, *n.*; Hansard, *Parl. Debates*, XXIV., 584.

CHAPTER VI

ON TO CANADA

(1812–1814)

THE war-makers of 1812 had no other purpose than to make an aggressive campaign from the start. The main reliance was to be upon the land forces, and consequently the only object of attack was Canada; hence it was along the long boundary-line stretching from Mackinac to Lake Champlain that the chief military operations took place, up to the summer of 1814. The conquest of Canada was one of the first and most important objects urged by men like Clay, to whom it had appeared for two years as the blow which England would feel almost as keenly as she had felt the loss of the thirteen colonies in the Revolutionary War. Either as a conquered province or as a hostage for securing from Britain the demands of the United States, it seemed supremely desirable. "The conquest of Canada is in your power," Clay announced to the House in February, 1810. "I trust I shall not be deemed presumptuous when I state that I verily believe that the militia of Kentucky are alone competent to place Montreal and Upper Canada at your feet. Is it nothing to the

British nation; is it nothing to the pride of her monarch, to have the last of the immense North American possessions held by him in the commencement of his reign wrested from his dominions? Is it nothing to us to extinguish the torch that lights up savage warfare?"[1]

In fact, so obtrusive was this aim that Randolph sarcastically declared: "Agrarian cupidity, not maritime right, urges the war. Ever since the report of the Committee on Foreign Relations came into the House, we have heard but one word,— like the whippoorwill, but one eternal monotonous tone—Canada, Canada, Canada!" Even Jefferson, who ought to have known better, wrote to Duane in August, 1812: "The acquisition of Canada this year as far as the neighborhood of Quebec, will be a mere matter of marching, and will give us experience for the attack on Halifax the next, and the final expulsion of England from the American continent." It may be recalled, however, that Jefferson was even less of an authority on military and naval matters than he was upon financial affairs. Very dearly were the Republicans to pay in terms of pain, loss, and pride for the jaunty way in which they attacked the British in Canada.[2]

Such a campaign was quite advisable and according to precedent. Successful attacks had been re-

---

[1] *Annals of Cong.*, 11 Cong., 1 Sess., 580.
[2] *Ibid,.* 12 Cong., 1 Sess., 533; Jefferson, *Works* (Federal ed.), XI., 265.

peatedly made upon the French provinces between 1689 and 1763, but always from the sea; the land expeditions against Quebec before and during the Revolution were dismal failures. The provinces, which stretched for twelve hundred miles from Quebec to Lake Superior, contained four hundred thousand souls, one-third of whom were English immigrants or American loyalists and their descendants. West of Montreal the competition for the fur-trade was keen and strong; the Americans outside the commercial centres felt bitterness and animosity for the British as a tradition. The west, which most hated the British, was the section which was most bent on the war, and it was fitting that the assault on the British power should come from that quarter. Dearborn submitted to the war department before the war broke out a plan of campaign which called for a main attack along the route leading past Lake Champlain to Montreal, with its easy access by way of the Hudson and Lake George. In support of this main attack, he planned three other invasions, from Sackett's Harbor, from Niagara, and from Detroit. The whole was to be undertaken by forces to be made up chiefly of militia.[1]

No one worked out the details of these plans, nor were the necessary men available for immediate action. Still, the general plan was wise: there was reason to expect that by the capture of Malden at the western end of Lake Erie, of Niagara at the east-

---

[1] H. A. Dearborn, *Defence of Gen. Dearborn*, 3.

ern, of Kingston, and then of Montreal, the British power would be squeezed out of Canada. But such a task needed first of all a commander of ability, training, and tenacity, and such a man did not so much as show himself upon the horizon either in Washington or on the frontier. The operations of 1812 were, in the language of a contemporary British officer, beneath criticism; those of 1813 much criticised and unsuccessful, save at the Thames; those of 1814 slightly relieved of the monotony of unsuccess by the American victory at Lundy's Lane and by the turning back of Prevost's army at Plattsburg.

The essential difficulties of the campaigns against Canada were not appreciated by any one connected with the administration; close study of the geography of the country and the systems of trails, waterways, and highways makes it almost incredible that a nation or a party could have committed itself to any war with such nonchalance. The frontiers were too thinly populated to supply an army with even coarse provisions, and no military posts or storehouses of consequence existed. There were no good roads in Michigan, Ohio, or western and northern New York over which to carry men, guns, ammunition, and supplies of food, clothing, and medicines. So difficult was transportation that it cost sixty dollars to get a barrel of flour from Philadelphia or New York to Detroit, and fifty cents to transport every pound of shot, cannon-balls, and ammunition sent over the same route.[1]

Other difficulties thrust themselves forward as foes against which enthusiasm, military experience, and patriotism would avail little: forests threaded only by a trail; rivers swollen by frequent rains; swamps fever-laden and pest-breeding in summer and treacherous in winter; and the omnipresent enmity of the Indians. The fight against these foes within her own territory cost the United States in the end almost as much in money, suffering, and life as did the actual struggle against adversaries wearing the uniform of his Majesty's service. A large part of the demand for internal improvements, which increased so rapidly after 1815, can be traced to the experiences of the government and the soldiers during the second war with Great Britain.[2]

The first blow of the campaign was to be struck at the British posts at Malden and Fort Amherstburg, and to the men of the west was assigned this, as the first of many easy victories. The capture of Malden would mean much more than the mere possession of an important post: it would awe the hostile and restless Indians of Michigan and Indiana at least into neutrality in the war, for it is the Indian nature not to be found on what is expected to be the losing side. This first campaign so well illustrates the

[1] McAfee, *Late War in the Western Country*, 50, 54, 183-187 (an excellent account of the hardships of the army); Kendall, *Autobiography*, 93 et seq.   [2] See chap. xv., below.

system of a nucleus of regulars with a force of volunteers and militia, under a political general, that it is worth while to go into some detail regarding it.

General William Hull, who finally accepted, in April, 1812, a brigadier's commission after much urging by Madison, was a man of Revolutionary experience, and since 1805 governor of the territory of Michigan. He was sixty years old at the time of his appointment. He set out from Washington for his post without any very definite instructions or directions; late in May he took command of his troops at Dayton, Ohio; and when war was declared he was already on his two-hundred mile march through the forest towards Detroit, with a force of nearly two thousand men. The British commander was Major-General Isaac Brock, lieutenant-governor of Upper Canada, a man of remarkable energy, courage, resourcefulness, and military efficiency, who, in nearly every point, was the opposite of his enemy across the lake. Communication in the western country was bad, and of course neither general could get any very definite information as to the plans or strength of the other. Regardless of the fact that the British were in naval control of Lake Erie, when Hull reached the Maumee River he sent off his baggage, hospital stores, intrenching tools, and, through a blunder, his muster-rolls and instructions, by a schooner to Detroit. The capture of this vessel by the British, gave them their first clear notion of the American purposes: "I had no idea," wrote General Brock to Prevost, "until I received ——'s letter [and these documents], a few days ago, that General Hull was advancing with so large a force." The British general lost no time in marshalling his little army, and in securing the co-operation of the Indians; but in numbers, and in possible reinforcements to his army, he was distinctly inferior to Hull.[1]

Hull reached Detroit in early July, and under orders from Washington crossed the river to attack Malden, issuing a boastful proclamation to the Canadians. With his superior force he should have attacked at once, taking the chances of war, before the reinforcement of the enemy should make the contest more nearly equal. But while the British grew daily stronger, the American forces lost heart and respect for their general; and the Indians, now allied under Tecumseh with the British, were able to make vicious slashes at the line of Hull's communications between Detroit and the Maumee. Most disheartening of all was the news Hull received after he had settled down to the siege of Malden, that the British had taken Michilimackinac, thus, as he believed, unleashing "a vast number of chiefs who led hostile bands" of Indians from the northern frontier and from western Michigan. Overcome by his difficulties and his fears, Hull weakly retreated from before Malden, and recrossed to Detroit,

[1] Clarke, *Campaign of 1812*, 305, 326, 328 *n.*; Tupper, *Brock* (2d ed.), 212.

August 8. Brock promptly turned the tables by following him. Hull sent off some six hundred men to try to open communication with the Ohio, and when they returned, unsuccessful, he wrote plaintively to Secretary Eustis: " It is a painful consideration that the blood of seventy-five men could only open the communications as far as the points of their bayonets extended." The truth was that Hull's officers and men had lost all confidence in him, and despondency prevailed. In most unmilitary conspiracy, the colonels of the little army offered to make Lieutenant-Colonel Miller, of the regulars, commander in place of Hull, but he declined to receive his promotion in that manner.[1]

Brock decided, two days after his arrival, to move against the fort at Detroit; and on August 15 he summoned Hull to surrender, playing skilfully upon the old man's fears of the tomahawk and scalping-knife, by expressing doubts of his ability to restrain his Indian allies when once the battle began. For the moment Hull refused to surrender, but when the British moved forward to attack the fort, with artillery, infantry, Indian allies, and the two armed vessels, Hull's last grain of courage slipped away. He sent out a white flag and offered terms. To the infinite and almost mutinous chagrin of the Americans, and to the utter amazement of the British themselves, Detroit was within a few hours in

---

[1] *Niles' Register*, II., 357, III., 37, 53 (Hull's Report); **McAfee,** *War in the Western Country*, 71, 81–83.

possession of Brock and his men. A force of about twenty-five hundred men, the fort and village of Detroit, and with it the whole of Michigan territory, thus passed into the hands of an enemy numbering only three hundred and thirty regulars, four hundred militia, and about six hundred Indians. Then and thereafter, Hull tried to justify his surrender by claiming that his troops were already on short rations, and that ultimate surrender was so certain that resistance was unjustifiable. It was true that he was isolated, and that his provisions on short issue would not have lasted more than a month, but Hull seems never to have realized that in war a good many things may happen in a month.[1]

Thus the anticipated victory turned out a most disastrous and shameful defeat. In the bitterness of disappointment and injured pride, the American public and even American statesmen made no allowance for the conditions which made the loss of Detroit practically inevitable — the raw, undisciplined troops, swarms of hostile Indians on flank and rear, broken communications, the lake in control of the British. Scorn and vituperation were heaped upon Hull. Jefferson called him a coward and an imbecile, and compared him to Benedict Arnold.[2] A year and a half later, he was tried by court-martial on charges of treason, cowardice, and neglect of duty. He was convicted on the last two

[1] Tupper, *Brock*, 246–252; *Niles' Register*, III., 53, VI., 345 et seq.   [2] Jefferson, *Works* (Federal ed.), XI., 268.

charges, and sentenced to be shot, though the court recommended him to the mercy of the president. Madison approved the verdict, but remitted the execution of the sentence on account of the former services of the old man.[1]

This brief story of the loss of an army, a fortified town, and a territory, might almost serve as the type of campaign which the United States, except in the few cases where the army was reinforced by the navy, as at Lake Erie and Plattsburg, was to carry on upon land, from the commencement of the war to the "crowning mercy" at New Orleans. Over and over again, at Niagara, in northern New York, in Maryland, was demonstrated the inadequacy of the militia, the stupidity and jealousy of the officers, the ignorance and inertia of the secretaries of war, the insufficiency of preparation at every stage of the war, and the unwillingness of American citizens to enter the regular army or enlist for long terms. Individual commanders like Brown, Scott, and Jackson, and single battles like Lundy's Lane, redeem in some measure the reputation of the army.

Meanwhile, Dearborn was trying with indifferent success to raise an army for the campaigns against Montreal and Niagara. His movements were sluggish and his plans hazy; and for a time he seemed to be on the eve of an accommodation which would end the war. The British certainly desired to avert

[1] *Niles' Register*, VI., 154 et seq., 162 (an account of the trial); Hull, *Defence* (autobiographical).

war, and after the repeal of the orders in council Minister Foster was instructed to arrange an armistice. The governor-general of Canada and Admiral Warren were given similar orders. Hence, Dearborn at Albany, in August, received and accepted an offer from General Prevost to confine his efforts to defensive operations, pending official acceptance by the United States of the offer of the British government. While these negotiations were going on in America, the representative of the United States in London, Jonathan Russell, was authorized to propose a suspension of hostilities, provided Great Britain would make an informal agreement against impressments and blockades. Since such assurance could not be obtained, Madison was unable to sanction Dearborn's arrangement, which was accordingly disavowed, and he was directed to resume hostilities, while Monroe explained the situation to the British minister. Dearborn, however, made little progress towards Montreal, though in November he marched a large force from Plattsburg up to the Canadian line. There the militia refused to leave their own country, and the senior major-general of the armies of the United States marched back to Plattsburg and winter quarters.[1]

Even more disgraceful was the third part of the campaign against Canada, the struggle to conquer

---

[1] *Niles' Register*, III., 153 (correspondence between Warren and Monroe); *Am. State Paps., Foreign*, III., 587; *MSS.* in war department, quoted by Adams, *United States*, VI., 340, 360.

the Niagara country. In August, Major-General Stephen Van Rensselaer of the New York militia, a "weak and incompetent man of high pretensions," as Monroe characterized him, was in command of a thousand men at Lewiston. He was the Federalist candidate for the governorship of New York against Tompkins, and it was incumbent on him to show his qualities by winning a victory in the field. The situation was so critical, especially after the release of British forces by the surrender of Hull at Detroit, that, by the middle of October, Dearborn sent to Niagara about five thousand regulars, volunteers, and militia. Yet the result of an attack on the heights of Queenstown, October 13, was a serious defeat, in which Van Rensselaer lost a thousand men killed, wounded, and prisoners.[1]

Part of the blame was due to his unseemly quarrel with General Smyth of the regular army, which caused the regulars to render little assistance in the fight. Van Rensselaer, relieved at his own request, was succeeded by Smyth, "an Irish temperament with a Virginia education,"[2] who proved even less respectable than Van Rensselaer as a commander. His attack upon the Canadian side in late November was a complete fiasco; his subordinate, Colonel Peter B. Porter, a "war-hawk" who entered the army, characterized the withdrawal of the troops as "a scene of confusion . . . which is difficult to

---

[1] Adams, *United States*, VI., 353 (from Jefferson *MSS*).
[2] *Ibid.*, 396.

describe. About four thousand men without order or restraint discharging their muskets in every direction"; nor did Porter hesitate, in a letter to the *Buffalo Gazette*, to attribute the "late disgrace on this frontier to the cowardice of General Smyth." For this the two men exchanged shots; Smyth soon got leave of absence, and in the spring was dropped from the army roll. Dearborn ought to have gone into retirement along with the rest of the vanishing incompetents of 1812, but political considerations dictated his retention until the following July, when he also was relieved of command.[1]

The incompetency of both the secretary of the navy and the secretary of war became so scandalous that Madison was glad to accept the resignation of each of them in December, 1812. In place of Hamilton he appointed William Jones, a ship-owner of Philadelphia who could at least manage the business of the department; to succeed Eustis, the president appointed John Armstrong of New York, who had been in the Revolutionary army, and who had but recently returned from service as minister to France. Monroe desired the war portfolio, since the state department did not furnish sufficient scope for his talents while the most active field of diplomacy was closed by the war. Although for political reasons Madison did not comply, jealousy and sus-

[1] *Niles' Register*, III., 138 (Van Rensselaer's Report); 264, 285 (Porter's letter).

picion between Monroe and Armstrong had a detrimental effect upon the military service.[1]

The real blame for the appointment of such men as Armstrong in the cabinet, and Hull, Dearborn, Wilkinson, and Pinckney in the army, must be placed squarely upon the president, whose responsibility for the failure of the armies in the north and west has been too much obscured. Madison knew these men well; their records and personalities were not closed books. In the case of Armstrong, he admitted that he hoped for, rather than expected, satisfactory relations.[2] From the start he gave him neither respect nor confidence.

The campaign of 1813 showed some gain for the United States in the extreme west, where General Harrison succeeded to the command. By his success at Tippecanoe in 1811, he had won the confidence and admiration of the men of Kentucky and the northwest; and though Madison actually nominated James Winchester, a rich old Tennessee planter, to the command of the western army, the pressure was so strong from Kentucky that he withdrew Winchester's name and appointed Harrison. The west rallied around the new commander for the purpose of wiping out the disgrace of Hull's surrender, for Harrison had military instincts and knowledge which won respect. But with an army many times larger than Hull's, there was no improvement in organization of commissary or of transporta-

[1] Adams, *Gallatin*, 470.   [2] Madison, *Works*, III., 384.

tion arrangements. All through the wet autumn and early winter the army floundered along in the mud of western Ohio or camped in the woods and swamps.[1]

When the frost of winter made the country passable, a force of thirteen hundred men under the command of Winchester, with provisions and artillery, pushed on towards the mouth of the Maumee, preparatory to an attack on Malden by crossing on the ice. While the troops waited for Harrison to come up, a call came to relieve the village of Frenchtown on the Raisin River, which was held by the British. In a chivalrous, adventurous spirit, Winchester sent off some six hundred and sixty of his best Kentucky troops to take the place, following a little later himself with two hundred and fifty more, thus separating his division from the rest of the army by thirty miles; while eighteen miles away on the other side were perhaps two thousand of the enemy in forts. The Americans were attacked, January 22, 1813, by more than a thousand men from Malden, under Proctor, and the battle, or "massacre of the Raisin" followed. More than five hundred Americans were made prisoners, while about four hundred were killed in battle or massacred by the Indians after the withdrawal of Proctor. Less than forty made their escape to the main body of the American army.[2]

[1] McAfee, *War in the Western Country*, 184; Dawson, *Harrison*, 293, 374, App. *n.* 8.
[2] *Niles' Register*, IV., 83 (Statement of Harrison's officers); James, *Military Occurrences*, I., 189, 420.

Weakened by this great loss, Harrison was at once compelled to retreat from the Maumee; his army was reduced to a handful by the expiration of the terms of enlistment of the militia in February, and the remainder would have been unsafe had a real leader commanded the British forces. With all the sacrifice of men and money, Harrison had gained nothing, and had added the gloom and discouragement of one more defeat. Nevertheless, he set himself to the difficult task of getting together another force, while he waited for Perry to secure control of Lake Erie. When at last, on September 12, he received the famous message from Perry: "We have met the enemy, and they are ours," he had assembled a force ample for the invasion of Upper Canada, and had reasonable hopes of success, now that the support of Perry's fleet for transport and protection was assured.[1]

The last of September, 1813, found Harrison's main force of forty-five hundred men safely landed near Malden, and the British retreating from the charred ruins of Malden and Detroit. Proctor's decision to abandon these places greatly disgusted Tecumseh, who contemptuously compared Proctor, in his presence, "to a fat animal that carries its tail upon its back, but when affrighted it drops it between its legs and runs off." The Americans were soon in pursuit of the fugitive army, and on October 5 overtook it on the banks of the Thames River, where a signal

---

[1] *Niles' Register*, V., 60, 99.

victory was won by Harrison and his able, energetic young lieutenant, Richard M. Johnson.[1]

Among the Indians slain in this short, sharp little battle, was Tecumseh, who, after all, represented the real force which made the British western campaign possible. Henry Adams graphically sums up the influence of this Indian element in the war in the northwest thus: "Not more than seven or eight hundred British soldiers ever crossed the Detroit River; but the United States raised fully twenty thousand men, and spent at least five million dollars and many lives in expelling them. The Indians alone made this outlay necessary. The campaign of Tippecanoe, the surrender of Detroit and Mackinac, the massacres at Fort Dearborn, the River Raisin, and Fort Meigs, the murders along the frontier, and the campaign of 1813, were the price paid for the Indian lands in the Wabash Valley."[2] By the victory of the Thames, the west was at length secure; the British forces driven out, beyond hope of return, and their Indian allies powerless. The United States felt so secure in its repossession of Michigan and the northwest, that Harrison dismissed most of his troops.

From this successful recovery of Lake Erie and the west, one turns to the miserable story of renewed campaigns in northern and western New

---

[1] Richardson, *War of 1812* (1902 ed.), 206 (Tecumseh's speech), 208 et seq.; *Niles' Register*, V., 130 (Harrison's report).

[2] Adams, *United States*, VII., 141.

York. Nothing could come from Dearborn's strategy; but when he was succeeded in July by General James Wilkinson, the prospect did not improve. Wilkinson was perhaps the scurviest knave who ever wore the straps of a general in the United States army; a man of low morality and shady reputation, conceited, insubordinate, and untrustworthy, who happened to have been friendly with Armstrong in the Revolutionary army. Scott in later years referred to him as an "unprincipled imbecile."[1] Alongside him, but not subordinate to him, was Major General Wade Hampton, who was to command the army on the Champlain route, receiving his orders directly from the war department. Hampton was a high-strung, proud, capable, sensitive South Carolina planter, and an able general. He hated Wilkinson with a fine and worthy hatred, and despised him with all his ardent soul. Had he known the relations with Wilkinson into which his acceptance of the northern command would put him, he would probably never have accepted it. Yet it was this utterly ill-mated pair who were set to a co-operative movement against Canada. Armstrong so well understood the situation that he even went to the front and joined Wilkinson's forces, in the endeavor to keep the generals to the execution of the plans of the department, which called for an attack on Kingston, followed by a descent of the St. Lawrence; and a union of the two armies in an attack

[1] Winfield Scott, *Memoirs*, I., 94 *n.*

on the strongly protected city of Montreal, which had at this time, in and around it, nearly fifteen thousand men under arms.[1]

With capable generals co-operating cordially in the campaign there would have been some prospect of success, but as it was there was nothing to illumine the failure of Wilkinson's expedition down the river from Sackett's Harbor with three thousand men, in October and November, 1813; while such skirmishes as that at Chrystler's Farm, in which two thousand Americans were defeated by eight hundred Canadians, were nothing short of a downright disgrace.[2] Hampton had marched according to orders, with his four thousand men, from Plattsburg north to the boundary, and then west to Chateaugay to hold the British in check. After waiting in this isolated and dangerous position until he was convinced that Wilkinson meant no real attack that winter upon the city of the Royal Mount, he marched his men back to Plattsburg without orders. Wilkinson returned to northern New York and also went into winter quarters, thus ending an entirely fruitless and almost bloodless campaign. The twelve thousand men then in the camps in the north had scarcely earned the quiet and safety of their rough quarters.[3]

Hampton resigned in March; Wilkinson asked for

[1] Wilkinson, *Memoirs*, III., 449, and App. xxiv.
[2] Cf. Winsor, VII., 458; H. Adams, VII., 188.
[3] *Am. State Paps., Military*, I., 461.

and received in March and April one more court-martial with the usual coat of whitewash. Armstrong went on his haughty and harsh way until forced out by the capture of Washington.[1] In place of these incompetents and mutual enemies, Madison appointed two new major-generals, George Izard and Jacob Brown, and six new brigadiers, including Winfield Scott, Macomb, and Gaines, to carry on the northern campaigns of 1814. All of these appointments were rewards of merit and in recognition of demonstrated ability. Improvement in the operations for 1814 naturally followed, though the results were not of the first magnitude in importance. Brown was of Quaker parentage, without military training, but he proved himself everywhere a soldier who believed that war meant fighting. He marched first to Sackett's Harbor in the spring of 1814, then on to the Niagara frontier, where he found an efficient little army which the energy and skill of Scott had succeeded in making out of the raw material furnished. The total American force present and ready for duty under General Brown in June, 1814, was not far from thirty-five hundred men. Opposing him the British forces on the Niagara numbered less than three thousand.[2]

The test of force came speedily. July 5, Scott's thirteen hundred men met Riall's fifteen hundred at

---

[1] See below, p. 141.
[2] *Niles' Register*, VII., 32; Adams, *United States*, VII., 407–410.

Chippewa, and won a signal victory, the American loss being 297, the British loss, because of the superiority of the marksmanship of the Americans, 515.[1] The work of a real soldier like Scott made its unmistakable showing, justifying his recent promotion. Three weeks later, in the murderous battle at Lundy's Lane, the result, after five hours of fierce fighting, was practically a victory for the Americans, though the field eventually remained in possession of the British. Again the losses showed the quality of the troops engaged and the spirit which animated them. The Americans "do not know when they are beaten," said one of the English officers who had seen service in the Peninsula; "they do not know when they ought to go away."[2] Lieutenant-General Drummond reported the losses of the British as a total of 879 out of an army of three thousand, while General Brown reckoned a loss of 853 out of two thousand rank and file.[3] Drummond, Riall, Brown, and Scott were all wounded in action.

The net results of the Niagara campaign were quite disproportionate to the efforts and sacrifices of the Americans, for the arrival of new troops to reinforce the English forces more than offset the advantages which came to the men under Brown and Scott from their experience and drilling. At the end

---

[1] James, *Military Occurrences*, II., 431, 434; Winfield Scott, *Memoirs*, 130 et seq.

[2] *Niles' Register*, VII., 410 (letter from a Halifax paper).

[3] Adams, *United States*, VIII., 62.

of the campaign the United States held no considerable post on the Canadian side, for they had been obliged to abandon Fort Erie, which they held for a short time. Madison wrote to Jefferson, October 23: "The most that can fairly be hoped for by us now is that the campaign may end where it is."[1] The defeat of the British expedition which under General Prevost, attempted to penetrate New York by the Lake Champlain route, was in reality so much a naval victory that its features are discussed in the following chapter.

[1] Madison, *Works* (Congress ed.), II., 591.

CHAPTER VII

THE NAVAL WAR

(1812–1814)

THE hope of the war party at the breaking out of hostilities was in the army — regulars supplemented by volunteers and militia. Though the war was to be made against the greatest commercial and naval power of the world, little or no thought was devoted to the preparation of the navy. The policy of the Jeffersonian Republicans towards this arm of the service had long been one of neglect and disdain; the navy was a Federalist institution, chiefly recruited from the Federal states of New England and from New York. Jefferson had once proposed to put all the naval vessels out of commission, hauling them up into fresh-water coves, and putting them under cover; at another time the Republicans pinned their faith in a navy upon a hundred and seventy gunboats which were more dangerous to their crews than to the enemy, and which hardly dared to go upon the high seas without securely stowing away the single gun which each carried. In 1812 there were more officers than ships, and, in justice to all, rotation in command was established

at the beginning of the war, so that each officer might
have his chance to win fame and glory for the nation
and for himself.

The navy in commission at the beginning of the
war consisted of three "vessels of the first class"
—the *President,* Commodore Rodgers, the *United
States*, Captain Decatur, and the *Constitution;* three
"vessels of the second class"— the *Congress*, the
Essex, and the *Adams;* three sloops and five brigs,
besides two hundred and fifty-seven small gunboats
mounting usually a single gun. A few other vessels
were undergoing repairs, while three or four hulks
were beyond that possibility. Two policies were
open to the administration in handling this little
navy: to harbor it and husband it, or to scatter it
and use it against the enemy wherever possible.
Most of the naval officers urged the latter, and they
were right. Sailing in companies of two or three,
or even singly, they would compel the British to
maintain a large number of vessels in convoy service,
and in the blockade of such ports as the British
meant to invest. Fortunately this policy was
adopted, and war had scarcely been declared when
Commodore Rodgers with three ships hurried to
sea from New York to try his chances against the
Jamaica convoy. While his cruise of seventy days
produced neither great victory nor rich prize it did
have the effect of restricting the movements of
British naval vessels.[1]

[1] Maclay, *Hist. of the Navy* (ed. of 1901), I., 317, 530, 531.

The chief events which characterized the fighting upon the ocean during 1812 were the four victories of the Americans in great sea-duels. Three days after Hull's disgraceful surrender of Detroit, his nephew, Captain Hull, from whom he must be carefully distinguished, commanding the ship *Constitution*, of forty-four guns, met the *Guerrière*, a frigate of thirty-eight guns, Captain Dacres, some three hundred miles off the coast of Nova Scotia. In half an hour the British ship was lying "a helpless hulk in the trough of heavy sea, rolling the muzzles of her guns under." After surrendering to her American victor she was found to be so badly damaged that it was impossible to take her into port as a prize, and she was burned. If General Hull had lost a province, Captain Hull had won a realm of vastly greater importance. In their ecstasy and exultation, the American people did not stop to consider the distinct superiority (estimated at thirty per cent.) of the *Constitution* in size, armament, and crew.[1] It was enough for them that the "sacred spell of the invincibility of the British navy was broken" by this first surrender of a British ship of war to a scorned and despised enemy whose navy was a "few fir-built frigates, manned by a handful of bastards and outlaws."[2]

[1] Mahan, "War of 1812," in *Scribner's Mag.*, XXXV., 344.
[2] Hansard, *Parl. Debates*, XXIV., 643, Canning's speech in the Commons, 1813; *Niles' Register*, III., 271, quoting London *Evening Star.*

The second of these ship-duels occurred in the middle of October, and though the *Wasp* defeated the British ship *Frolic*, both vessels were taken by another British man-of-war and carried to the Bermuda Islands. A week later Captain Decatur of the frigate *United States*, forty-four guns, defeated the *Macedonian*, thirty-eight guns, off the Madeira Islands, and took the prize to Newport. In late December, Captain Bainbridge of the *Constitution*, defeated the *Java*, thirty-eight guns, off the Brazilian coast, and destroyed the vessel. Among the prisoners found aboard were ten impressed American seamen. Bainbridge paroled the remainder of the prisoners at San Salvador, and reached Boston in February.

The loss of the three war vessels in itself was to the British government a trifling matter, but the humiliation of British pride resulting from this series of American victories produced in England a depression almost as exaggerated as the American jubilation. Canning declared in 1813, from the Opposition benches, to be sure, that the loss of these vessels "produced a sensation in the country scarcely to be equalled by the most violent convulsion of nature."[1] England was invaded by sea; she was attacked in her most boasted strength. Though the feeling was that of a tingling, insulting blow, rather than a serious shock, irritating and disconcerting rather than dangerous, the British recognized that

[1] Hansard, *Parl. Debates*, XXIV., 643.

the effect upon America would be far-reaching, stimulating American patriotism, awakening pride in the navy and exultation in its achievements after the disasters at Detroit and Niagara, and making probable a more united support of the war. The London papers endeavored to minimize the effect of the American successes by declaring that the American vessels were really line-of-battle ships in disguise.

Gratification of the people of the United States over these successful attacks on that agency which England had most used to oppress and degrade American citizens and American authority and to violate American rights, led to almost hysterical manifestations of joy. The heroes of the fights were given great banquets, were voted medals and swords, and listened to innumerable eulogistic orations. Even the Republicans felt compelled to adopt the navy as their own and to make provisions for its support and enlargement. An act of January, 1813, provided for the construction of four seventy-fours and six first-class frigates; and two months later the construction of six more war vessels was authorized, and the president given authority in his discretion to add ships of war on the Lakes. Pennsylvania and South Carolina even proposed to construct war vessels to be presented to the Union.[1]

The United States could not expect to continue

---

[1] *Niles' Register*, III., 268, 269; *U. S. Statutes at Large*, II., 789, 821.

the record of the victories of 1812. As soon as the British navy should really bestir itself, by very force of numbers and the weight of metal the American fleet would be overwhelmed; still, in duels between vessels of approximately even size, victories continued to be won by the United States. Captain Lawrence of the *Hornet* defeated the British sloop *Peacock*, eighteen guns, in a fifteen - minute contest in February, 1813. For this victory he was promoted to the command of the *Chesapeake*, then in Boston Harbor, and while blockaded there by the British vessels he accepted the invitation of Captain Broke of the *Shannon* to a fight outside of Boston Harbor, ship for ship. In spite of the fact that the *Chesapeake* had new officers and a green, untrained crew, part of whom had but just arrived on board, Lawrence, with more courage than judgment, prepared for battle. In a fifteen-minute fight on June 1, the raking fire of the *Shannon* disabled the *Chesapeake* and mortally wounded Captain Lawrence, whose last order, "Don't give up the ship," became a famous watchword during the war and after. The loss of the *Chesapeake*, and the death of Lawrence, "a very Bayard of the sea," were serious matters for the United States, for it signified the renewal of British vigor in blockading and in attacking American vessels.[1]

---

[1] Roosevelt, *Naval War* (3d ed.), 178–194; James, *Naval Occurrences*, chap. ix., App. No. 36; *Niles' Register*, IV., 102, 276.

From the work of the regular navy, attention must be turned to the irregular naval warfare. The large shipping interests of the United States, which had been developed in the prosperous years before 1806, had in several ways prepared both men and vessels for a successful attack upon British commerce. The coasting trade, the West India trade, the trade with Europe, and the fisheries, called forth and disciplined multitudes of sailors. During the embargo and non-intercourse struggles, much attention was given to the building of swift-sailing clipper-ships, to engage in the carrying trade with colonies of European belligerents, in spite of the war of decrees and orders. It was unquestionably true at the outbreak of the war that the American ships were the best-built and best-manned in the world. Furthermore, the restrictive policy of the year preceding the war had been the best possible foundation for building up privateering. Capital was idle, many ships were temporarily out of commission, and many a shipowner and sailor was eager for a chance to make prize of the enemy's ships.

From the beginning, therefore, the American navy sought to strike at the enemy's enormous commerce, which was "strictly analogous to the impairing of an enemy's communications, of the line of supplies connecting an army with its base of operations, upon the maintenance of which the life of the army depends. Money, credit, is the life of war; lessen it, and vigor flags; destroy it, and resistance dies."[1] Measured by the number of vessels in the navy, the Americans were twenty to six hundred and twenty; but in power to inflict damage upon the enemy's commerce by means of war vessels and privateers, the disparity was by no means so great. In the first place, Great Britain's enormous trade with the West Indies, carried on in large, slow going vessels, must pass for a long distance parallel with the shore of the United States, an easy prey to cruisers and privateers. In the second place, swift, elusive, audacious vessels, flying a piece of striped bunting, soon found their way almost to the docks of England.

The navy, however, was too small, too subject to systematic attack, and too reduced as the war wore on, to keep up the work of destruction. Hence, coincident with the beginning of the war, privateers began to appear along the American coasts, though privateering was distinctly less respectable than it was before the agitation at the close of the preceding century. The sections from which privateers would be most naturally expected by reason of the occupation of its people, New England, New York, and Maryland, had the least hostility for the British; and it was not at first clear to the New England mind that it was just to despoil the property of his honorable British correspondent, merely because the Republicans of Virginia, South Carolina, and the west had chosen to declare war on England rather

[1] Mahan, "War of 1812," in *Scribner's Mag.*, XXXV., 191.

than on equally criminal and offensive France, with whom America had little trade.

But the combined motives of necessity, plunder, and revenge soon overcame all scruples, and prompted the sending out of numerous privateers from Salem, Boston, New York, Philadelphia, and Baltimore. Idle vessels, idle pilot-boats, and idle sailors, the result of British orders and French decrees and American embargoes and non-intercourse acts, found immediate occupation. The vessels themselves had been built to evade British cruisers; they were fast-sailing, easily handled craft, and over and over again demonstrated that it took more than one cruiser to catch and hold them. "If pursued (they) 'put on their sea-wings' and laughed at the clumsy English pursuers," said the London *Times* in February, 1815.[1] The very names themselves indicate something of the spirit prompting this form of attack upon British interests: *Orders in Council; The Right of Search; Bunker Hill; True-Blooded Yankee; United We Stand.* A month after the declaration of war, sixty-five privateers were in search of British merchantmen; and within six months three hundred prizes had been taken by public and private vessels of the United States. *Niles' Weekly Register* from the beginning of the war until late in 1814, published a regular list of American prizes, and maintained steadily as a heading for the list as it mounted up past the thousand mark, this quotation from the *British Naval Register:*

[1] Quoted in Adams, *United States*, VIII., 210.

"The winds and seas are Britain's wide domain,
And not a sail, but by *permission*, spreads!"[1]

Privateering was by no means all profit; the risks were large and the recapture of prizes not infrequent. Long cruises were made without falling in with any prince, and frequently the sale of prizes was so low as to leave no profit at all. Of the total of five hundred and twenty-six privateers sent out from the United States during the war, only two hundred and seven are reported as taking any prizes, and at the end of the war only about sixty were still afloat under the American flag. For these reasons the privateersmen petitioned Congress for remission of the duty upon the goods which they brought into America. When the British began to maintain a rigorous blockade of the American ports by British cruisers, the privateersmen betook themselves to British waters, especially the English Channel and the Irish Sea.[2]

The second year of the war saw a distinct diminution in the number of privateers; but at no time during the war were these naval auxiliaries absent, or deficient in daring, or in the seriousness of their attacks upon British commerce. The career of the *General Armstrong* illustrates the distinction some of them attained, almost entitling the schooner to

---

[1] *Niles' Register*, III., 120, 270 (list of privateers).
[2] *Ibid.*, 187, 276; Maclay, *Am. Privateers*, 506, places the total number at 515.

rank as a ship of the line.[1] The *Governor Tompkins* burned fourteen vessels in the British Channel, and the assaults upon British ships almost in sight of the English ports from which they had sailed, compelled the London *Morning Chronicle*, in August, 1814, to admit that the Irish coast "from Wexford round by Cape Clear and Carrickfergus" was blockaded by "a few petty fly-by-nights."[2] The London *Times*, which seven years before had threatened that Americans would not be able to go from Staten Island to New York without British permission, had now to record that British vessels sailing across the Irish Channel must either get leave from American privateers or pay an insurance of thirteen guineas in the hundred pounds.[3]

Captain Boyle of the privateer *Chasseur*, which put thirty prizes to his credit, including the schooner *St. Lawrence* of the royal navy, sent to London in 1814, for posting at Lloyds' Coffee-House, a proclamation in imitation of those issued by Sir John Warren and Sir Alexander Cochrane, in which he announced "by virtue of the power and authority in me vested (possessing sufficient force) [I] declare all the ports, harbors, bays, creeks, rivers, inlets, outlets, islands and sea coasts of the United Kingdom . . . in a state of strict and rigorous blockade."[4] Glasgow

[1] Maclay, *Am. Privateers*, chaps. xiii., xiv.; *Am. State Paps.*, *Naval*, I., 493.   [2] Adams, *United States*, VIII., 197.

[3] *Niles' Register*, VII., 190; *Parl. Papers*, 1814–1815, IX., No. 45.

[4] *Niles' Register*, VII., 290; Coggeshall, *Am. Privateers*, 358 (sketch of Boyle's work).

and London merchants, ship - owners and under-writers memorialized the admiralty in September, 1814, for better protection against this "new system of warfare," declaring that in two years "above eight hundred vessels have been captured by the power whose maritime strength we have hitherto impoliticly held in contempt."[1] The damage done by this fleet of privateers was not a vital matter to British commerce, for, compared to the whole trade of the nation, it could not have been great. But the irritation of the continual menace to her ships and merchants, especially after the close of the Napoleonic wars had opened so many new markets to British trade, made the British shipping interests less tolerant of the lax administration of the admiralty. In certain industries like cotton manufacturing, there was real distress. Early in 1814 the quotation for sea-island cotton reached four shillings and one penny per pound, while a little later the freight from America to Europe rose to ten pence per pound.[2] "Doubtless the privateer contributed more than the regular navy to bring about a disposition for peace in the British classes most responsible for the war."[3]

To return to the operations of the regular navies, a manifesto of the prince-regent of England, issued

[1] *Parl. Papers*, 1814–1815, IX., Nos. 45, 60 (memorials and the replies of the admiralty).
[2] Williams, *Liverpool Privateers*, 452.
[3] Adams, *United States*, VII., 331.

in January, 1813, was a sort of counter-declaration of war, reciting the history of the causes and stating the principles by which the conduct of Great Britain was governed. It showed plainly that henceforth Great Britain meant to put forth renewed effort to blockade the ports of the United States, thus protecting British commerce and compelling the United States to divert part of its strength from the Canadian frontier. In other words, England was to invade from the sea as well as from the Canadian provinces.[1] Rear-Admiral Sir George Cockburn was sent out to command the expedition against the most important and vulnerable part of the coast south of New York. His attention was principally fixed upon the Chesapeake Bay with its rare combination of interests in Washington, the capital of the nation; Norfolk, a prominent naval station; and Baltimore, an important commercial centre. Furthermore, two American frigates, one at Norfolk and one in the Potomac, were to be captured or shut in, just as the *United States* and *Macedonian* were rendered useless by the British blockade of New London and Narragansett Bay.

By October, 1813, the blockade of the American coast south of Cape Cod was so effective that not a single American man-of-war was free to protect the Atlantic coast, and scarcely a vessel flying the American flag was able to enter or leave a port. The whole situation was summed up in the bitter wail

[1] Hansard, *Parl. Debates*, XXIV., 363.

of a Boston Federalist in November: "Our coasts are not navigable to ourselves though free to the enemies and money-making neutral; our harbors blocked, our shipping destroyed or rotting at the docks; silence and stillness in our cities, grass growing on the public wharves." [1] Out of forty-four vessels clearing Boston for foreign ports in three weeks of December, only five were American.[2]

The whole story of the British blockade of the American coast during 1813–1814 is singularly free from striking incidents or conflicts, with the exception of attacks on Washington and Baltimore. The American ships-of-war were either bottled up, or afloat in distant waters, like the *Essex* in the Pacific; the commercial vessels were either floating idly at the wharves, or had turned privateers seeking British shipping in the West Indies or on the European side of the Atlantic. The most that could be done by the blockading squadrons was to seize, carry off, or burn everything that floated, and to destroy all that could contribute to national resistance. The harassing of the shores, however, was carried on in a mild and gentlemanly fashion— private property being respected, or if it were levied upon, payment was made, unless the owners offered resistance. The opposition to the great numbers of line-of-battle ships, frigates, sloops, and

[1] Mahan, "War of 1812," in *Scribner's Mag.*, XXXVI., 495.
[2] *Niles' Register*, V., 311.

transports which entered the Chesapeake, was confined to a flotilla of gunboats consisting of three or four sloops and schooners and a miscellaneous collection of barges, sometimes hardly larger than a ship's boat.[1] This effectiveness of blockade is confirmed by the statement of a writer in *Niles' Weekly Register*, December 3, 1814, that there had not been an arrival in Baltimore from a foreign port for a twelvemonth.[2]

The cruise of the *Essex*, thirty-two guns, Captain Porter, was illustrative both of the quality of American seamanship and the method by which naval war was carried on after the severe blockade began. At the outbreak of the war the *Essex* was in New York Harbor for repairs. Putting to sea a month later, Captain Porter cruised the Atlantic for the remainder of the year, endeavoring to cut out his share of the convoyed merchant-vessels of Great Britain. The results of this cruise were ten prizes with four hundred and twenty-three men. The next cruise took the *Essex* to the south Atlantic, and finally around Cape Horn, where Porter made attacks upon British whaling interests centring about the Galapagos Islands. After destroying a dozen whalers, and in consequence driving all others from that part of the ocean, he went to the south Pacific islands to refit his ship. In February, 1814, he reached Valparaiso, where his ships were block-

[1] Roosevelt, *Naval War* (3d ed.), 317.
[2] *Niles' Register*, VII., 194.

aded and captured in March.[1] Among the prisoners taken by the British from the *Essex* and *Essex Jr.*, a refitted prize, was David G. Farragut, a midshipman then thirteen years old, who fought so gallantly in the civil war nearly fifty years later.

This cruise of a year and a half in enemy's waters, or in open sea far from any harbor of the United States, is one of the unique episodes of modern naval warfare. The *Essex* was obliged to live off the enemy, providing herself with everything needed, cordage and sails, guns and anchors, provisions, medicines, and even money to pay the officers and men. The story of this vessel is the American counterpart of the voyages of Sir Francis Drake in the Pacific in the sixteenth century, with the exception that Porter was unable to return home with the results of his spoiling of the enemy.[2]

The naval war upon the Lakes was scarcely second in importance to the naval contests upon the Atlantic. The success of the American attack upon Canada was dependent upon control of lakes Erie, Ontario, and Champlain. Both parties recognized this fact, and made prompt and vigorous efforts to establish fleets for the control of these inland waters. At the beginning of the war, the two Lake fleets were about equal in strength. The Americans had a slight predominance upon Lake Ontario, while the

[1] Cf. Porter, *Journal of a Cruise made to the Pacific Ocean;* Roosevelt, *Naval War* (3d ed.), 78, 134, 164, 291.

[2] Maclay, *Hist. of the Navy* (1901 ed.), I., 575.

British were substantially in control of Lake Erie. With the loss of a small American brig to the British at the capture of Detroit, there was on Lake Erie no war-vessel flying the American flag. The co-operation of the American fleet from Sackett's Harbor, at the eastern end of Lake Ontario, with the armies intended to operate against Niagara and Montreal, was one of the essential features of the northern campaign. The transportation of more men from Buffalo and Cleveland to Detroit for its recapture, after its surrender by Hull, was so vitally important that measures for the construction of a new fleet upon Lake Erie were taken before the end of 1812. Commodore Chauncey to this end sent Commander Jesse Elliot to Buffalo, to create a naval force by construction or by purchase of Lake schooners. He made his beginning, however, by capturing a small Canadian brig, the *Caledonia*, which had anchored at Fort Erie, two miles from Buffalo.[1]

The work of constructing a fleet upon Lake Erie was a slow and difficult task; it was therefore fortunate that a man of the energy and resourcefulness of Captain Oliver Hazard Perry, a young officer in gunboat service at Newport, was sent to take charge on Lake Erie. When he reached Presqu'isle, now known as Erie, the ship-carpenters had on the stocks two twenty-gun brigs, a schooner, and three gunboats, besides several other craft in preparation

---

[1] Roosevelt, *Naval War* (3d ed.), chap. iv.

at Black Rock, near Buffalo. With the exception of timber, nearly everything had to be brought by slow and difficult transportation from Philadelphia by way of Pittsburg, there being water-transport from the latter place by way of the Alleghany River and its tributaries to within fifteen miles of Lake Erie. So came the iron, guns, ammunition, sails, cordage, and provisions. Some of the iron for construction was gathered in scraps from stores, warehouses, and farms; wagon-tires, hinges, and pots, all counted. Buffalo contributed a thousand pounds, and Pittsburg still more. Most of the workmen came from Philadelphia.

Through the summer of 1813 the work went on vigorously; and when the British fleet, moved by lack of provisions, attacked Perry in September, his improvised fleet created by capture, purchase, and construction, consisted of six vessels, which in tonnage, men, and metal outranked the British. The victory which he won over the British on September 10, 1813, was fraught with immense political and military consequences.[1] The result was summed up in his laconic despatch to General Harrison: "We have met the enemy and they are ours. Two ships, two brigs, one schooner, and one sloop."[2]

The destruction of the British fleet gave the United States supremacy on Lake Erie and compelled the abandonment of Malden and Detroit; it recovered

---

[1] Roosevelt, *Naval War* (3d ed.), 254–281.
[2] *Niles' Register*, V., 60.

Michigan, and made a real invasion of Canada once more a possibility, for by means of the control of the Lakes thus given, Harrison was enabled to enter at once upon an aggressive campaign on the Canadian side of Lake Erie. His men were easily transported to the north side, and his line of communication was no longer threatened by a British fleet. Its effect too upon the American people was decidedly important; for the first time an American fleet had met a British fleet and defeated it. Nor was it fair to discount the significance of the victory by saying that the vessels were small and of hasty construction. The charm of British invincibility had been broken in the great ship duels which made the names of Decatur, Bainbridge, and Hull household words. To this list was now added the name of Perry, who was looked upon by the Americans as a hero of the same class as Nelson; and he in his turn received their adulation, evidenced by receptions, illuminations, and presentation swords.

Other events on the Lakes during 1813 were of small consequence. Commodore Chauncey and Sir James Yeo divided control of Lake Ontario, first one and then the other turning the balance in his favor by building a new vessel. In similar fashion, the following year saw the capture of Oswego and the blockade of Sackett's Harbor by the British; and the capture of Toronto in 1813 was matched in 1814 by the blockade of Kingston. The only large and significant event upon the Lakes during 1814 was the splendid victory of the Americans on Lake Champlain. Sir George Prevost, in command of an army of eleven thousand men, the most formidable which Great Britain ever sent to America, undertook in the summer of 1814 the invasion of New York by the route which General Burgoyne had taken thirty-seven years before. The success of this expedition naturally depended upon control of Lake Champlain, since the existence of a hostile fleet on this water would be a continual menace to the flank and rear of the British column, and to its necessary connection with Canada.[1]

The British already possessed upon the lake a fleet consisting of one brig, two sloops, and about a dozen gunboats, and the construction of a large frigate to be known as the *Confiance*, thirty-seven guns, was begun. The Americans realized the vital importance of the control of the lake, for they were unable to place in the field a force sufficient to impede the progress of the British army, much less to defeat such veterans as made up its regiments. General McComb, in command of the troops at Plattsburg, could muster not more than two thousand effectives.[2] Supporting the army, the Americans had on the lake a fleet consisting of one heavy corvette, two smaller vessels, and ten gunboats or galleys, with a large brig in process of construction. In command of this little squadron was Captain

[1] *Niles' Register*, VII., 41–45; James, *Military Occurrences*, II., 206.　　　　　　　[2] *Niles' Register*, VII., 60.

Thomas Macdonough, a young man of thirty years who had received his training in the Mediterranean wars. Both fleets on the lake were more or less deficient in stores and equipment, and the gunboats on both sides were in part manned by soldiers. By any fair measurement, the advantage of the British in guns and equipment was almost as great as that which characterized the army.

The plans for the battle showed Macdonough's superiority over the common run of commanders. He carefully provided against possible disaster, placing his vessels in such a way as to utilize to the full the advantages of the geographical situation. In fact, it might be called a naval battle with a natural land backing. The most dramatic incident of the fight illustrates the quality of Macdonough's ability. After two hours of fighting, the British squadron had a very distinct advantage and was on the point of taking the whole American fleet because Macdonough's chief vessel, the *Saratoga*, became disabled. He promptly devised means for turning the vessel half-way round by the operation known as "winding ship," so as to present to the enemy what was substantially a new and fresh vessel. This resourcefulness saved the day, and during the folfowing half-hour the *Confiance* struck her colors, and was followed by other vessels of the squadron.[1]

This battle resulting in such a distinguished American victory was one of the most stubbornly con-

---

[1] *Niles' Register*, VII., 41; James, *Naval Occurrences*, 401 et seq.

tested of the war, and added one more hero who could rank with Perry in public estimation. He received a vote of thanks and a gold medal from Congress, and later the state of Vermont gave him a farm overlooking the scene of his victory. The decisiveness of this battle was evident at once to the British. Hardly was the result known, when measures were taken for the retreat of Prevost's army into Canada.[1] At best, Prevost's assault upon the land forces had been so poor as to give little aid to the fleet; and for this failure and his prompt retreat, Prevost was ordered to trial by court-martial, but died before the trial could take place. The war was practically ended by this retreat of the British army from Plattsburg into Canada. It would seem as though the persistent mismanagement of the American forces in northern New York, the incompetency of Dearborn and Wilkinson, the strange interference of Secretary Armstrong, the diversion of the forces of Izard from the front of Prevost's army, were all atoned for by the brilliancy of the accomplishment of Commodore Macdonough and his handful of sailors and soldiers on Lake Champlain.

[1] James, *Military Occurrences*, II., 461 (Prevost's report); *Niles' Register*, VII., 44, 60; Roosevelt, *Naval War* (3d ed.), 398.

CHAPTER VIII

THE SOUTHWEST AND THE CENTRE
(1813-1815)

IN another quarter the campaigns of 1813 and 1814 were important — in the southwest. The people of Tennessee, Georgia, and Mississippi territory expected that Florida would be their share of the spoils of war, just as Canada would be the reward of the north and west. Had not the United States already taken West Florida and occupied Amelia Island, as evidences of its attitude towards the strip of Spanish territory north of the Gulf? In the winter of 1812-1813, at the call of the war department, the governor of Tennessee despatched Andrew Jackson, major-general of the militia of that state, with two thousand men down the Mississippi to Natchez, there to wait for marching orders, which would, it was expected, direct a movement against Mobile and the "lower country." Congress was already considering the relation of Florida to the course of the war, and the first proposal discussed in the Senate was to sanction the occupation of all or any part of East Florida. But Congress was not willing to go quite so far even in secret session, as it had gone in 1811; and finally authorized the president, by the special act of February 12, 1813, to take possession of Mobile and the portion of Florida west of the Perdido.[1]

Thus once more Madison's enemies in the Senate thwarted his desires; and since the troops under Jackson could not be used to occupy Pensacola and St. Augustine, they were ordered dismissed at Natchez, five hundred miles from home. Jackson was angry with the administration, at what seemed to be deception on its part, or what might be a device for coercing the militia to enter the volunteer service; and he marched his troops back to Tennessee on his own guarantee of their rations and pay. Secretary Armstrong later explained the matter to Jackson in a letter in which he thanked the Tennesseeans for their services, which would have been needed "had the Executive policy of occupying the two Floridas been adopted by the national legislature." He further mollified the irascible general by allowing the claims for the expenses of his troops on their return march. While the actual occupation of West Florida to the Perdido, and the erection of Fort Bowyer on Mobile Bay, was carried out by General Wilkinson during the spring of 1813, another year was to elapse before General Jackson could make his longed-for assault on the Spanish

---

[1] See above, p. 27; *Annals of Cong.*, 12 Cong., 2 Sess., 124–127; *U. S. Statutes at Large*, III., 472.

province and plant the American flag at Pensacola.[1]

The part of the campaign in the southwest most directly connected with the welfare of the United States was the subjugation of the Indians of the Alabama country. The state of Georgia had long set the fashion of maltreating those Indians within her borders who were settled upon lands which the white man coveted both passively and actively. As the settlements spread to the westward and came in contact with the Creeks and other partly civilized tribes, the irritation of the Indians became acute. The half-civilized tribes took deeper and deeper root as they developed, under the guidance of the federal government, away from the hunting stage to the cultivation of fields; and every piece of evidence that the Indians might remain in the region permanently, roused fresh antagonism among the Georgians and Tennesseeans. The Creeks and Seminoles were by temperament and by their nearness to the weak and poverty - stricken Spaniards, at a disadvantage in their fight against the white "civilization," when compared with the aggressive Indians of the northwest, who profited by the strength of their accommodating British neighbors. The spirit of resistance in the southwest was stirred especially by the visit of Tecumseh in 1811, and by the movements of warriors

[1] *MSS.* in war department, quoted by Adams, *United States*, VII., 210; Parton, *Jackson*, I., 377-382, 384 (Benton's account).

back and forth between the Shawnees and Creeks in the two years thereafter. By August, 1813, the Creek country was aroused: two thousand Indians were brandishing their war-clubs—hence the epithet of Red Clubs or Red Sticks often applied to these Indians and frequent attacks were made on the white settlers.

The climax was reached in the massacre of two hundred and fifty whites at Fort Mims, August 30. A veritable Macedonian cry for help struck a responsive chord in Tennessee, and within six weeks, with his usual energy and promptness, Jackson was at Huntsville in northern Alabama with twenty-five hundred Tennessee militiamen, ready to push into the Creek region. But the army was one of those kaleidoscopic militia forces which changed almost daily with the expiration of service of different sections, so that the year ended with little accomplished beyond the killing of seven or eight hundred of the northern Creeks, certainly the least offending division of the tribe. All through the spring and early summer of 1814, Jackson and his little army, which now reached five thousand men, were fighting the Creeks, killing them off by the hundreds, though not always without paying well for their victories. For example, at the Horseshoe, in March, Jackson lost fifty-one killed and about one hundred and fifty wounded, many of them by arrows, so primitive was still the mode of fighting among these Creeks who warred against the United States.

The dead Indians numbered at least eight hundred and fifty.[1]

The campaign closed with the signing by the Creeks of the hard treaty of capitulation of August 9, 1814, in which Jackson compelled them to cede to the United States, as an indemnity for the expenses of the war — and for the benefit of the whites of Georgia, Alabama, and Tennessee in their westward progress—two-thirds of their vast territory; and to withdraw from the southern and western parts of Alabama, thus surrounding themselves with white settlers.[2] For the future of the southwest this conquest of the Creeks was cardinally important, opening up as it did a great tract of new country to settlement and to the expansion of slavery after the war. Jackson's reward for his successes in this Indian campaign was, in May, 1814, a major-generalship in the regular army and the command of the district which included Mobile and New Orleans. Thus many mighty issues for Jackson and for the United States depended on the outcome of this Creek war— the defence of New Orleans, the later Seminole War, Florida, and the presidency of Jackson.

Meanwhile, the British were ready to take the offensive on land as well as by sea; and the year 1814 saw at three points the well-planned attacks of

[1] Parton, *Jackson*, I., 423 et seq.; *Am. State Paps., Indian*, I., 858; *Niles' Register*, V., 218, 240, 427.
[2] See map **p. 276**; U. S. Bureau of Ethnology, *Eighteenth Report*, pt. ii., 678, and maps Nos. 1, 15; *U. S. Statutes at Large*, VII., 120.

land forces supported by the navy—Lake Champlain, the Chesapeake, and the Gulf. The first of these has already been described.[1] The second and third were in part made possible by a new feature of the war —viz., the reinforcement of the British armies in America by large bodies of veteran troops released in Europe by the overthrow of Napoleon.

The blockade was also to be made more effective, but that at best was a negative sort of warfare and not suited to impress vividly upon all classes in America the might of their enemy and the impotence of their government. The continuance of the struggle for control of the lakes, especially Ontario and Champlain, was marked by no new methods or change of leadership, though General Brown and General Scott became the real directors of the movements of the troops in the north.

Great Britain naturally expected much from the experienced soldiers and officers who were sent from the victorious fields of Europe to carry on war against a crude and undisciplined half-militia army of artisans, farmers, and backwoodsmen. In June and July, 1814, enough troops were sent to Canada to raise the effective strength of Prevost's armies from sixteen thousand to twenty-nine thousand. Another division of some four thousand was sent under Major-General Ross of the Peninsular army "to effect a diversion on the coasts of the United States of America in favor of the army employed in the

[1] See above, p. 102.

defence of Upper and Lower Canada," at a point to be determined by Ross and Vice-Admiral Cochrane, who selected the cities of the Chesapeake. Still later in the year an army of ten thousand men who had seen seven years of service in the Peninsular campaigns was sent out under the leadership of Major-General Sir Edward Pakenham, a brother-in-law of the Duke of Wellington, and one of his ablest and most courageous lieutenants, to take the city of New Orleans. These preparations for the campaign of 1814, in their extent and carefulness, may well be compared with those made for the expedition of Burgoyne in 1777, when the British expected to divide the colonies and end the war of the Revolution.[1]

The blockade of Chesapeake Bay, which was maintained with more or less vigor after February, 1813, so that Maryland's export trade of four million five hundred thousand dollars in 1811 fell to two hundred and thirty-eight thousand dollars in 1814, did no positive damage to the cities on the bay, beyond the stoppage of their commerce. Attacks on Craney Island and Norfolk, where there was a navy-yard, were unsuccessful; but with the coming of Ross and his troops in August, 1814, the campaign took on new vigor and definiteness. The immediate object of attack was determined largely by events in a remote frontier region. More than a year before, during the campaign against York, or Toronto,

[1] Adams, *United States*, VIII., 124.

the capital of Upper Canada, the parliament buildings were burned by private soldiers quite without authority, so Dearborn declared at a later day. A similar and less excusable act of vandalism took place in May, 1814, when a handful of American soldiers, acting on their own responsibility, crossed over Lake Erie to Long Point, and destroyed some mills, distilleries, and houses. Though the officer commanding was afterwards tried by court-martial and censured for the raid, General Prevost wrote to Admiral Cochrane, who had succeeded Admiral Warren in command in American waters, suggesting that the latter should "assist in inflicting that measure of retaliation which shall deter the enemy from a repetition of similar outrages." The admiral promptly issued to the blockading squadrons instructions "to destroy and lay waste such towns and districts upon the coasts as you may find assailable," these orders to be in force until the American government should make proper restitution to the injured Canadians. He also notified Secretary Monroe of these orders to his fleet, under date of August 18, and received a rather tart reply after the secretary returned to the devastated capital.[1]

In the Chesapeake the British commanders might attack Baltimore, destroying its shipping, and could hope to annihilate the flotilla of gunboats com-

---

[1] Pitkin, *Statistical View* (2d ed.), 56; Adams, *United States*, VIII., 126, 128; *Am. State Paps., Foreign*, III., 693 (Monroe-Cochrane letters); *Niles' Register*, VII., 18.

manded by Captain Barney, which blockaded the Patuxent River. They were, however, most strongly attracted by the capital of the nation, for the dispersion of the great officers of the government and the suspension of administration are not only in themselves serious calamities, but they have a great moral effect upon any people. In the War of 1812 it was one of the prime objects of the British to bring the Republican government into such disrepute and scorn that it would have to make peace on British terms, or yield to a revolution favorable to British interests. Therefore, by the rules of war and of political strategy, the Chesapeake expedition in itself was wise and proper, though some of its incidents cannot be justified on any grounds.

The preparations of the United States to meet the invasion of the British were ridiculously inadequate. The hostile fleet had been in full command of the Chesapeake for nearly a year and a half, yet there was neither fortification of consequence nor army of appreciable size or efficiency for the protection of the capital. Though the cabinet had discussed the defence of Washington in early July, there was not a fort, a breastwork, a trench, or a battery, even on paper. The officer in command, General W. H. Winder, appointed for political rather than military reasons, was worse than useless, the very incarnation of incompetency, a fussy, nerveless man, who owed his appointment as brigadier-general in command of the military district to his kinship with the Federalist governor of Maryland. To make matters worse, Monroe, then secretary of state, had a penchant for military affairs, and undertook to interfere with the arrangements made under the orders of the secretary of war, who graciously called him a "busy and blundering tactician." [1]

The news of the landing of General Ross at Benedict, in Maryland, August 19, created a panic at Washington. To meet four thousand British veterans, requisitions for militia were hastily sent to the neighboring states, and all the troops in the vicinity were ordered out—an improvised army of raw militia, a Jeffersonian reliance. The usual hortatory proclamations were of course issued. The leisurely march of the British across a country described by the secretary of war as "covered with wood, and offering at every step strong positions for defence," was, except for the heat, almost a summer-holiday affair. The Americans selected Bladensburg as the place where opposition should be made to the advance of the enemy, and thither flowed an absurd array of secretaries, clerks, cabinet officers, the president himself, regulars, militia, and four hundred sailors from Barney's little fleet. Before the battle began, however, the president remarked to Monroe, "It would now be proper for us to retire in the rear, leaving the military movement to military men," the retirement being exe-

[1] *Am. State Paps., Military*, I., 524, 538; Armstrong, *Notices*, II., 140.

cuted with celerity barely sufficient to prevent their capture by the British.[1]

The motley crowd of seven thousand Americans which faced the British on August 24 can hardly be called an army, though its nucleus was about one thousand regulars and sailors. As seen by the British "Subaltern in America," they were mostly "country-people, who would have been more appropriately employed in attending to their agricultural occupations than in standing with muskets in their hands on the brow of a bare, green hill"; while Winder describes them as "a mass of men suddenly assembled, without organization, discipline, or officers of any, the least, knowledge of service." Twice did the Americans fire artillery and musket volleys at the enemy, and thus administer a slight check before retreating towards Georgetown. A few companies fell back in good order, but for the most part it was the retreat of a panic-stricken mob.

It was the presence of Barney's fighting sailors which alone dignifies the field of Bladensburg with the name of battle. Posted on a hill-side a mile from the village, along the route of the British towards Washington, under the independent command of Barney, and quite undismayed alike by the flight of their friends and the advance of their enemies, they made a fine, firm resistance, until the

[1] *Am. State Paps.*, *Military*, I., 536, 537, 596; Gleig, *Campaigns* (ed. of 1821), 102, 109.

British got in their rear, when they were compelled to give up the struggle, leaving their wounded commander a prisoner. "The rapid flight of the enemy and his knowledge of the country," wrote General Ross after the fight, "precluded the possibility of many prisoners being taken." So acute was the panic among the Americans fleeing westward beyond Washington and into Virginia that a fresh alarm on the second night drove the president from his bed into the Virginia woods for refuge. The course and condition of the president were typical of the whole government: the officers were metaphorically wandering in the woods without direction or co-operation, the victims of their own incapacity.[1]

The British troops marched directly from Bladensburg to Washington, camping just outside the city on the evening of August 24. A detachment of soldiers under orders burned the Capitol and department buildings while another body proceeded to burn the White House. A messenger sent by the French minister to ask a British guard for his house found General Ross in the act of piling up furniture in the White House drawing-room preparatory to setting it on fire. A third conflagration took place at the navy-yard, where the buildings and vessels were burned by order of the secretary of the navy. While the burning of the Capitol and other

[1] *Am. State Paps., Military*, I., 552, 556, 579 (Barney's report); James, *Military Occurrences*, II., 496 (official report of Ross); *A Subaltern in America*, 67.

public buildings in Washington was a piece of pure, unmitigated vandalism, deliberately committed by high officers in the British service and afterwards applauded by the prince regent and Lord Bathurst, the administration of Madison cannot escape the severest censure for its ridiculous unpreparedness for defence. The British officer, Gleig, was right in saying that the capture of Washington "was owing more to the faults of the Americans themselves, than to any other cause." Jomini, a contemporary European military critic, expresses the great surprise of military men that a handful of British soldiers could take and burn the capital of a nation with ten million people.[1]

Having accomplished their purposes at the capital, destroying public property estimated to have been worth more than one million five hundred thousand dollars, the British promptly withdrew to their fleet at Benedict without firing a single musket at their enemy; thus the Washington campaign was completed in a little more than a week, from landing to re-embarkation. The officials and people of Washington filtered back, while part of the American army turned towards Baltimore.[2]

---

[1] *Niles' Register*, VI., 442 et seq.; British account, in Gleig, *Campaigns* (ed. of 1821), 158 et seq.; Serrurier's account, in Adams, *United States*, VIII., 146; Jomini, *L'Art de la Guerre* (ed. of 1894), II., 456; the myth of the White House banquet, King, in *Mag. of Am. Hist.*, XIV., 450, XV., 509.

[2] *Am. State Paps.*, *Military*, I., 532 (report of special House committee); James, *Military Occurrences*, II., 297.

One of the most important political results of the capture of the capital was the forced resignation of the secretary of war. John Armstrong had probably borne himself with more dignity during the trying days of the campaign than had any other officer of the administration; but dignity does not organize battalions, build defences, or inspire commanders. On the other hand, no secretary could make bricks without straw or clay, and that was about what Armstrong, with an empty national treasury and with emergency militia companies for an army, had been required to do. Madison's attitude towards Armstrong, in an interview after their return to Washington, suggests strongly the dismissal of Robert Smith in 1811: Madison proposed as a compromise that Armstrong should retire temporarily, until the storm of criticism of the president and his secretary of war on account of the mismanagement of the war, should blow over. But Armstrong declined this arrangement, resigned his portfolio, and published the reasons for his act in a plain-speaking letter in the Baltimore *Patriot*. After some delay, Monroe was made secretary of war, continuing also as secretary of state, since in the latter office there was comparatively little to do at that time.[1]

The British next turned their attention to Balti-

[1] Madison, *Writings* (Congress ed.), III., 424; Monroe, *Writings* (Hamilton's ed.), V., 293; *Niles' Register*, VII., 6 (quoting Armstrong's letter); *Am. State Paps., Military*, I., 538.

more, in the expectation of levying a heavy contribution on its commerce and shipping, just as they had done at the little city of Alexandria, where they had received and carried off on their ships goods estimated to be worth one hundred thousand dollars. The fleet moved up the bay to the attack of Baltimore, and anchored off the mouth of the Patapsco River, September 11. Troops to the number of four or five thousand were landed for the attack, while the ships were to proceed to the bombardment of Fort McHenry. The distance in either case was only twelve or fourteen miles, and the approach much easier than in the attack on Washington. But Baltimore had made good use of the time since the British determined to make the first attack on Washington. Her citizens and mayor had not left their defence to the incapacity of government generals and engineers; they took matters in their own hands, and when the Englishmen arrived before the city there were good intrenchments and batteries mounted with cannon, forming a line of redoubts manned by an army of respectable size. In fact, the returns showed a force of nearly fourteen thousand present, under command of Senator Samuel Smith, now a major-general of militia. Fort McHenry was occupied by a force of regulars, sailors, and volunteers reaching nearly one thousand.[1]

In a skirmish on September 12, General Ross was

---

[1] *Niles' Register*, VII., 13; *Am. State Paps.*, *Military*, I., 591; Gleig, *Campaigns* (ed. of 1821), letters xiii., xiv.

killed; and when the bombardment by the fleet and
the movements of the troops on the following day
proved ineffective, it was evident that the intrenchments of the Americans, combined with the shallow-
ness of the water and a line of sunken vessels off the
fort, which prevented near approach of the British
fleet, were obstacles which the British could not
overcome with the men under their command.
Cochrane sent word to the military commander
that he could do no more, and the invading army
retreated to the shore and embarked on the transports. In a few days the ships dropped down the
bay, and by the middle of October Chesapeake Bay
was unvexed by the keel of a single British block-
ader, and its shores once more undisturbed. The
members of the administration were back in Washington, and Congress, which met in special session
September 19, was naïvely considering Giles's resolution for an inquiry into the state of the defences
of the city of Washington.[1]

Operations against the coast of Maine were going
on at the same time as those on the shores of the
Chesapeake. In July the British took Moose Island
and the town of Eastport, which, however, had been
in dispute since the treaty of 1783. A later successful expedition against the fort at Castine, at
the mouth of the Penobscot, left no doubt of the
intention of Great Britain to possess herself of so

---

[1] *Niles' Register*, VII., 23–30, 40; James, *Military Occurrences*,
II., chap. xx.; *Annals of Cong.*, 13 Cong., 3 Sess., 17, 18.

much of the territory of the United States as would give her free and convenient transit by land from Montreal to the Atlantic coast. General Sherbrooke, governor of Nova Scotia, with an army of two thousand men, took possession of the Massachusetts counties lying about the Penobscot in September, 1814, without encountering any resistance, though their military population was not far from twelve thousand. The people of this hundred miles of Maine coast were required to take the oath of allegiance to King George III., and took it seemingly without reluctance, with every prospect of remaining permanent subjects of the tyrant of 1776.[1]

By the terms of a despatch sent to Ross in July, the expedition, after the completion of the Chesapeake campaign, was to proceed to Jamaica, and there await further orders looking towards the reduction of the Gulf coast with the aid of reinforcements which would be sent to him from England. But Admiral Cochrane reported that "he had no doubt in his mind that three thousand troops landed at Mobile, where they would be joined by all the Indians with the disaffected French and Spaniards, would drive the Americans entirely out of Louisiana and the Floridas." Accordingly, the Ross expedition, under modified orders, was directed to co-operate with Cochrane in the Gulf. It seems strange that this undertaking had not earlier been set on

[1] James, *Military Occurrences*, II., 475 et seq. (British side); *Niles' Register*, VII., 51, 117 (American version).

foot, for the excellent reasons set forth in this despatch.

The control of the mouth of the Mississippi and of the rivers to the east flowing into the Gulf would be a most serious blow to the interests of the west, which had been so much endangered by the restrictions of Spain ten years earlier that the United States had been led to purchase Louisiana. If the stronger hand of Great Britain should seize control of these waterways, which the weak grasp of the Spaniards had given up, it would be no foolish prophet of evil who would expect the ultimate separation of the western part of the American republic. In fact, Great Britain might reasonably anticipate that with the control of the Mississippi would come again control of the Indian trade and Indian lands of the west and northwest. Or if this problematic advantage were not desirable, the occupation of the Gulf coast would be an "important and valuable possession by the restoration of which we may improve the conditions of peace, or which may entitle us to exact its cession as the price of peace." [1]

The Gulf expedition of the British left Jamaica November 26—a fleet of fifty vessels including five seventy-fours, and an army of nearly ten thousand veterans in command of two able generals, Pakenham and Gibbs, who had been trained in the best

---

[1] Above despatches from *MSS.* in the British archives, quoted by Adams, *United States*, VIII., chap. xii.

of military schools, the campaigns of Wellington in Spain. With such a force they anticipated an easy victory with abundant spoil. If the Americans had desired to have their resistance dignified and their coming victory magnified, this fleet and this army would have well served their purpose.[1]

The defence of the city of New Orleans, with its twenty thousand people and its strategic location, was seemingly almost as neglected as that of Washington in the preceding August. But there were two important differences: Andrew Jackson was in May, 1814, put in command of the military district, and the secretary of war had ordered munitions of war and companies of militia from Tennessee and Mississippi to the support of Jackson. Jackson spent the months of the summer in subjugating the Creeks in Alabama, and, even after it was well known that the British would attack the Gulf coast, he lingered in Mobile, going late in the autumn on an unauthorized—in fact, forbidden—expedition against the town of Pensacola in Spanish Florida. With no evident comprehension of the urgency of the occasion, he at length reached New Orleans, December 2, about a week before the British fleet cast anchor off the Louisiana coast. Three weeks more passed, and then the advance-guard of the enemy, two thousand strong, entered Lake Borgne and emerged from the Villeré Canal on the banks of the Mississippi,

---

[1] Gleig, *Campaigns* (ed. of 1821), 255, 304, 421; James, *Military Occurrences*, II., 339.

seven miles below the city, on December 23; but not a soldier nor a gun nor an intrenchment of any kind stood between them and the city which they coveted.[1]

Jackson's energy never shone to better advantage than when he recognized this emergency, which was in considerable degree due to his own neglect and misunderstanding of the meaning of the movements of the enemy. With a superior force of regulars, militia, and volunteers, aided by the twelve-gun war-schooner the *Carolina*, he promptly attacked the British advance-guard, and in a sharp skirmish on December 24 succeeded in giving the invaders such a severe check that they decided to wait for the main army and their light artillery before advancing on New Orleans. This was Jackson's opportunity. He halted his troops five miles from the city, on the edge of a dry canal. With the aid of negroes, his men deepened the canal and threw up a high parapet, which in three days was so formidable that it deterred the British from open assault. General Pakenham again waited, this time for his heavy artillery to be landed from the ships and hauled through the winter mud of the swamps with distressing efforts, in order to command the American position and to destroy the *Carolina*, whose fire in his flank or rear would be disastrous. On New Year's Day an artillery battle took place. Jackson's long line of breastworks mounted fifteen guns, while the

[1] Latour, *War in Florida and Louisiana*, 44, 52, 145.

British could present twenty-four; but to the great chagrin of the English officers, the work of the American artillerymen was distinctly superior, and after losing several guns the enemy withdrew from this form of contest. Two odd expedients for strengthening the defences were equally ineffective: "the cotton bales which formed the cheeks of the embrasures [of the Americans] proved as little serviceable as the hogsheads of sugar in the British river battery." [1]

By January 8, 1815, strong reinforcements had arrived for both commanders. Jackson chose wisely not to risk his militia in an open attack, but to wait for the British general to assault his works. On both sides of the river the American forces numbered about four thousand men, the great body lying behind the long line of earthworks with their mounted cannon, flanked on one side by the river and on the other by the cypress swamp. Here Pakenham made his main assault with more than five thousand men, instead of flanking his enemy by an advance up the river. The main attack failed at every point, for the fire of Jackson's riflemen and artillery drove back the British with fearful effectiveness. Three of the British major-generals, including Pakenham, were killed, and the total losses in killed, wounded, and missing were more than two thousand. The American loss proved to be seventy-one, though Jackson

---

[1] Latour, *War in Florida and Louisiana*, 124, 132; Gleig, *Campaigns* (ed. of 1821), 319; Adams, *United States*, VIII., 364.

on the 9th estimated it at ten killed and as many more wounded. The British made immediate preparations for retreat, and by the end of the month they were embarked on their ships and en route to Mobile Bay, where they succeeded in reducing the crude forts on February 11, before receiving news of peace. [1]

The battle of New Orleans had no effect whatever on the termination of the war, for the treaty of peace was signed two weeks before it was fought; but, as a closing act to a contest which on land had brought almost nothing but shame and disaster to the American arms, it was most gratifying. It covered a multitude of sins of omission and commission on the part of the government and the commanders. It reinforced the pride of the people, which had been so often and so sorely wounded. It gave the United States a military hero who appealed to the west as no naval hero could appeal.[2]

[1] *Niles' Register*, VII., 357, 373, 385 (Jackson's official reports); Gleig, *Campaigns*, 355, 424; James, *Military Occurrences*, II., 371, 382, 542, 550 (Lambert's and Cochrane's reports).
[2] Roosevelt, *Naval War* (3d ed.).

CHAPTER IX

NEW ENGLAND AND THE WAR
(1811–1815)

THE conduct of Federalist New England from the declaration of war in 1812 to the proclamation of peace in 1815 was marked by a fine Puritan consistency and resourcefulness. Men like Pickering, Otis, Quincy, Cabot, and Strong failed neither in their logic nor in the courage to carry out their convictions. But consistency must not be required to stretch over too long a time. Fifteen years earlier there had been Federalist declarations which were hard to reconcile with those later utterances. The famous speech of Josiah Quincy on the Louisiana bill in 1811 made clear the logical extremity to which New England was willing to go in support of her principles—"as it will be the right of all, so it will be the duty of some, definitely to prepare for a separation, amicably if they can, violently if they must." A high-priest of the Federalist faith had spoken; it remained for loyal adherents to stand by the pronouncement with grim and unswerving determination.[1]

[1] *Annals of Cong.*, 11 Cong., 3 Sess., 525.

The debates on the war measures during the spring and early summer of 1812 demonstrated that the New-Englanders, while opposed to war, were not in favor of tame submission. They wanted adequate protection for the commerce and citizenship of the nation, but they preferred on the whole to work out their own salvation rather than to accept the Jeffersonian Republican brand which was to be forced upon them. They voted for the increase of the army to thirty-five thousand quite as much to embarrass their opponents as to promote the intended war; but when it came to the actual declaration they voted almost to a man against it.[1]

The legislature of Massachusetts presented to Congress a moderate memorial against the declaration of war; after the passage of the fateful act, thirty-four of the forty-nine members of the national House who had voted against the declaration, issued a protest or "Address . . . to their Constituents," in which they severely arraigned the policy and motives of the Republican majority.[2] These documents did not augur well for that unity and harmony for which Niles looked when war was declared: "At a time like the present, every *honest* diversity of sentiment will be sacrificed, or, at least, suffered to rest in peace for a season, on the ALTAR

---

[1] Adams, *United States*, VI., 171–175; *Annals of Cong.*, 12 Cong., 1 Sess., 1599.

[2] *Mass. Acts and Resolves*, 1812–1815, p. 331; *Niles' Register*, II., 309 (the "Address").

OF UNION. . . . A little time and patience with prudence, will bring about a perfect union when the war *really* begins."[1]

In January, 1812, Congress voted thirteen new regiments of regulars; in February the president was authorized to accept fifty thousand one-year volunteers; and in April he was authorized to call out one hundred thousand of the state militia. Let Madison tell of the enthusiasm of the response to these acts up to August 8, 1812: "The enlistments for the regular army fall short of the most moderate calculation; the Volunteer Act is extremely unproductive. And even the militia detachments are either obstructed by the disaffected governors or chilled by the Federalist spirit diffused throughout the region most convenient to the theatre."[2] The sorry truth was that the governors of several of the New England states had refused to comply with the call for militia in the manner desired by the administration.

Major - General Dearborn, acting under the authority of the secretary of war, asked for detachments of the militia of Massachusetts and Connecticut on June 22, directing that part of the companies be sent to various posts in these states, part to Rhode Island, and part—four companies—to be placed under the commanding officer of the United States army at Fort Trumbull. Governor Griswold of Connecticut at once convened the council of that state in extra session, and requested its advice on the

[1] *Niles' Register*, II., 284, 285. [2] Gallatin, *Writings*, I., 524.

two important questions raised by the requisition of General Dearborn: Could the militia be legally demanded until one of the three contingencies named in the Constitution had arisen—to "execute the laws of the Union, suppress insurrection, and repel invasion"? Could the militia be placed "under the command of a continental officer"? The council and the governor were agreed in a negative answer to both of these important questions, and accordingly the request for militia was refused. The legislature, however, voted to raise and arm twenty-six hundred men for the defence of the state. In Massachusetts the same issue was submitted to three judges of the supreme court and answered in the same way.[1]

It was evident the militia was not needed to execute the laws, nor was there any insurrection to suppress, but on the question of invasion the case was not quite so clear. Offensive warfare from the British side was imminent but not actual; and any but a strongly partisan mind would have recognized the wisdom of thorough, timely preparation for the probable invasion. President Madison well said in his message to Congress, November 4, 1812, "The refusal was founded on a novel and unfortunate exposition of the provisions of the Constitution relating to the militia. . . . It is obvious that if the authority of the United States to call into service and com-

---

[1] *Am. State Paps.*, *Military*, I., 321, 324 (opinion of the Massachusetts judges).

mand the militia for the public defense can be thus frustrated, even in a state of declared war and of course under apprehensions of invasion preceding war, they are not one nation for the purpose most of all requiring it, and that the public safety may have no other resource than in those large and permanent military establishments which are forbidden by the principles of our free government, and against the necessity of which the militia were meant to be a constitutional bulwark." The final word as to the correctness of the president's view was said by the supreme court of the United States in 1827, in the case of Martin *vs.* Mott: "We are all of the opinion that the authority to decide whether the exigency [of calling out the militia] has arisen belongs exclusively to the President, and that his decision is conclusive upon all other persons."[1]

The question of the control and use of the militia was more or less acute during the whole war. Not merely did the New England states object to the first war-call, and to putting their companies under United States officers, but the men refused to march beyond the borders of the United States, and even in some cases beyond the borders of their own state. It would be an error to suppose that the militia took no active or important part in the war. Though the federal government came finally to the policy of leaving the New England states to take care of themselves, the states to the eastward frequently acted

[1] Richardson, *Messages and Papers*, I., 516; 12 Wheaton, 30.

under orders from Washington; yet for the most part they constituted state armies more or less independent of the federal authorities, and sometimes they caused almost as much anxiety to those in office at Washington as did the enemy. The militia of Massachusetts, seventy thousand in enrolment, well-drilled and well-equipped, was definitely withdrawn from the service of the United States in September, 1814 — that is, two weeks after the capture of Washington, and one week after portions of Maine had been taken by the British and the inhabitants had taken the oath of allegiance to the king of Great Britain.[1]

The general orders of Governor Strong, dated September 6, placed the militia under a state major-general, and when the governor asked Monroe, then acting secretary of war, "whether the expenses thus necessarily incurred for our protection will be ultimately reimbursed to this state by the general government," he got the curt reply that the state's measures were the state's affairs, not the affairs of the nation, and that the expenses were chargeable to the state, not to the United States. Accordingly, the state legislature authorized a loan of one million dollars, and six hundred and thirty-one thousand dollars was actually realized for defence.[2] Con-

---

[1] Dwight, *Hartford Convention*, 282–285; *Am. State Paps., Military*, I., 613 (Governor Strong to secretary of war).
[2] *Niles' Register*, VII., 148; *Mass. Acts and Resolves*, 1812–1815, p. 569.

necticut withdrew her militia force from federal control even before Massachusetts took the step. Rhode Island and Massachusetts exchanged notes, like two European powers, offering assurances of aid in case of invasion of the territory of either state.

The same restraint of effort which marked New England's compliance with the military demands of the United States marked also her course regarding financial aid to the government during the years of the war. Measured by almost any standard of financial strength, Massachusetts, Rhode Island, and Connecticut were better able than any other three states (leaving Pennsylvania out of the question) to aid in financing the war. Timothy Pitkin of Connecticut, a reliable statistician, estimated that in 1812 the paid-up banking capital of the whole country was sixty million dollars, of which New England had about eighteen millions, while Massachusetts alone had about ten millions. The conservative management of their circulation and their heavy reserves of specie made the banks of Massachusetts and Connecticut the strongest in the Union.[1]

As early as 1810, when the adoption of manufacturing was forced upon New England as a temporary substitute for the commerce which had made that section so rich and solid, New England began to supply the rest of the country with the manufactured goods which were shut out by national legislation; and in return specie flowed in an accelerated stream

---

[1] *Annals of Cong.*, 13 Cong., 1 Sess., 1297.

into her coffers. The war embargo and blockade almost shut off the marketing in New England of the produce of the middle and southern states, so specie accumulated in the vaults of the eastern banks. Massachusetts banks reported specie deposits in 1811, $1,709,000; in 1812, $3,915,000; in 1813, $6,171,000; and in 1814, $7,326,000. The New England banks had probably about one-half the specie in the country at the end of 1814.[1] The only way to get this money back into circulation in the states from which it had been drawn was through the medium of government loans, the proceeds of which would in the course of events be paid out to soldiers, carriers, and farmers.

At this critical point the New England Federalists found means to oppose the war without the least violation of any law or the straining of any constitutional interpretation. With grim reserve they almost withheld subscriptions to the national loans, no matter how urgent the needs of the administration: the south and west had made the war— "Mr. Madison's War"—let them pay for it! Of the $11,000,000 loan of the spring of 1812, New England took less than $1,000,000; and during the whole war her total subscription to national loans was less than $3,000,000, while the middle states paid in nearly $35,000,000.[2] In other words, in a time of

---

[1] Gallatin, *Writings*, III., 283; Adams, *United States*, VII., 388, gives slightly different figures.
[2] Gallatin, *Writings*, III., 284.

great financial difficulty the government of the United States was deprived of almost a third of the financial accumulations which might have been its reliance, just when the winding-up of the Bank of the United States bore away another resource.

The moneyed interests of the east were not content with passive resistance; they bought British drafts at a discount with specie sent to Canada; they supplied beef to the British armies in Canada, and furnished subsistence to British fleets off the eastern coasts—all for highly profitable considerations. Madison wrote sharply of this practice in his message of December 9, 1813, and the British commander wrote to the home government of the continuance of the same conditions in the following August: "Two-thirds of the army in Canada are at this moment eating beef provided by American contractors. . . . This circumstance, as well as that of the introduction of large sums of specie into this province, being notorious in the United States, it is to be expected Congress will take steps to deprive us of those resources, and under that apprehension large droves are daily crossing the lines coming into Lower Canada." [1]

New England could not be coerced into subscription to national loans, but she might be prevented from trading with the enemy. Accordingly, a new and rigid embargo was enacted in December, 1813. Hardly was it on the statute-book when it had to

---

[1] Adams, *United States*, VII., 146 (Prevost to Bathurst).

be modified to prevent the people of the island of Nantucket from starving, because of the rigid enforcement of the prohibition of intercourse with the mainland.[1] A fortnight after the passage of this embargo came news of the overwhelming defeat of Napoleon at Leipzig, which meant that all the continent of Europe was now open to British commerce. The Federalists saw the meaning of the situation and keyed their opposition higher. The year which followed demonstrated that they would not hesitate to move steadily along in their resistance to the measures of the Madisonians, even if the end of the route lay outside the Union. The withdrawal of the militia from the service of the Federal government and the establishment of state armies, already described, were part of the campaign. By April the futility of the embargo was clear: it was not serviceable either abroad or at home, and on Madison's recommendation it was repealed, April 14; but its effect in increasing the aggravation of the Federalists was not to be effaced.[2]

The progress of events during 1814 seemed to make clearer and clearer to the Federalists the need of some final, decisive action for their protection. The organization of state troops was not confined to New England. New York voted the establishment of an army of twenty thousand; Pennsylvania followed; even Virginia voted a state army with two

[1] *U. S. Statutes at Large*, III., 88, 123.
[2] Richardson, *Messages and Papers*, I., 540.

major-generals, and Kentucky took steps for a similar army of ten thousand men. The treasury was so reduced by January, 1815, that the drafts of General Jackson could not be met, and the secretary of war, Monroe, who never during his whole life had sufficient money for his private needs, was obliged to give his personal security in the banks of Washington and Georgetown for small loans for his department. "That the Treasury is empty I admit," said Artemas Ward to the House in December, "that the ranks of the regular army are thin I believe to be true; and that our country must be defended in all events, I not only admit, but affirm."[1] Miller, of New York, went even further: "The States must and will take care of themselves; and they will preserve the resources of the States for the safety of the States."[2]

New England logic led from these various premises to the conclusion that the war must be brought to an end, and that Madison and the administration at Washington must be coerced to this object or else secession would take place. Joseph Story, himself a New-Englander, but a moderate Republican, had written as early as August, 1812, at the very beginning of the war: "I am thoroughly convinced that the leading Federalists meditate a severance of the Union, and that if public opinion can be brought to support them they will hazard a public avowal

[1] *Annals of Cong.*, 13 Cong., 3 Sess., 907.
[2] *Ibid.*, 790.

of it." [1] Pickering, the most radical of the Federalists, declared in a letter to Gouverneur Morris, in October, 1814: "I have even gone so far as to say that the separation of the Northern section of the States would be ultimately advantageous." [2] In justice to those men who wrote about and talked about secession, it should be said that during the first thirty-five years of the federal government under the Constitution it was a possibility often suggested; to assert it was not really terrifying, and called for no governmental action. [3]

Early in the year 1814 memorials were sent up to the Massachusetts legislature from many towns, suggesting a convention of delegates from the different states to "obtain such amendments and explanations of the Constitution, as will secure them from further evils." [4] The House took the lead in the movement when the legislature met in extra session to enact measures for the defence of the state, and on October 16 voted to appoint twelve delegates to meet at Hartford and confer with delegates from other New England states upon the subject of their public grievances and concerns. The Senate concurred, and among the delegates elected were George Cabot, Harrison Gray Otis, and Nathan Dane. A memorial was drawn up and forwarded to the legislatures of Connecticut and Rhode Island, which

[1] Story, *Story*, I., 229.   [2] Lodge, *Cabot*, 535.
[3] John Adams, *Works*, VI., 629.
[4] Dwight, *Hartford Convention*, 341.

in turn appointed delegates to the convention. A Massachusetts Federalist newspaper published news of the action of Connecticut under the significant head, "Second Pillar of a New Federal Edifice Reared."[1] Rhode Island was the "Third Pillar Raised." The convention thus provided for, which met in Hartford, December 15, 1814, was made up of twelve men from Massachusetts, seven from Connecticut, four from Rhode Island, besides three unofficial delegates from New Hampshire and one from Vermont, chosen by local conventions. After a session of three weeks, under the obligation of strictest secrecy, the convention adjourned on January 15, 1815, issuing a report to its constituents. The language of this report is in part deliberately copied from the Virginia resolutions of 1798, which had been written by the pen of Madison himself — "in cases of deliberate, dangerous, and palpable infractions of the Constitution, affecting the sovereignty of a State and liberties of the people; it is not only the right but the duty of such a State to interpose its authority for their protection, in the manner best calculated to secure that end."[2]

The report of the convention closed with a series of resolutions calling for the following measures:

1. The states represented to take the necessary steps to protect their citizens from the provisions of all acts of Congress providing for the draft, con-

---

[1] *Columbian Centinel* (Boston), November 9, 1814.
[2] Dwight, *Hartford Convention*, 361.

scription, or impressment of the militia or other citizens of the states, unauthorized by the Constitution.

2. These same states, through their legislatures, should seek to obtain from the federal government an arrangement by which the states might assume the defence of their own territory, and have reimbursement by means of a portion of the federal revenue collected within these states, such portion to be paid into the state treasury.

3. The states to pass laws which would permit the use of their militia in assisting other states.

4. The states to endeavor to secure seven amendments to the Constitution: apportionment of representation and direct taxes among the several states according to their respective numbers of free persons; no new states to be admitted without the concurrence of two-thirds of both Houses of Congress; prohibition of all embargoes exceeding sixty days; no interdiction of foreign intercourse without a two-thirds vote of both Houses; no declaration of war, save by a similar vote; no naturalized citizens to hold civil office under the authority of the United States; ineligibility of the president for two terms; and a prohibition of successive elections from the same state.

In case of the failure of this application for amendment of the Constitution, or of neglect of the defence of the New England states, it was voted expedient for the legislatures of the states to appoint delegates to another convention to meet in June, "with such powers and instructions as the exigencies of a crisis so momentous may require." [1]

The parallel between the course of this convention and the course of the first Continental Congress is suggestive of revolutionary proceedings. Doubtless the report was a compromise between conservative Federalists like Cabot and Otis, who draughted it, and a hot-headed element which stood ready to go to any length of resistance to the war and to the administration. In Boston "Epaminondas," representing this latter class, announced in an address to the convention that "The once venerable Constitution has expired by dissolution. . . . At your hands therefore we demand deliverance. New England is unanimous, and we announce our irrevocable decree, that the tyrannical oppression of those who at present usurp the power of the Constitution is beyond endurance, and we will resist it." [2] Even Gouverneur Morris wrote from his quiet New Jersey home to Pickering in Congress: "I care nothing now about your actions and doings. Your decree of conscriptions and your tremendous levy of contributions . . . are alike indifferent to one whose eyes are fixed on a star in the East, which he believes to be the star of freedom and glory. The mad-men and traitors assembled at Hartford will, I believe, if not too tame and timid, be hailed here-

[1] Dwight, *Hartford Convention*, 378.
[2] *Columbian Centinel*, December 28, 1812.

after as the patriots and sages of their day and generation." [1]

These evidences of New England sedition, together with all the other discouragements, profoundly depressed an administration "without force, without money, without talents, and generally despised." [2] Months earlier William Wirt had called on the president and reported: "He looks miserably shattered and woe-begone. . . . His mind is full of the New England sedition. He introduced the subject and continued to press it, painful as it obviously was to him." [3] Monroe, however, was less pessimistic. Late in December he wrote: "The gentry will, I suspect, find they have over acted their part. They cannot dismember the Union, or league with the enemy. . . . I hope that the leaders will soon take rank in society with Burr, and others of that stamp." [4] To the more advanced Republicans like Grundy and Calhoun, the Federalist opposition culminating in the Hartford Convention amounted to moral treason, while John Quincy Adams passionately asserted, in 1829, that the Hartford Convention was unconstitutional and treasonable, wholly abnormal, hideous, and wicked. [5]

A committee was appointed by the Hartford

---

[1] Morris, *Gouverneur Morris*, II., 575.
[2] *Ibid.*, 578 (Morris to King, January, 1815).
[3] Kennedy, *Wirt*, I., 339.
[4] Monroe, *Writings* (Hamilton's ed.), IV., 305.
[5] Lodge, *Cabot*, 413 (summarizing an unpublished MS. of Adams).

Convention to present its resolutions for constitutional amendments to Congress, and early in February the committee was in Washington ready to negotiate with the national government. Had Jackson been defeated at New Orleans, or had news of the failure of the negotiations at Ghent been received, the overthrow of the government at Washington and the establishment of a New England confederacy, and possibly an alliance with Great Britain, would seem to have been inevitable. The news of peace and of victory saved Madison, and perhaps the Union. The committee of the Hartford Convention slipped out of Washington as quietly as possible, and made its way home amid the jeers of Republicans and the reproaches of conservative Federalists.

The complete overthrow of the Federalist plans for coercing the national government left the convention and its members under a cloud from which they were never able to emerge. The triumphant Republicans lost no opportunity to cast reproach upon all connected with that secret body. The report of the convention, dignified, able, and unobjectionable as it was, did not overcome the suspicions of the public generally. Strange tales were told of the debates of the convention; and, as the journal was sealed and placed in the hands of the president, no contradiction of these mischievous declarations could be made. When published by the secretary, Theodore Dwight, in 1833, it was found to contain nothing treasonable, but it was always suspected that this journal reflected neither the temper nor the decisions of the convention. Individual expressions and explanations were useless. No man connected with the convention ever entirely recovered his political standing. The new and invigorated Republican party speedily absorbed all but the most irreconcilable Federalists, so that the opprobrium of sedition rested chiefly upon the handful of leaders like Pickering, Strong, and Cabot. New England's conversion to manufacturing completed her transformation from incorrigible Federalism to temperate Republicanism.

CHAPTER X

PEACE NEGOTIATIONS

(1813–1815)

THE declaration of war by no means silenced the advocates of peace; the news of the repeal of the orders in council added point to their formal protests, and encouraged all efforts to bring pressure for a cessation of hostilities. The war was forced upon the country in much the same way as in the Revolution the war and independence were forced by an energetic, enthusiastic minority upon a conservative majority. Within the Republican party there was a large element opposed to the war, while the Federalists almost to a man denounced it, insisting that peace be made at once, and declaring their intention to reduce their support to the barest legal minimum.[1]

Pressure for peace was not confined to America; for the war between the United States and England had a very important bearing upon the relations of European nations in their mighty struggle against

[1] Webster, *Writings* (National ed.), XV., 583, 599 (Portsmouth speech, July 4, 1812, and Rockingham Memorial, August, 1812).

Napoleon. The Americans fully realized that their national and commercial interests were entangled in the meshes of the European system, yet the diplomacy of the United States as an independent power can hardly be said to have passed the apprenticeship stage in this period of passion and violent disregard of neutral rights. The complaints, protests, and innumerable representations of the United States ever since 1803 were to England and France little more than annoying foot-notes or irritating distractions in the warfare of decrees, orders, and proclamations.

Four days after the United States declared war upon Great Britain, Napoleon declared war upon Russia. By the middle of August he reached the Dnieper River, and a month later he was in Moscow. England and Russia were allied, and whatever weakened England in this crisis added just so much to the chances for Napoleon's success. Russia had been friendly to the United States since the Revolution; and John Quincy Adams, minister of the republic at St. Petersburg since 1810, was treated with special consideration. The fact that he represented a nation entering upon a war with England would have diminished his influence at the court had he not been carrying on his negotiations with Count Roumanzoff, the Russian chancellor and minister of foreign affairs, who was in reality in favor of France rather than England in the European contest, and whose influence, for this very reason, was waning with the czar since the French made war on Russia. But Alexander still gave him substantially his own way. The intrigues in the Russian ministry thus worked in the end to add strength to Adams's influence.[1]

The Czar Alexander was much disturbed by the news of the American declaration of war against his important ally, and in the latter part of September, 1812, the directed Count Roumanzoff to sound Mr. Adams on the question of Russian mediation between the United States and Great Britain. Although without instructions in the matter, Adams declared that he felt sure the United States would welcome the mediation if England would consent. Without waiting for a reply to a similar proposal made to England through the British ambassador, the Russian *chargé d'affaires* at Washington was instructed to lay the proposal before the secretary of state. Monroe received the offer of mediation March 8, 1813, and promptly accepted it in a note full of compliments to the czar.[2]

With the same precipitation and injudicious eagerness that marked the negotiations with Erskine, and with France in 1810, both Madison and Monroe assumed that the offer would not have been made without the consent of England. They decided, after consultation with Jefferson, to give weight and political effect to the negotiations, by appointing a

[1] Adams, *United States*, VII., 26–32, 339–358.
[2] J. Q. Adams, *Memoirs*, II., 401; *Am. State Paps., Foreign*, III., 624.

commission to consist of Adams and two other men of prominence. As an evidence of the desire for peace, James A. Bayard of Delaware, a Federalist, was appointed, and a third commissioner was to have been a western man, to secure the confidence and acquiescence of that section in the treaty which might be formulated; but when Gallatin asked for the appointment, the president acceded to his request. Gallatin believed that his usefulness in the treasury department was at an end, for his efforts were steadily thwarted and his recommendations disregarded. He foresaw the direst confusion and perhaps bankruptcy of the treasury within a few months, and he rightly concluded that he might better serve the country by turning his high order of abilities into the channels of diplomacy than by remaining as the chief of the clerks of the treasury department.[1]

Gallatin's intimate knowledge of Europe, his long experience in the cabinet, his reserve, patience, resourcefulness, and penetration, made him quite the ideal man for dealing with England or Russia at this time. Madison was unwilling to accept Gallatin's resignation as secretary of the treasury, but, appointing the secretary of the navy, William Jones, as acting secretary of the treasury, he sent Gallatin on his foreign mission just as Washington had sent Chief-Justice John Jay to negotiate the treaty of 1794 with England, and as John Adams had sent

[1] Adams, *Gallatin*, 483.

Chief-Justice Ellsworth on a mission to France in 1800. It was May before Gallatin had completed the fiscal arrangements for the coming year: the loan of sixteen million dollars was placed, provision made for the issue of treasury notes, the tax bills were made ready, and the draught of a charter for a new Bank of the United States was completed.

The Senate, to which the nomination was sent after the two commissioners had sailed, investigated the appointment, resolved that the holding of two offices was inadvisable, and finally rejected the nomination. Once more the enemies of Gallatin fed the ancient grudge they bore him, and he remained secretary *de jure*, but envoy *de facto*, until early in February, 1814, when he was nominated for the new commission, and was succeeded in the treasury by G. W. Campbell. The commissioners bore elaborate instructions, the gist of which was that in case of failure to secure a treaty with clear provision for the relinquishment of the right of search and the abandonment of impressments, they should make no peace, but return home.[1]

When Adams called on Roumanzoff, June 22, 1813, to announce the appointment and departure of the two additional negotiators, he was informed that Lord Castlereagh had very politely rejected the czar's offer, on the ground that the questions at issue between England and the United States "were of a

[1] *Am. State Paps., Foreign*, III., 695; Madison, *Writings* (Congress ed.), III., 566.

nature which they did not think suitable to be settled by mediation."[1] Roumanzoff, however, was not
willing to let the matter drop, and finally for his own
purposes secured from the czar a renewal of his offer
to England.

In the mean time Gallatin and Bayard had arrived
at Gottenburg en route to the Russian capital. The
news of the presence and purpose of the two American commissioners in Europe so greatly disturbed
Lord Castlereagh that he despatched two letters to
Ambassador Cathcart at St. Petersburg, in July,
declaring that the czar ought not to "push his personal interference on this point [of mediation] further," even if the commission were already on the
ground; and that Great Britain was ready to treat
directly with the United States at London or Gottenburg. The same news reached Gallatin from
his friend Alexander Baring, the London banker, to
whom he had early announced his arrival in Europe,
and whose assistance in forwarding the mediation he
had asked. But from July, 1813, to January, 1814,
the commissioners waited at St. Petersburg in per-
plexing uncertainty.[2]

This important suggestion of direct negotiations
was many months in reaching the United States.
Not till January 3, 1814, did Monroe receive a note
from Lord Castlereagh (dated November 4), an-

---

[1] J. Q. Adams, *Memoirs*, II., 479.
[2] Adams, *United States*, VII., 340–348; Gallatin, *Writings*, I.,
546.

nouncing officially England's willingness "to enter upon direct negotiations for the restoration of peace between the two states." He accepted the offer two days later; the whole correspondence was laid before Congress, and it was decided to enlarge the number of commissioners by adding Henry Clay and Jonathan Russell. Since the envoys were to treat with England and not with Russia, new commissions and new instructions had to be issued.[1]

Meantime Gallatin was permitted to go on to London, to forward if possible the direct negotiations which the two governments had agreed upon. He arrived in the midst of the celebration over the fall of Napoleon; but though the world was at peace once more, save for the war between England and America, it was not an opportune moment for proposing a settlement of the difficulties between the two belligerents. With Napoleon overthrown and Great Britain in undisputed control of the seas, the English newspapers, if not her statesmen, were indulging in arrogance and abuse of America. There should be no peace, they declared, until the disgrace of defeats upon Lake Erie, at the Thames, and on the ocean had been wiped out; there should be a review of the title of the United States to Louisiana; Madison's "dirty, swindling manœuvers" in Florida should be punished; the fishing rights of the United States off the British coasts should be cancelled; control of the St. Lawrence and Niagara should

---

[1] *Niles' Register*, V., 319.

pass to Great Britain, and an Indian territory north
and west of a line drawn from Sandusky to Kas-
kaskia should be created for the benefit of the savage allies of Great Britain. Small wonder that
Gallatin was profoundly depressed by the prospect.
He even went so far as to hold a personal interview
with the czar in London to persuade him to intercede
with the prince-regent for a modification of England's demands, but the czar gave him no encouragement. In June he wrote to Monroe that the best
to be expected would be the *status quo ante bellum*,
without any settlement of the blockade or impressment questions.[1]

England was, however, in no hurry to begin the
direct negotiations to which Castlereagh had committed himself. Her armies on the continent were
relieved, and fifteen or twenty thousand men were
to be sent to America. Her ships no longer need patrol the coasts of France and France's more or less
willing allies. Her people wanted to continue the
war; but the government knew that England needed rest, that the occasion for defying American national sentiment on impressment had disappeared,
and that England would lose prestige in Europe if
she refused fair terms of adjustment.

The five American envoys had been waiting six
weeks at Ghent, the place finally chosen for the joint
meetings, when the British commissioners arrived,
early in August, 1814. The make-up of the British

[1] Adams, *Gallatin*, 514; Adams, *United States*, VII., 356–363.

commission surprised even London, for it showed an almost ill - bred contempt for the Americans: Lord Gambier, a naval officer, raised to the peerage for his participation in the shelling and burning of Copenhagen; Henry Goulburn, a young man scarcely beyond cadet rank in diplomacy, though he had served as under-secretary of state for Lord Bathurst; and William Adams, a doctor of civil law—these commonplace men made up a commission which neither commanded respect at home nor carried weight abroad. Individually and as a body they lacked tact, experience, and breadth of view, and in the end they had served as little more than clerks to record the changing moods and concessions of the British ministry.

Against this weak and nerveless commission were arrayed five men who made up the strongest, most vigorous, and most representative group that Madison could have selected. John Quincy Adams, the head of the commission, at the age of forty-seven, was intimately acquainted with the vital problems of Europe, a scholarly man of the best training and tradition in American politics. In keenness, mental vigor, and high devotion to duty, he has had few equals in American history. But he was also a man of cold and repellent temper, prone to carry things with a high hand, and for the present mission he was handicapped by the fact that he was almost a free lance in politics, an apostate Federalist who came from a state bitterly opposed to the war.

While Adams was nominally head of the commission, Gallatin was really the member to whose authority the others bowed, even though by the later date of his appointment he was at the bottom of the list. Besides the advantages of great and recognized ability, and a temper not easily ruffled, he represented in a peculiar way the views of the president with whom he had been intimately associated for more than a dozen years as a member of the cabinet. It is not too much to say that the commission would have probably broken up from its own disagreements had not Gallatin's singular tact, patience, and good-nature been used in his noble fashion.[1]

Henry Clay, ten years the junior of Adams, was quite the opposite in every quality save patriotism and native ability. He was no Puritan in mental, moral, or physical habits; he was high-spirited, impulsive, impatient of opposition, and gifted with great social charms. In the commission he proved the most difficult to control, especially in dealing with questions affecting the west or the honor of the nation, such as the fisheries or the navigation of the Mississippi, on which he and Adams were tenaciously opposed. James A. Bayard, a moderate, or half-Republican Federalist, was a judicious, high-minded gentleman. The fifth member was Jonathan Russell, a well-educated Rhode Island merchant of or-

[1] J. Q. Adams, *MSS.*, quoted in H. Adams, *United States*, IX., 51.

dinary ability, who had served in minor diplomatic posts.

Each side began by insisting absolutely on certain demands. The English instructions authorized the discussion of the right of impressment and allegiance; made the admission of the Indians to a part in the general pacification a *sine qua non;* and included the revision of the Canadian boundary and the general subject of shore fishing rights. To this the Americans replied that they had no instructions regarding Indians and fisheries, since these subjects had never been in dispute, but that they had very explicit instructions regarding impressments, allegiance, Canadian boundaries, blockade, and indemnity to private citizens.[1]

The Indian question, therefore, came near producing a complete rupture of the negotiations—perhaps the real purpose of the proposal; for the Americans declined even to consider the creation of an Indian buffer-state out of the soil and sovereignty of the United States. At this juncture the British commissioners asked for a suspension of the meetings so that they might refer the matter to the home government. After ten days of delay came new and astonishing instructions, fresh from the hand of Castlereagh, then on his way to the Congress at Vienna to assist in determining the destinies of Europe. In place of the previous instructions on the Indian question was a proposition for the establish-

---

[1] *Am. State Paps., Foreign,* III., 705.

ment of a permanent barrier between the western settlements of the United States and the possessions of Great Britain. This was really an offset to the effort of the United States to conquer Canada; and to Mr. Gallatin's inquiry as to what was proposed to be done with the hundred thousand citizens of the United States in Michigan, Illinois, and part of Ohio, Dr. Adams said "that undoubtedly they must shift for themselves." In addition a new boundary between Canada and the United States was to leave clear communication between Quebec and Halifax; a new line was to be drawn from Lake Superior to the Mississippi River with the right of navigating that river. With it was coupled the dismantling of Fort Niagara and Sackett's Harbor, and an agreement that no ships of war of the United States should be permitted on the Great Lakes.[1]

These demands were presented in writing at the request of Mr. Adams, who draughted the reply which was worked over by the whole commission "sifting, erasing, patching, and amending," till no more than one-fifth of Adams's original memorandum was left. The result was an admirably fine, strong, forceful, dignified paper, in which the commissioners declared it was useless to refer the British proposals to the United States government. They refused again to consider the question of Indian boundaries submitted by the British commission, and, believing that

[1] J. Q. Adams, *Memoirs*, III., 19–25; *Am. State Paps., Foreign*, III., 710.

negotiations were at an end, they prepared to leave Ghent. Adams planned to go back to St. Petersburg; Russell would set out for his new post at Stockholm; Clay for Paris; Gallatin and Bayard would return to the United States. A messenger from the commissioners bearing despatches to the United States announcing the failure of the mission sailed from the Texel, August 31.[1]

The news of the British demands reached America in early October, while the air was ringing with the shouts of rejoicing over the victories of Macdonough, Gaines, and Brown. By vote of the House of Representatives ten thousand copies of the correspondence were printed and spread over the country. When Castlereagh at Paris learned of the American reply to the British demand, he read clearly the meaning of the Americans. He ordered his commissioners to await instructions from London, informing them that they had greatly misunderstood the policy of Great Britain, that certain matters were not *sine qua non*, but were set forth to prolong discussion.[2] The new instructions which arrived September 4 were distinctly concessional. They conceded that the Indian lands, Canadian boundary, and the occupation of the lakes had nothing to do with the maritime rights, to protect which the United States began the war; but the aggressive spirit of the United States evidenced in the en-

---

[1] J. Q. Adams, *Memoirs*, III., 22; *Am. State Paps.*, *Foreign*, III., 711.   [2] Adams, *United States*, IX.. 26.

croachment upon Indian lands, the acquisition of Louisiana, the dismemberment of the province of Florida, and the declared purpose to conquer Canada obliged Great Britain to protect her own interests.

In reality the ministry was trying to gain time in the hope that affairs in America would turn in England's favor. The Americans firmly refused to discuss the Indian question, to consider a provisional article, or to refer it to Washington. Another reference to London brought instructions to drop the Indian territorial question and the control of the lakes, but to insist upon admitting the Indians to the peace treaty. This the American commission flatly refused, but offered as the only possible substitute amnesty to all Indians who had taken arms against the United States. This concession, being referred to London, was accepted, another victory for the American commission.

The next matter which came up for discussion related to the territorial status of certain portions of the border country which had changed hands during the war. The United States contended for the *status quo ante bellum*—a restoration of the territorial conditions preceding the war; while the British commission urged *uti possidetis*—the continuation of possession as it existed at the time of signing the treaty. Unfortunately for the latter contention it was presented for consideration on the day of the receipt of the news of the victory at Baltimore and on Lake Champlain, and of the retreat of Prevost's army. The United States commission promptly rejected the British proposal.

Smarting under military defeat, the British ministry was moved strongly to continue the war, even though the cost for the year would be ten million pounds. The ministers, however, had to face several uncomfortable facts: negotiations at Vienna were not proceeding smoothly; the reports from America were unfavorable; the continuance of the war would prevent the reduction of taxation already oppressively high, a reduction which the taxpayers of Great Britain had a right to expect after the defeat of Napoleon. Wellington was asked to go to America to assume command in order to bring about such victories as would enable England to end the war with honor. Wellington on his side gave the ministry very cold comfort; he would go to America if ordered, but it was useless to attempt a land campaign without control of the lakes, and that seemed remote. He furthermore stated that Great Britain was not justified in insisting upon the *uti possidetis*. So the cabinet yielded, negotiations went on, and the British commissioners asked the Americans to submit a project of a treaty.[1]

During the early summer of 1814 the question of impressments loomed up as an insuperable obstacle to peace. The original instructions of April, 1813, made the abandonment of impressments by Great

[1] Adams, *United States*, IX., 40 (Wellington to Castlereagh, November 9, 1814).

Britain a *sine qua non* for a treaty; failing to secure this, wrote Monroe, "all further negotiations will cease and you will return home without delay." By the new instructions of February, 1814, abandonment was made "important" but not "indispensable"; finally, when the commissioners were assured that no treaty could be made if they insisted on a renunciation by Great Britain of the right to impress, and that as a matter of fact impressments must cease since the royal navy was to be reduced, they asked for new instructions. Under the date of July 27, 1814, Monroe yielded the whole matter by writing to the commission: "You may omit any stipulation on the subject of impressments, if found indispensably necessary to terminate it [the war]." [1]

Still, the formulation of an acceptable treaty in response to the request of the British, developed almost irreconcilable differences among the American commissioners. Those from the east were interested in the preservation of the right to fish off the coasts of British America. The west, whose sentiments were voiced by Clay, desired the nullification of the present right of Great Britain, based on the treaty of 1783, to free navigation of the Mississippi. If the treaty of 1783 was of a nature to be terminated by the result of the breaking out of war between the parties, then the navigation of the Mississippi and the fishing privileges or rights, both had automatically ceased to be. If, on the other hand, the treaty of

---

[1] *Am. State Paps., Foreign*, III., 700, 703, 704.

1783 was of an extraordinary nature, not nullified by war, which was the contention of Adams, and probably sound in international law, then the right to the fisheries was unimpaired, but the navigation of the Mississippi was still open to Great Britain. It was in the violent discussions which took place upon these questions that Gallatin was especially helpful in harmonizing the differences between Clay and Russell on the one hand and Adams and Bayard on the other. A humorous allusion, a witty thrust, or a keen sally more than once produced a laugh and saved the commission.

The draught treaty as finally sent to the British commissioners, November 10, contained no stipulations either as to the Mississippi or to the fisheries. The British returned the document with many notes and modifications, including the addition of a specific provision conceding their right to navigate the Mississippi. Again protracted debates and sharp contentions between Clay and Adams required the services of Gallatin as peacemaker among peacemakers. But the anxiety of the British cabinet for peace steadily increased; the Americans refused to consent to a clause reserving for further negotiations all questions relating to the fisheries and the Mississippi, since such a wording might have unwelcome implications; and the two commissions mutually agreed to omit all reference to both these questions. The treaty was thus reduced to lowest terms; each party consented to the elimination of all clauses on the questions which had produced the war, and which at the beginning of the negotiations had been considered of vital importance.[1]

The treaty in this expurgated form, as signed December 24, 1814, provided for a cessation of hostilities, for the release of prisoners, for the appointment of commissioners to settle the disputed boundary, for the restoration of all conquests, for the termination of Indian hostilities, and for steps looking towards the abolition of the slave-trade. Not a word about impressments, the right of search, blockades, neutral rights or indemnities; no mention of neutral Indian territories, the control of the Great Lakes, the navigation of the Mississippi, or the fisheries. It was peace in its simplest form, but no more dishonorable to one than the other. It was, as Gallatin wrote to Monroe, "as favorable as could be expected under existing circumstances, so far as they were known to us."[2]

The news of the signing of the treaty reached New York, February 11, 1815; the effect was immediately seen on every hand. Federalists and Republicans alike welcomed the treaty with satisfaction more or less tempered with regret. The Republicans were humiliated at its terms, which fell so far short of their party boasts when the war began, but they solaced themselves with the bare fact of peace.

[1] J. Q. Adams, *Memoirs*, III., 66 et seq.
[2] *U. S. Treaties and Conventions*, 399–405; Gallatin, *Writings*, I., 645.

Madison officially declared to Congress that the treaty terminated "with peculiar felicity a campaign signalized by the most brilliant successes," and a war which had "been waged with a success which is the natural result of the wisdom of the Legislative Councils, of the patriotism of the people, of the public spirit of the Militia, and of the valor of the military and naval forces of the country." Presidential euphemism could hardly go further, even in addressing Congress. The Republicans drew great lessons from the war and looked forward eagerly to the prosperity which would surely be realized with the coming of peace. The Federalists reluctantly admitted their gratification at the treaty —"bad as it is we hail it with delight." The stock market in New York and Philadelphia reflected the satisfaction, for stocks rose ten and even eighteen per cent. during the week after the announcement of peace.[1]

The treaty was submitted to the Senate on February 15, unanimously ratified, and by proclamation of the president on the 17th, it became the law of the land. "Perhaps at the moment the Americans were the chief losers; but they gained their greatest triumph in referring all their disputes to be settled by time, the final negotiator, whose decision they could safely trust."[2]

[1] Richardson, *Messages and Papers*, I., 552; Adams, *United States*, IX., 62.   [2] Adams, *United States*, IX., 53.

CHAPTER XI

THE RESULTS OF THE WAR

(1815)

WHEN measured by any standard of material or immediate advantage, the results of the War of 1812 were all negative. For two years and a half the United States had waged war upon land and upon sea, yet had not added a square mile of territory nor a ton to her commerce; she had not settled one dispute as to boundaries nor obtained definite recognition for a single right for which she had contended. On the other hand, the losses of men, money, and property were positive and distinct, while the derangement of the finances was not outgrown for some years. But however great the material losses, they were temporary and soon forgotten. The immaterial or spiritual results upon the nation and national policy were not so immediately obvious, but in reality they were second only to those of the Revolution: the first war segregated the materials for an independent nation; the second gave them new form and effective unity.

The cost of the war in men, as wars go, was moderate. The population of the country was about eight and a quarter millions, yet the effectives in the army never exceeded thirty thousand, and the number actually engaged in any one battle never reached four thousand. The number killed in battle was estimated to be about fifteen hundred, the total of killed and wounded in land battles not far from five thousand, and the grand total of losses, including prisoners, nine thousand seven hundred.[1] The most liberal estimate of the loss of men, in battle on sea and land, in camp, in hospital, and in prisons, places it at thirty thousand. In other words, the loss of men could not have exceeded two per cent. of the military population, a loss which seems almost insignificant when compared with South Carolina's sacrifice of twenty-five per cent. of her military population during the Civil War.

In terms of money, the cost of the war was about two hundred million dollars, which cannot be considered exceedingly burdensome. The issue of bonds and treasury notes had added over eighty millions to the previous debt, which thus rose to one hundred and twenty-seven millions, or about fifteen dollars a head for the population, as against about twenty dollars a head in 1791.[2] Had the currency been in good order and taxation equalized, no one would have complained of the burden of the federal debt.

The people felt the war most severely in the high prices of such commodities as groceries and iron, and in the low prices of the staple products like

[1] *Niles' Register*, X., 154.
[2] Dallas, Report, in *Am. State Paps., Finance*, VIII., 8.

wheat, flour, tobacco, and cotton, for which there was little or no market while the war lasted. The extent of these difficulties was illustrated by the sudden reversal of conditions after peace was proclaimed, when the price of sugar was cut in two and the price of flour rose fitty per cent.[1] The figures of the export trade of the country told the same story: 1811, forty-five million dollars; 1813, twenty-five million dollars; 1814, seven million dollars. New England suffered least, because the British in the early stages of the war refrained from harassing that section, and because the New-Englanders defied the laws of the United States by trading with the armies of the enemy on the Canadian frontier and in Maine, and by taking advantage of British permits for trading at sea. Yet Boston's trade in foreign products, first imported, and then exported to Europe, fell from nearly six million dollars in 1811, to slightly more than three hundred thousand dollars in 1813. Virginia, on the other hand, suffered most from lack of market for her flour and for her tobacco, which, Jefferson declared, "is not worth the pipe it is smoked in." Coasting-trade was practically suspended and land transportation so difficult that flour, in August, 1813, was worth $4.50 a barrel in Richmond and $11.87 in Boston.[2]

[1] Adams, *United States*, IX., 61.
[2] Jefferson, *Works* (Washington's ed.), VI., 398; *Niles' Register*, V., 41, gives a very valuable table of prices current, showing prices in cities from Boston to New Orleans.

Considering the extent of the American seaboard and the lack of provision for defence, it is rather surprising that the United States escaped with so little damage to her coasts and cities. Washington was the only city of importance that suffered severely, while the shores of Chesapeake Bay and of Georgia, and the Niagara frontier, were the only regions plundered. The commercial and shipping interests were hardly in a different situation after the war began from that in which they had been for the greater part of the preceding five years. Their losses probably were no greater by capture in war than they had been by French sequestration and English prize courts. At the Boston docks in September, 1813, two hundred and forty-nine sea-going vessels were lying idle, ninety-one being of the largest class. When the war was ended, one hundred and forty-four vessels sailed from Boston within a month, while the entries into Charleston, South Carolina, in three weeks of April, 1815, showed one hundred and fifty-eight vessels exclusive of coasters. That the year 1815 did bring great relief to American commerce is undeniable, but it cannot safely be asserted that this relief was a result of the war, though Clay, in a fine frenzy, in 1813, had said that the United States was "fighting for FREE TRADE AND SAILORS' RIGHTS." The rise of manufacturing as one of the results of the war on commerce between 1806 and 1812, and of the war of battalions and of vessels between

1812 and 1815, will be treated at length in another chapter.[1]

After the war and the peace of Ghent, rather than because of these events, the United States was in a new sense free to work out her destinies. By a stroke of good-fortune and a rare combination of circumstances in Europe and America, comparable with those which existed in 1783 and 1793, the United States was free from entangling connections with England or France and from subserviency to their animosities. Save for the brief period between 1789 and 1793, she had known no such freedom before. Old things had passed away—questions of neutral rights, impressments, embargoes, orders in council, French decrees, Napoleonic treachery. The new world was to be a domestic world. Its questions would be too big for the states to solve alone; national settlement and national action would be required on such issues as the currency, banking, the tariff, internal improvements, public lands, the extension of slavery, immigration, and the development of the west.

All but unconsciously the nation at the close of the war heard and obeyed the call to face about. Hitherto it had looked towards the sea; for years it had scanned the horizon anxiously, lest the coming ship should be unfriendly or the bearer of ill tidings

[1] Mahan, "War of 1812," in *Scribner's Mag.*, XXXVI., 495–497; Clay, *Speeches* (Colton's ed., 1857), I., 70; Ingersoll, *Second War*, 2d series, II., 360.

for merchant and statesman. Now its face was set towards the west and the frontier, of which the illimitable possibilities were beginning to dawn upon the national consciousness, as they had been borne in upon Washington and Jefferson in the days of the fathers. The breezy exuberance and the high optimism of the first products of this western life had been felt with vague and uncertain forebodings by the leaders of the old school, when the "war hawks" took it upon themselves in 1811 and 1812 to settle for the nation the long-threshed question of peace or war. Now that the war was over, the same energy and optimism were to be devoted freely for a generation to the new problems. Surely in land areas and in politics there was to be a new earth if not a new heaven.

In dealing with these new affairs, or old affairs on a vaster scale, the ideal and spirit of the nation were to be of vital importance. There was no body of traditions to guide, no solid backing of experience to which to appeal, no adequate conception of the magnificence of the future for which the foundations must be deeply laid. Experimentation, reorganization, readjustment, expansion—these were the processes by which the youthful fibre of the republic was to be hardened for its ever-enlarging work in the world. "We are great," exclaimed Calhoun in 1816, "and rapidly—I was about to say fearfully—growing. This is our pride and danger, our weakness and our strength."[1]

---

[1] *Annals of Cong.*, 14 Cong., 2 Sess., 853.

The consciousness of nationality which came out of the second war with Great Britain was the chief political result, the one most far-reaching in its effects. Before the war the alignment of parties was determined quite as much by the sympathies of the voter with England or with France as by his attitude towards the Constitution or towards the rights of the states. The British party (Jefferson's Anglomen) and the French party (the Federalists' Mobocrats), could not, of course, change all their stripes in a single five years; but common pride in the navy and its achievements, exultation in the peace which brought with it such immediate prosperity, and· the fact that the Republicans of 1815 had absorbed a good number of Federalist principles in their fourteen years of power, tended to soften, if not to obliterate, party lines.

Up to the declaration of war, the United States was practically still in colonial relation to Europe, and was treated accordingly by Great Britain and France. The war in America and the closing of an era in Europe changed all this, and made steady progress in nationalism possible. The narrowness of the escape from exactly the opposite condition— the collapse of the national government in 1815— has not been given proper emphasis. The historian who begins to spin from the distaff of what might have been, may spin forever; but it seems clear that Madison's administration, and with it the fate of the federal government, was in the balance in 1815.

Men waited anxiously for news from New Orleans, anticipating defeat for Jackson at the hands of the veterans from the Continental wars; they were prepared to learn from the next packet from Europe that negotiations at Ghent had failed; the committee from the Hartford Convention, with its ominous suggestions, was already in Washington to treat with Congress and the administration. The shock of severe defeat at New Orleans, or complete rupture at Ghent, might have loosed even the slender ties holding the administration together, and sent the fragments of the discredited government flying from the capitol just as the march of the British had dispersed the president and his cabinet in the preceding summer. With victory favoring the United States at Ghent and at the mouth of the Mississippi, the Federalists might well believe that the stars in their courses fought for the Republicans; for it seemed that no degree of incapacity or imbecility in the government and no excess of incompetency in its generals could overbalance good fortune, the fortune of peace.

The government and party thus saved had come into power by the "revolution of 1801," strongly emphasizing democratic principles, state rights, and strict construction of the Constitution; it emerged from the war in 1815 greatly changed, if not greatly chastened, by fourteen years of experience in administration, including three years of war. Every deviation from the strict principles of 1801 had been

in the direction of nationalism — the purchase of
Louisiana, the embargo, the seizure of West Florida,
and the imposition of a direct tax along with the
revival of excises. Hamilton himself would have
hesitated to take some of the steps which the Jeffersonian Republicans took trippingly. It was this
new, nationalized democracy, purged of most of its
impractical theories, which found itself triumphant
as the result of the war, and apparently endowed
with a long lease of power. Nationalism and democracy were to grow together, both reinforced by the
development of the west, by the diversion of the
attention of the east from commerce to manufacturing, and by the change from attachment to European
interests to devotion to internal development.

In several respects the two parties had exchanged
places. The Federalists threatened secession in
1811, because the party responsible for the Virginia
and Kentucky resolutions of 1798 and 1799 was
about to admit part of the Louisiana purchase as
the state of Louisiana, without the consent of all the
original states. Later on, the Hartford Convention
seemed to make preparations for breaking up the
Union. The extent to which Republicans had
adopted Federalist positions is perhaps best illustrated by the suggestions in Madison's annual
message of 1815; for none but a strong government
with liberal endowment of powers could carry out
his programme: liberal provisions for defence, an enlarged navy, protection to manufacturers, national

roads and canals, a national university, more military academies, and—very cautiously—a national bank.[1]

Even before this message was prepared, Congress gave evidence of the conversion of the Republicans to better views regarding the army and navy. The ratification of the treaty of Ghent made it necessary to put the two services on a peace footing. Monroe, the secretary of war, recommended to the Senate committee on military affairs the establishment of an army of twenty thousand men, involving an annual expense of five million dollars. But this was too much for either House; after various votes for ten, six, and fifteen thousand men, ten thousand was agreed upon in conference, and in this form the bill became a law. Though no large provision was made for the future of the navy, the whole war establishment was maintained unreduced, and an appropriation of four million four hundred thousand dollars made for its support.[2]

A little war upon the dey of Algiers might be called one of the results of the war against England. In almost the same breath by which Congress had voted to continue the whole war establishment of the navy, it authorized the use of that navy for punishing the dey for his depredations upon Amer-

---

[1] Story, Story, I., 284, quotes a remarkable letter by Justice Story, written in 1815, on the "glorious opportunity" before the Republicans; Richardson, Messages and Papers, I., 562 et seq.

[2] Monroe, Writings, V., 321; U. S. Statutes at Large, III., 222, 223, 224.

ican commerce. In the annual tribute which the United States had paid for seventeen years to the piratical Algerine, he alleged there was a deficiency of twenty-seven thousand dollars, and, taking advantage of the war with England, he captured American ships and enslaved American citizens In accordance with the act of Congress, Captain Decatur sailed with ten vessels in May, 1815, to punish the dey and exact a new treaty. After destroying a forty - six - gun frigate and a smaller vessel, he sailed boldly into the harbor of Algiers, and finally extracted from the dey the renunciation of all tribute for the future, the release of all American prisoners without ransom, and a guarantee that the commerce of the United States should never again be molested by the Algerians. "You told us," one of the dey's courtiers is reported as saying to the British consul, "that the American navy would be destroyed in *six months* by *you*, and *now* they make war upon *us* with *three of your own vessels* which they have taken from you." A visit to Tunis and Tripoli with the same grim purpose resulted in similar guarantees of safety to American commerce in the Mediterranean.[1]

Not the least of the results of the war was the prominence gained by three of the younger military commanders, each of whom, in consequence, eventu-

[1] *Am. State Paps., Foreign,* III., 748; *Ibid., Naval,* I., 396; Maclay, *Hist. of the Navy,* II., chap. i.; Waldo, *Decatur* (ed. of 1822), 278.

ally was nominated for the presidency, and two of them elected. The American people, while essentially peace-loving and unmilitary by temperament, have shown a curious hero-worship of the successful military leader. The "availability" of Jackson, Harrison, Taylor, and Grant for the presidency rested almost entirely upon their records as military commanders. Ever after 1815 Andrew Jackson was known as the "Hero of New Orleans," and in a few years he became a presidential possibility. William Henry Harrison was a man of good family, education, and political experience, but except as the victor at Tippecanoe in 1811, and at the Thames in 1813, he would hardly have been a highly eligible candidate for the presidency at the age of sixty-seven. Winfield Scott entered the war as a young lieutenant - colonel, but at the close he bore the epaulets of a major-general and a gold medal voted by Congress; promotion and the opportunities of the Mexican War made him the logical Whig military candidate in 1852. Another presidential candidate, a civilian, was John Quincy Adams, whose advancement came as a result of his part in the negotiations at Ghent — a fine recognition of real merit, undiminished by any suggestion of personal or party "pull." Madison transferred him from St. Petersburg to London at the close of the war, and from that post he was called to be secretary of state in 1817 and president in 1825.

Social results of any particular event or series of

events, like those of a war, are not easy to disentangle
or measure. Such results cannot be traced like a
nerve-fibre from the brain to a particular organ.
What changes might have appeared in American
society, even had there been no war with England,
simply as a result of the expansion of the country,
the development of slavery, and the pacification of
Europe, are matters for infinite speculation. This
much, however, may be set down as an effect of
the war: a new, almost intoxicating sense of self-
respect on the part of the people and the governing
powers in state and nation. The young men of
1815, who had heard so much depreciation of American character during the years of depression and
subservience to France and England, gloried in the
demonstration of the courage—and good fortune—
of the nation; nor did even the Federalists analyze
too carefully the validity of the grounds for this
personal and national uplift. All were quite ready
to forget those things which were behind, and press
towards the realization of a new high calling.

The effect of this fresh, free impulse, this fine
sense of detachment and of opportunity, affected
the literary and religious life of America almost as
profoundly as it did the political and economic ideals
and activities of the nation. It aided the "theolog-
ical thaw" which had already begun before 1815.
The emotional side of the revolt from the hardness
of the old orthodoxy found its expression in the attempts of Campbell in the west and of Hosea Ballou

in the east to reduce religion to a simpler and more inclusive matter, as over against the complex, severely logical exclusiveness of Calvinism and its modifications. The Unitarian movement in New England, centring about Harvard Unive sity, had been spreading for a decade when the peace of Ghent was made. Its strong emphasis on the worth of man and the naturalness of his living a loving, sober, righteous, and godly life, according to the dictates of a mind carefully instructed in the comprehensible things of the spirit and of doctrine, fell in with the new national sense of the political worth of the people of the nation. Even where these two movements did not cause organized changes in the churches, their influence was clearly felt, though the era of good feeling in the religious world was slow in succeeding the war of faction and doctrine.[1]

In literature the new life began to manifest itself in this second decade of the century, but it seems to be rather a part of the large movement in the English-speaking race than a merely local or national affair, for the international ferment of the American Revolution and of the French Revolution and the Napoleonic period had not exhausted its influence at the end of the generation of those who took part in these mighty events. Still it was perhaps due in no small degree to the conditions of the time, that, within a period of twelve years following 1810, there

[1] Adams, *United States*, IX., chap. viii.

were graduated from Harvard University alone a group of men whose achievements, each in his own field of activity, were to be great: Edward Everett, Henry Ware, William H. Prescott, John G. Palfrey, George Bancroft, Caleb Cushing, and Ralph Waldo Emerson.[1] Bryant was beginning his literary career with the striking " Lines to a Waterfowl" and "Thanatopsis." Irving published his uniquely fresh *History of New York, by Diedrich Knickerbocker*, in 1809. The *North American Review* began its long and honorable career in 1815. The rise of a group of political and occasional orators of great power and of brilliant diction must not be forgotten in any estimate of the intellectual and social characteristics of the period after 1811; their efforts were as distinctly literary and stimulating as were the efforts of Ware or Irving. Clay, Calhoun, Webster, and Everett found their original inspiration in the national idea, and with one exception maintained it with cumulative power and grace.

[1] *Harvard Quinquennial Catalogue* (1905), 154–165.

CHAPTER XII

PARTY DIVISIONS AND PERSONALITIES
(1815-1819)

BEFORE going on to trace the direct political and diplomatic effects of the new national spirit, something should be said of the parties and the men who led the new movement. The political re-arrangement which was so much facilitated by the disappearance of old questions after the close of the war, reached a sort of climax in the election of 1816. Rufus King, the Federalist candidate, was senator from New York and quite the last of the great Federalists still in active service—representative of the conservative rather than the aggressive wing of his party. For the regular Republican nomination there was a lively contest between Monroe, who represented the Virginia dynasty, and Crawford, representative of the young Republicans. In the Congressional caucus of 119 (including proxies) out of 141 Republican members then in Washington, Monroe received 65 votes against 54 for Crawford. Monroe was beyond question the choice of the administration, and probably had been accepted by Madison as his political legatee when Monroe entered the cabinet in 1811. In the election, the Federalists, already reduced to an innocuous minority, succeeded in securing only 34 votes in the electoral college, against 183 for Monroe. King carried but three states, even New York going for Monroe, whose election was without doubt in accordance with popular desire.[1]

Monroe had many qualities which fitted him for the presidency, especially in a time of transition from old conditions to new, when steadiness rather than brilliancy and ambitious initiative was a quality much needed. He was a man of great personal dignity, of unquestionable integrity and devotion to public service, and of wide, if not highly successful, legislative, diplomatic, and administrative experience. Most important of all, for the occasion, he was not closely associated with the factional quarrels of the Republicans. Though he was a man of such cautious, painstaking judgment and conciliatory disposition as to command public confidence and respect, he was far behind the rank of great statesmen; while the severer of his critics put him down as a third-rate man, neither capable nor judicious. Even in those labors where his opportunities were largest, he certainly fell short of real achievement: with Livingston he shared in making the Louisiana treaty, but his course in France under Washington, and in England under Jefferson, was

[1] *Niles' Register*, X., 59, XI., 409; Stanwood, *Hist. of the Presidency*, chap. ix.

disavowed by his superiors. With the ripeness and solidity of experience and later years, the quality which Calhoun described as Monroe's "wonderful intellectual patience" came out strongly in his dealings with the members of his cabinet, with Jackson, and with Clay.[1]

The first place in the new cabinet was given to John Quincy Adams, the most experienced and able of the American diplomats of his time, with the possible exception of Gallatin; and although his appointment was probably made on political grounds, his services during Monroe's first administration more than justified his selection. Monroe knew perfectly well the sharp criticism which had been passed upon the Virginia dynasty because of its tendency to become a close corporation. Regarding this selection of a secretary of state, he wrote to Jefferson: "I am inclined to believe that if I nominate anyone from this quarter [south and west] . . . I should embody against the approaching administration, principally to defeat the suspected arrangement for the succession, the whole of the country north of the Delaware immediately, and the rest [north] of the Potomac would be likely to follow it. My wish is to prevent such a combination. . . . With this view I have thought it advisable to select a person for the Department of State, from the Eastern States."[2]

As secretary of the treasury, Monroe continued

---

[1] Calhoun's letter of 1831, in Monroe MSS., quoted by Schouler, United States, III., 204.   [2] Monroe, Writings, VI., 3.

William H. Crawford, of Georgia, who had been his chief rival for the nomination as president, a man of great energy and unusual ability, but somewhat lacking in the highest sense of loyalty and honor among his colleagues. Gallatin described him as one "who united to a powerful mind a most correct judgment and inflexible integrity,—which last quality, not sufficiently tempered by indulgence and civility, has prevented his acquiring general popularity," and, he might have added, also prevented his reaching the presidency.[1]

The first offer of the war department was to Clay, who refused it with some show of temper because Adams had been preferred to him for the more conspicuous and honorable place of secretary of state; thus Clay followed the example of Monroe himself, who had refused to accept office under Madison in 1809, save as secretary of state. Crawford wrote to Gallatin: "It is understood that he [Clay] objects to entering the Cabinet in what he considers subordinate rank. . . . How the conflict between his ambition and his dread of retirement will terminate remains to be seen. I think there are but few men who have less relish for retirement than Mr. Clay."[2] Ex-governor Isaac Shelby, of Kentucky, was then nominated and confirmed as secretary of war, but declined on account of age. Calhoun was thereupon offered that department, and accepted. William Wirt

[1] Gallatin to Badollet, July 29, 1824, Adams, *Gallatin*, 598.
[2] Gallatin, *Writings*, II., 36.

became attorney-general, succeeding Richard Rush, who was sent as Adams's successor as minister to England.

Since Clay could not enter the cabinet, he sought and found in the speakership of the House an opportunity of power and influence superior to that of any cabinet office, and he remained there, a thorn in the side of Monroe to the end of that president's term.[1] His speakership was a guarantee against the return of old-line methods, even if the fifteenth Congress, elected in 1816, had not shown such a large proportion of new men. Time and rotation in office had eliminated many of the older leaders, and only thirty-three members of the new Congress had enjoyed so much as ten years of congressional experience. The execution of the new measures already enacted—the national bank, the resumption of specie payments, the protective tariff, and appropriations for internal improvements — were all sure of sympathetic reinforcement.

Monroe certainly cherished the honorable ambition of Jefferson so to carry on his administration as to reduce party antagonisms to a minimum. The circumstances and conditions of 1817 were infinitely more favorable for the realization of this ambition than they had been when Jefferson spoke the memorable words of his first inaugural.[2] So far as the great parties were concerned, the first administra-

---

[1] Follett, *Speaker of the House*, §§ 45, 46.
[2] Richardson, *Messages and Papers*, I., 321.

tion of Monroe was apparently an "era of good feeling," though underneath this superficial unanimity and agreement there lay smoldering the fires of bitter personal animosity which within twenty years would flame up to scorch the reputation of more than one man of the group of presidential aspirants.

To promote the tendency to good feeling, and to harmonize the already mollified Federalists and Republicans of New England and the Middle States, Monroe undertook a long tour to the east during the summer of 1817. The ostensible purpose was "to inspect the national defences," but the incidents of the long journey, and the tone of the speeches, would make it fair to call it a tour to forget political offences.[1] He was everywhere received with unusual cordiality and respect, and mutual observation and contact profited both the president and the New-Englanders. "I have seen enough to satisfy me," wrote Monroe to Jefferson in July, "that the great mass of our fellow-citizens in the eastern states are as firmly attached to the Union and to Republican government as I have always believed or could desire them to be."[2] Crawford's view of the eastern tour — somewhat tinged, of course, by his secret jealousy of Monroe—was expressed in a letter to Gallatin in October: "The President's tour through the East has produced something like a political

---

[1] *Narrative of a Tour of Observation.*
[2] Monroe, *Writings*, VI., 27.

jubilee. They were in the land of steady habits, at least for the time, 'all Federalists, all Republicans.' If the bondmen and bondwomen were not set free, and individual debts released, a general absolution of political sins seems to have been mutually agreed upon. . . . The carping, the malevolent men in the Ancient Dominion are ready to denounce him for his apparent acquiescence in the seeming *man-worship* with which he was venerated by the *wise men of the East*. Seriously, I think the President has lost as much as he has gained by this tour, at least in popularity." [1]

Some of the characteristics of John Quincy Adams have already been described. He was without any considerable personal following, for his qualities were not those to attract individual men—"a virtuous man, whose temper . . . is not the best," wrote Gallatin.[2] By dint of his fiery devotion to public service, in high conscientiousness in all that pertained to the work of his office, and in capacity for keen, incisive statement of principles and purposes, Adams was superior to any other man in the public service during Monroe's administration. The successful negotiations with Spain and with England, and the resistance which he established to the encroachments of European powers in America, admirably illustrated these qualities, and commanded for him sufficient support to make him the successor of Monroe, in spite of a certain personal severity of

---

[1] Gallatin, *Writings*, II., 55.   [2] Adams, *Gallatin*, 599.

manner, and a tendency to carry things with a high hand.

The character of Henry Clay offers many striking contrasts to that of Monroe or Adams. What the latter lacked in popular qualities and good-fellowship, in the power to attract men and hold them, Clay possessed in a degree rarely equalled in American politics. Frank, suave, courteous, emotional, rarely thinking out his conclusions with clear logic unmixed with passion, he received the confidence and support of men. Nor did they tax him with gross inconsistency when he honestly and completely changed his mind, as he did on the question of the bank. This facile adaptability, combined with his ready mastery in debate, his dash, and telling vigor of style, were no mean factors in his political success. His best work was not done, like Adams's, in the quiet of his study or in the sharp contests of logical arguments; it was done rather in the public gaze, with the inspiration of an audience, but always under the impulse of genuine patriotism. His long success was undoubtedly due to a rare balance of admirable qualities. While other men might greatly excel him in any one of them—in solid learning, in logical power, in shrewd political judgment, in purity and loftiness of eloquence, the harmonious union of such faculties combined with subtle personal magnetism made Clay a power of the first class, to be reckoned with in all matters political, for four decades from 1811. His chief defect was in a certain dictatorial assurance which on occasions became condescension towards those who ventured to oppose his views.[1]

Clay was precisely the man around whom might crystallize those liberal elements of the Republican party which were held in solution during the era of good feeling. The work of organizing the material out of which the Whig party would later be formed was already going on under his deft hands during Monroe's first administration. The ardent advocacy of the bank and the tariff, the preaching of the gospel of western expansion and internal improvements at federal expense, the recognition of the revolted Spanish American republics, which seemed to be following in the footsteps of the northern republic—these were matters into which Clay threw himself heart and soul. In a word, whatever tended to magnify the importance of the nation and to increase its prestige was sure to receive the enthusiastic support of the versatile speaker of the House, who represented not merely the aggressive, optimistic spirit of Kentucky and the west, but also the positive, exuberant nationalism of the new generation.

The sons of the Federalists in New England failed in many cases to follow in the footsteps of their fathers. The defection of such men as John Quincy Adams was typical of the movement which produced the amalgamation of the parties. Daniel Webster, who had entered the political arena as a

[1] Cf. Turner, *New West* (*Am. Nation*, XIV.), chap. vii.

Federalist of the younger generation, gradually went over to the national wing of the Republican party, though it was with much difficulty that he made the readjustment. He opposed war against Great Britain, as became an orthodox Federalist, but if there was to be war he favored a naval war. He proposed a bank scheme of his own in 1814, but voted against the bill of 1816; he opposed the protective duties of 1816, in the expectation that New England capital would return to commerce; but later became a stanch supporter of the Whig platform of protection. In 1816 he removed to Massachusetts, withdrew from politics in a large degree, devoting himself to his law practice, so that for some years his political influence was comparatively slight.

His commanding abilities as an orator and leader were already recognized by men like Monroe, who were convinced that it must be under young men that New England would be brought into harmony with the rest of the nation. Webster's superb intellectual endowments were really ripening and accumulating power during this period of temporary retirement from public life; and when the new national spirit just coming to consciousness under Monroe should need a defender of giant stature, Webster would be ready to take up the rôle.[1]

The figure of Calhoun in the decade under discussion is one of peculiar attractiveness, if not one of greatest influence. A young southerner of good

[1] Webster, *Writings* (National ed.), VI., 3, 181.

family, fine endowments, and fine education, he was an ardent nationalist, working for, arguing for, and dreaming of a great and powerful United States safely bound together for its work in the world. He was ambitious, but he could afford to wait for his promotion; he could serve diligently in the cabinet, without intrigue and without scrambling in unseemly fashion for the succession, as did Crawford, whose cordial dislike he reciprocated. Through all the quiet energy of his work and the luminous diction of his speeches runs a strain of passion and chivalrous sentiment. More nearly than any one else of this time did Calhoun fulfil the prophetic function for the south, showing forth its best spirit and noblest impulses, as yet unwarped and uncorroded by slavery. To be sure, De Witt Clinton of New York, with an acrid censoriousness reserved for those who opposed him, privately called Calhoun "treacherous" and "a thorough-paced political blackleg"; and Gallatin ten years later wrote him down "a smart young man, one of the first among second-rate men, but of lax political principles and a disordinate ambition." [1] But after four years and more of intimate association with him in the cabinet, John Quincy Adams, who differed from him as widely as Massachusetts differed from South Caro-

---

[1] John Bigelow, "De Witt Clinton as a Politician," *Harper's Monthly*, L., 417, notes that Clinton called Adams a political "apostate . . . and everything but amiable and honest," and the son of a "scamp"; cf. Adams, *Gallatin*, 599.

lina, wrote of Calhoun in his *Diary* in 1821: "A man of fair and candid mind, of honorable principles, of clear and quick understanding, of cool self-possession, of enlarged philosophical views, and of ardent patriotism." [1] With the changes which came over Calhoun after 1825, changes which struck to the bottom of his thinking and acting, giving him marvellous strength and ruinous weakness, this volume has nothing to do; but recognition cannot be withheld from his great enthusiasm and progressiveness as a young Republican, nor from his industry and skill in the war department in promoting national sentiment and strength.[2]

The last of the group of men whose personalities were to shape the destinies of the parties and of the nation during the thirty years after the war of 1812, was Andrew Jackson. In 1812, at the age of forty-five, he was apparently without political ambition, though he was locally prominent. He had served on the bench of Tennessee, in the United States Senate, and as major-general of militia, but at the opening of hostilities he was in no official position, a simple farmer-lawyer. What he lacked in education he made up in intensity. The strength and loyalty of his friendship was equalled only by the implacableness and intolerance of his enmity. As with most men bred on the frontier, breadth, the

---

[1] J. Q. Adams, *Memoirs*, V., 361.

[2] See Turner, *New West*, chap. xi; MacDonald, *Jacksonian Democracy*, chaps. v., vi., ix. (*Am. Nation*, XIV., XV.).

discipline of self-restraint, and fine powers of discrimination were not his strong qualities. Metamorphic heat had not produced marble in his character; he never became other than limestone, rough, strong, and useful. His opportunity for promotion in public favor must come when the nation was psychologically ready to appreciate and liberally reward virility, courage, self-assurance, and downrightness. In the terse sentence of Professor Sumner: "The outbreak of the second war with England afforded him an arena in which his faults became virtues." [1]

At the time when these strong personalities were striving with political principles to determine the alignment of parties, a new issue of an entirely different sort asserted itself. Twenty-five years earlier, the invention of a Connecticut Yankee schoolmaster had begun the transformation of slavery in the United States from a patriarchal institution to a social and economic system.[2] Where the institution had pressed its leisurely way, as a convenience more or less profitable, the system was to thrust itself aggressively and intolerantly, urged on by greed and sensitive pride of race and possession. As it expanded geographically, as its economic importance increased in domestic and international relations,

[1] Sumner, *Jackson*, 25; cf. Turner, *New West*, chap. xv., and MacDonald, *Jacksonian Democracy*, chap. ii. (*Am. Nation*, XIV., XV.).

[2] Bassett, *Federalist System*, chap. xii.; Channing, *Jeffersonian System*, chap. viii. (*Am. Nation*, XI., XII.).

just so its subtle influence on politics widened and deepened, until it seemed to dominate and dictate the political field. Personalities counted for less and less as the new issues became more clearly defined—the tariff, the bank, slavery. Not again until the twentieth century would conditions be so favorable for the influence of personalities as apart from the principles of parties as they were in the decade after the new birth of the nation in 1815.

The first parties under the Constitution were determined by human nature and by different ideas of the Constitution, and only slightly by geographical considerations; the second alignment showed less of personality and more of industrial difference, with sectionalism playing no small part when the commercial north strove with the agricultural south; the third differentiation was, in final analysis, essentially based on sectionalism, the slave-holding, agricultural south against the free, manufacturing, trading, and agricultural north and west. The nation, by 1819, had come to consciousness of itself, with a youthful pride in its growth and achievements and a sturdy, if somewhat belligerent, faith in its future. It could not, however, put away its black heritage of slavery, even if it wanted to do so, and until it should really desire emancipation from that burden the pride of section and the strife for sectional advantage would wage political war against nationalism.

CHAPTER XIII

WAR FINANCE AND THE SECOND BANK
(1816)

THE political theories of the Republicans, according to which the powers of the federal government were to be kept at a minimum, broke down when applied to finance and banking. Gallatin alone, from the accession of Jefferson to the end of the régime of Andrew Jackson in 1841, showed real financial genius. But Gallatin had, for the greater part of the time, the immense advantage of an expanding country, an increasing trade, and a fairly stable currency. The refusal of Congress to recharter the Bank of the United States in 1811, the epidemic of careless banking, the outbreak of war, the withdrawal of Gallatin from the treasury, the dull, unseeing incompetency of William Jones and George W. Campbell, who in turn succeeded him, united to produce a condition at the beginning of 1815 which was very tersely described by the new secretary of the treasury, A. J. Dallas: "The monied transactions of private life are at a stand, and the fiscal operations of the government labor with extreme inconvenience. It is impossible that such a state of things should long be endured." [1]

The condition of the currency was perhaps the most serious evil. Bad enough before the war, when hostilities began the result was direst confusion and irregularity. The Bank of the United States, up to 1811, exercised a powerful steadying influence over the currency of the nation; its bills were good the country over; its prompt transmission of money from one part of the United States to another equalized the pressure put upon the currency; and its facilitation of government business was a great, if little appreciated, benefit to all sections and all large business enterprises.

It was good Republican logic that if the profits of the bank were so large as to enable it to offer a magnificent bonus for recharter, such benefits ought to be distributed rather than centralized in one national institution which might be used for political purposes. Banking in general had come to be looked upon as immensely profitable, and this accounts in no small measure for the rapid increase of local banks from eighty-eight in 1811, to two hundred and eight in 1813. Pennsylvania is a good illustration of the working of the craze for banks and paper money. In March, 1813, Governor Snyder vetoed a bill creating twenty-five banks, with a capital of nine million five hundred and twenty-five thousand dollars, declaring that there were banks enough already for all

[1] *Annals of Cong.*, 13 Cong., 3 Sess., 403.

the business of the state.[1] At the next session another bill for forty-two banks was passed over the governor's veto, and thirty-seven of the banks went into operation in 1814. In this way did Pennsylvania make up for her virtue in resisting the offer of the Pennsylvania shareholders of the old bank to give the state a bonus of a half-million and a loan of another half-million for internal improvements, if the state would give them a new charter good for twenty years. Similarly, New York's legislature passed, in 1812, a charter for a bank capitalized for six million dollars, after the governor had in vain prorogued the legislature for fifty-five days, to give the members time to come to their senses.[2] Even Massachusetts, temporarily Republican in 1812, chartered twenty new banks in eighteen towns.

The shareholders in these new banks were individuals, companies, and even states themselves, as in the case of New Jersey and Kentucky. Nominally their notes, in denominations from one to five dollars, were redeemable in specie, but when the note issues were three times the capital of the bank, and the specie was steadily flowing into New England, the probability of redemption outside that section grew remote, and suspension of specie payment of the notes was inevitable. New England sold its manufactures and imported goods to the south, whose foreign market was almost hermetically sealed by the war; but the four thousand four-horse teams

[1] *Niles' Register*, IV., 58.   [2] *Ibid.*, II., 89, 90, 227.

said to be engaged in the trade between the east and south or west about 1814 could not move a very great quantity of cotton and tobacco from the plantations to the northern markets. So Boston called upon New York for specie, New York upon Philadelphia and Baltimore, and these cities in turn upon the south and west. In five years, from 1809 to 1814, the store of specie in Massachusetts banks multiplied nearly ninefold, and it might almost be said that the difficulties of trade outside New England rose in about the same ratio.[1] So great was the variety of local notes, and so uncertain their value, that Philadelphia banks refused to receive for deposit the notes of the banks of the west and south, which were at a discount of seven per cent. in Philadelphia; while the notes of the Boston banks were at nine and ten per cent. premium. New York notes in Boston were discounted as high as twenty per cent.[2]

The final plunge into the stream of irresponsibility was taken when the news of the capture of Washington and the dispersion of government officials reached the banking centres. By the end of 1814 every bank from the Hudson to the St. Mary's had suspended specie payments. The government was the chief sufferer by this suspension, for it had mill-

[1] *Mass. Senate Docs.*, 1838, 38; Adams, *United States*, VII., 388.

[2] McMaster, *United States*, IV., 299; *Niles' Register*, X., 79, 398, XI., 80.

ions of revenue deposited in the suspending banks, nearly all of it being in paper money, which it was useless to move even if there had been convenient means. Discharged soldiers, army contractors, and holders of the securities of the United States alike went unpaid. The treasury was temporarily bankrupt, and the secretary borrowed small sums in order to live from hand to mouth. By the suspension of specie payments the government probably lost outright not less than five million dollars, not to mention indirect losses.[1]

It was in the midst of financial distresses such as these that the movement for a new national bank gained headway. Back of it was a man of Gallatin's energy and wisdom. When Gallatin resigned the treasury portfolio, in 1814, Madison had desired to appoint A. J. Dallas, of Pennsylvania, to succeed him; but at that time the president dared not risk rejection of the nomination at the hands of Leib and Smith. The accumulation of financial distress following the burning of the Capitol, and the fortunate resignation of the nerveless, unrespected Campbell, enabled Madison to put Dallas to the task of bringing some order out of the chaos in the treasury. He was almost the last man who would have been thought of for the place under ordinary circumstances, for he was a most unrepublican Republican, aristocratic, dogmatic, unpopular with the leaders in his state, a firm friend of Gallatin, and never an

[1] Dewey, *Financial Hist. of the U. S.*, 145.

admirer of the Virginia school of statesmen; but, withal, he was a man of ability, convictions, and courage. Within a fortnight after he became secretary of the treasury he sent to the committee of ways and means a letter recommending a national bank with a capital of fifty million dollars, and the House, by the decisive vote of 93 to 54, on October 28, 1814, resolved "that it is expedient to establish a national bank with branches in the several states," and instructed the committee to bring in a bill for such a bank.[1]

This bill was introduced November 7, but contained an objectionable provision authorizing the president of the United States to suspend specie payments by the bank in his discretion. The wrangle over this provision ended in the rejection of the whole bill by a two-to-one vote of the House, and the Senate then took its turn at formulating a bank measure. Within a week it had passed and sent to the House a bill embodying substantially the recommendation of Dallas. The House passed it with certain amendments proposed by Daniel Webster, whose speech on the measure was one of his masterpieces.[2] Out of a long and tedious struggle between the two Houses over these amendments, the Representatives emerged victors, and the bill, as sent to the president, provided for a bank with a capital of thirty million dollars, of which the United

---

. [1] *Annals of Cong.*, 13 Cong., 2 Sess., 457.
[2] Webster, *Writings* (National ed.), V., 35.

States might subscribe five million dollars in government stock; the remainder, open to private subscription, must be paid one-sixth in coin, one-third in stock, one-half in treasury notes; and the bank could not loan to the United States more than five hundred thousand dollars, nor could it buy government indebtedness. No permission was given to suspend specie payments.[1]

Desperate as was the need of the government for relief, both Madison and Dallas disapproved of this bill, which furnished little or no aid in the disposition of the bonds of the United States, and was really intended to be a curb on the state banks. So the president sent to Congress a veto message, in which he set forth the objections of the administration to the measure. He began with an admission which showed how far he had advanced in Constitutional interpretation since 1791 and 1799, when he had cited the incorporation of the bank as an example of the usurping tendency of the federal government.[2] "Waiving the question of the constitutional authority of the Legislature to establish an incorporated bank, as being precluded in my judgment by repeated recognitions, under varied circumstances, of the validity of such an institution in acts of the legislative, executive, and judicial branches of the Government, accompanied by indications, in different

---

[1] *Annals of Cong.*, 13 Cong., 2 Sess., 126, 259, 998, 1025, 1030, 1044; Dunbar, *Currency, Finance and Banking*, 257.

[2] Elliott, *Debates*, IV., 550.

modes, of a concurrence of the general will of the nation, the proposed bank does not appear to be calculated to answer the purposes of reviving the public credit, of providing a national medium of circulation, and of aiding the Treasury by facilitating the indispensable anticipations of the revenue and by affording to the public more durable loans." [1] In other words, the bank could not loan sufficient sums to the government to make it a worthy ally; it must maintain specie payments as an alternative of loss of its charter; and its provisions for subscriptions in government stock were not likely to make any improvement in the quotations of such stock. The treasury was thus left hopeless, with its six-per-cents. worth only sixty cents on the dollar in gold, and its treasury notes, which were receivable for taxes, at seventy-five cents. Within a week peace was proclaimed, and with it better prospects for the embarrassed treasury, so that the chartering of a new bank went over to the next Congress.

In his annual message of 1815, Madison suggested to Congress with characteristic indirection that "if the operation of the State banks cannot produce this result [the restoration of a uniform national currency], the probable operation of a national bank will merit consideration." [2] His secretary of the treasury, Mr. Dallas, moved in a straight line to his object, in a letter of December 24 to Calhoun, the

---

[1] Richardson, *Messages and Papers*, I., 555.
[2] *Ibid.*, I., 566.

chairman of the committee on the national currency.[1] He submitted an outline of a plan for a national bank, and supplemented it with an able exposition of the points relating to the capital, organization, duties, and operation of the bank. Not a word appears in either the message of the president or the letter of Dallas about constitutional objections, and in the debate Calhoun disposed of this stumbling-block of the Jeffersonians by saying, almost contemptuously, that the discussion of the constitutional question was "useless consumption of time." Even Republican newspapers did not disdain to publish Hamilton's argument in favor of the bank. To the Federalists of the school of John Adams and Pickering this must have seemed very like the devil quoting Scripture. Curiously enough, in the shifting of party positions the Federalists were now lined up in opposition to the new bank measure, headed by Daniel Webster, the leader of the younger school of Federalists.

The bill introduced by Calhoun, January 8, 1816, followed closely the outline made by Dallas. It provided a capital of thirty-five million dollars, three and a half times that of the first bank; subscription of seven million dollars of this by the United States; individual subscriptions, payable in coin and the funded stock of the United States; and a bonus of one million five hundred thousand dollars to be paid by the bank to the government

[1] *Am. State Paps., Finance,* III., 57.

in return for the charter privileges. Three men were especially prominent in the debates on the bill—Calhoun, Clay, and Webster—and the future course of these leaders lends particular interest to the attitude taken by them in this debate. Calhoun was in charge of the bill, and argued at length to prove that it was the right and duty of Congress to regulate the currency, thus restoring specie payments; that the right to make money was not at that time exercised by the government as a matter of fact, but by the state banks, which numbered some two hundred and sixty, scattered over the Union, circulating paper money in irresponsible fashion to the amount of one hundred and seventy million dollars on the basis of not more than fifteen million dollars in their vaults. The only adequate remedy was a national specie-paying bank such as the bill would provide.[1]

Clay took the same position. But Clay had a record to explain. He had voted against the rechartering of the first bank in 1811, because, as he now descended from the speaker's chair to explain, he had been instructed by his state to oppose the bank, because he had believed the bank to be meddling in politics, and because he did not believe then that the power to grant the charter existed. Now, "the force of circumstances, and the lights of experience" made it clear to him that the institution was indispensably necessary, and that Congress did

[1] *Annals of Cong.*, 14 Cong., 1 Sess., 1062.

really have this "constructive power." [1] Surely the old order was changing, from the Republican president to the latest accession to the group of the leaders of the party. Even Samuel Smith, the leader of the old anti-Gallatin faction in the destruction of the first bank, pleaded for consideration for the state banks, without opposing the proposed national bank, and he finally voted for the bill. The state banks, during the war, so he averred, "had been the pillars of the nation, now they were the caterpillars." John Randolph, who, defeated by Jefferson's son-in-law in 1813, had regained his old seat, flung a handful of indiscriminate invectives and insinuations, in his unique manner: "Every man you meet in this House or out of it, with some rare exceptions . . . was either a stockholder, president, cashier, clerk, or doorkeeper, runner, engraver, papermaker, or mechanic in some way or other to a bank. . . . A man might as well go to Constantinople to preach Christianity as to get up here and preach against banks." [2] Webster argued that there was no need for banks to regulate the currency, for the currency of the United States was as good as any in the world—gold and silver. Let Congress forbid collectors of duties, taxes, and payments on land purchases to receive the notes of state banks, and the financial situation would be speedily and sufficiently improved. [3]

[1] *Annals of Cong.*, 14 Cong., 1 Sess., 1189.
[2] *Ibid.*, 1112, 1113.
[3] Webster, *Writings* (National ed.), V., 48.

Opposition was unavailing, though the combination of Federalists and unreconstructed Republicans, 38 and 31 respectively, made a minority of 69 against the majority vote of 80 by which the bill passed the House in March. The Senate concurred, and by Madison's approval the bill became a law, April 10, 1816.[1]

In July the subscription-books were opened in twenty of the large towns and cities from Portland to New Orleans. When the period set for closing the books arrived, about twenty-five of the twenty-eight millions had been subscribed, and the balance was at once taken up by Stephen Girard, of Philadelphia. The total number of shareholders was 31,334. New England still refused to come to the rescue of the administration, even for a consideration, and her total subscription was only about four million dollars, while Philadelphia's reached nearly nine millions and Georgia's one million two hundred thousand. The bank opened its doors in January, 1817, and within a year branches to the number of nineteen were established in the principal cities and large towns of the country.[2]

The government of the bank was vested in a board of twenty-five directors, of whom the president of the United States named five; it was obliged to

---

[1] *Annals of Cong.*, 14 Cong., 1 Sess., 282, 1219; *U. S. Statutes at Large*, III., 266.

[2] Catterall, *Second Bank*, chaps. i.–iii; Dewey, *Financial Hist. of the U. S.*, 143–160.

transfer the public funds without commission, and from the government was to receive deposits of its funds, subject to the direction of the secretary of the treasury. The management of the bank during its first year was so bad that it barely escaped wreck. Its president, William Jones, lately acting secretary of the treasury, was almost criminally lax and inefficient. The provisions of the charter were violated in numerous instances: payments of coin on subscriptions were not insisted on; personal notes were taken for stock; the officers speculated in the stock of the bank and in the stock of other banks; discounts were made with half - paid - for stock as collateral; the relations with the local state banks were inconsiderate and often oppressive, especially through the attempt to regulate the issues of notes by the local banks. The liberal policy regarding loans in the west and south, and the consequent issue of notes in a region where stability of finances was not remarkable, increased rather than reduced the derangements of the currency which the bank was particularly designed to remedy. The culmination of two years of mismanagement was reached when the collapse of the Baltimore branch caused a loss of three million dollars. In January, 1819, it was proposed in Congress to repeal the charter, but a reorganization of the management, by which Langdon Cheves was made president, saved the institution for the fulfilment of its proper mission, though it never outgrew the prejudice and suspicion which these first years generated. Under Cheves its loans and circulation were reduced promptly to a safe and business-like basis, though not without great difficulty.[1]

While the bank was the chief instrument designed to bring about the much-desired resumption of specie payments by the state banks, it was not the only means employed. In the same month in which the bank act was passed, Webster secured the passage of a resolution ordering that all taxes should be collected in specie, or some medium equivalent to specie, after February 20, 1817.[2] Dallas tried to hasten resumption by seeking the consent of the state banks in July, 1816, to a regulation by which collectors of revenues were to be directed to refuse to receive state-bank notes of five dollars and under after October 1, unless they were convertible into coin on demand; and to refuse likewise all notes of the banks which failed to redeem these small notes.[3] The banks did not take kindly to this suggestion, and countered it with another. They did not see how the resumption could be made before July, 1817, since it was improbable that the new national bank would be in operation before that date.[4] The administration was not to be defeated in this fashion; it would enforce the legal provision at the earliest possible date, and so informed the banks. In Jan-

[1] Am. Hist. Assoc., *Reports*, 1896, I., 364 et seq.
[2] *U. S. Statutes at Large*, III., 343.
[3] *Niles' Register*, X., 376.　　　*Ibid.*, 423.

uary, 1817, the bank was in operation, and the people were ready for resumption. Crawford, who had succeeded Dallas upon his voluntary retirement in October, notified the banks that in case they did not resume specie payment on the date set by Congress, February 20, he would direct the removal of government funds from the state banks to the branches of the Bank of the United States. This had the desired effect, and resumption took place in normal and uneventful fashion on the day set. The statesman-like plans of Dallas were thus realized. The bank was in operation, the currency was reformed, if not perfected, and in place of a bankrupt treasury, which was his heritage, Dallas bequeathed to his successor a surplus of about twenty million dollars.[1]

---

[1] *Am. State Paps., Finance*, III., 141.

CHAPTER XIV

THE TARIFF

(1815–1818)

THE return of the nation to peace in 1815 was by no means a return to the thought or to the economic status of the period before the struggle. As a matter of fact, so far as commercial interests were concerned, war began with the embargo of 1807; and for eight years the commerce of New England was compelled to resort to strategy and to violation of the law to maintain such relations abroad as would bring profit. But, even so, it was found necessary to divert large amounts of capital from old occupations to new. While this diversion was supposed to be temporary and more or less limited, a means to prevent loss of interest and perhaps of the capital itself, it was found in the end that such investments as were made could not in the nature of the case be promptly withdrawn, to put back the money into the old channels of trade and commerce. One reason was that the investment had proved in a great many cases to be profitable, so profitable, in fact, that Calhoun asserted in a speech in the House in April, 1816, "he had often heard it said both in and out of Congress that this effect [of the war] alone would indemnify the country for all its losses."[1]

Economic conditions during the five years preceding the war operated in a considerable degree to protect such manufactures as sprang up during that period. But added to this condition was the fact that the tariff laws enacted between 1789 and 1812 were in reality protective. Twelve measures of this sort slightly increased the duties on a number of articles. In July, 1812, the existing permanent duties upon goods, wares, and merchandise from foreign countries were doubled, and an additional ten per cent. put upon goods not imported in vessels of the United States; while an added tonnage duty of $1.50 per ton was put upon foreign vessels. These duties were to last during the war and for one year after peace. In 1813 a further imposition of duty on iron, wire, refined sugar, and salt operated to increase the existing protection. Under the stimulus of these acts and these conditions, the amount of capital invested reached, by 1816, probably a hundred million dollars.[2] In cotton manufacturing alone, in 1816, the capital was estimated to be forty million dollars, employing one hundred thousand men, women, and children, with wages reaching

---

[1] Stanwood, *Tariff Controversies*, I., chap. v.; Calhoun, *Works* (Crallé's ed.), II., 169.

[2] *U. S. Statutes at Large*, II., 768, III., 35, 49; *Niles' Register*, IX., 365, 441, publishing in full the report of the committee of commerce and manufactures, February, 1816.

fifteen millions yearly, and producing goods worth forty millions. The woollen manufactures absorbed capital amounting to twelve million dollars, employed fifty thousand men, utilized wool worth seven millions, and produced a product valued at nineteen millions.[1] The total product of manufacturing in New England, so early as 1812, had risen to the very respectable figure of fifteen or twenty million dollars per year. Within a radius of thirty miles from Providence, Rhode Island, according to a memorial to Congress in December, 1815, there were one hundred and forty manufacturers of cotton, while Connecticut almost monopolized the making of woollens.[2]

During the war these rising manufactures practically monopolized the market for their products in America, since importation from Europe was at a stand-still, and they prospered accordingly. But peace and the revival of European competition spelled ruin for them, for, while these establishments were multiplying in America, the products of the old manufactories in England were accumulating in their warehouses. One of the first results of peace was the attempt on the part of the English to place this accumulated stock of goods on the market without much consideration of the original cost of the articles, sending them to America at a venture, and disposing of them at auction sales. "It was

[1] Another report of the same committee, in *Niles' Register*, X., 82.   [2] *Annals of Cong.*, 14 Cong., 1 Sess., 1651.

well worth while," said Lord Brougham, in Parliament, in 1816, "to incur a loss upon the first exportation, in order, by a glut, to stifle in the cradle those rising manufactures in the United States which the war had forced into existence, contrary to the natural course of things. The enormous amount of, I believe, eighteen millions worth of goods was exported to North America in one year." [1]

The American manufacturer felt at once this competition, in spite of the high duty which the English goods had to pay on entering the American market. The New England capitalist, earlier in the game, might have welcomed these shipments, and would have been glad to relinquish to the Englishmen the whole manufacturing industry, provided the trade of the sea might again go freely in New England bottoms. The longer the development of manufacturing went on in Massachusetts, Rhode Island, and Connecticut, the clearer it became that capital could not return to its old channel. Hence petitions for protection to the rising manufactures poured into Congress from the eastern and middle states, and the newspapers devoted much space to the dangers threatening the new industries.[2] So serious was the menace to these large and important interests that the administration and Congress felt compelled to take up in a large way the suggestion of protection for them. Not the least of the converts was Thomas

---

[1] Hansard, *Parl. Debates*, XXXIII., 1099.
[2] *Niles' Register*, IX., 295, 297, 310, 418.

Jefferson, who had held firmly against manufacturing in the beginning of the government, believing that cities and manufacturing were alike essentially evil.[1] One can scarcely believe that so complete a transformation in his views could take place as would enable him to write: "To be independent for the comforts of life, we must fabricate them ourselves. We must now place the manufacturer by the side of the agriculturalist. . . . Shall we make our own comforts, or go without them, at the will of a foreign nation? He, therefore, who is against domestic manufacture must be for reducing us either to dependence on that foreign nation, or to be clothed in skins and live like wild beasts in dens and caverns. I am not one of these." [2]

Madison's annual message of 1815 voiced in similar language his change of views: "Manufacturing industry . . . has made among us a progress and exhibited an efficiency which justify the belief that with a protection not more than is due the enterprising citizens whose interests are now at stake, it will become at an early date not only safe against occasional competition from abroad, but a source of domestic wealth and even of external commerce." [3]

Secretary Dallas, of the treasury, in obedience to a

---

[1] Jefferson, *Works* (Federal ed.), IV., 85, 87 *n*, 449, 469.
[2] *Ibid.*, XI., 502 et seq. Another form of this letter is given in *Niles' Register*, IX., 451.
[3] Richardson, *Messages and Papers*, I., 567.

resolution of the House, presented, February 12, 1816, an extensive and detailed report on the subject of a general tariff.[1] In this report he frankly faced the new situation of the United States in regard to manufacturing: "From the peace of 1783 until the year 1808 the march of domestic manufactures was slow but steady. It has since been bold, rapid, and firm; until at the present period, considering the circumstances of time and pressure, it has reached a station of unexampled prosperity." Dallas divided the manufactures of the country into three classes: first, those firmly and permanently established and able to supply almost entirely the domestic demand; second, those which, being recently established, do not supply the domestic demand, but which, under proper cultivation, are capable of being matured to the whole extent of the demand; and, third, those so immaterial or so poorly cultivated that the demand of the country is still upon the foreign source for supply. In the second class he put cotton goods of the coarser kind, woollen goods, iron manufactures of the larger kinds, spirits, beer, and ale. It was upon goods of this second class that he urged the imposition of protecting duties for the promotion of their development and the hinderance of foreign competition.

A general bill which carried out the suggestions of Secretary Dallas was introduced March 12, 1816. This tariff can hardly be called a party measure, for

---

[1] *Niles' Register*, IX., 437.

it received votes from every state except North Carolina. New York and Pennsylvania voted 36 to 8 for high protection of cotton interests; while the states south of Pennsylvania voted 53 to 11 against the cotton schedule.[1] Webster, who represented the commercial interests of New England, opposed the protective measure, even though the manufacturers of that section were to be its beneficiaries. Calhoun, on the other hand, was an ardent advocate of the measure, a position which, by the strangest of reversals of opinion, he later controverted in his "Exposition" of 1828. He thus narrowed his views from national to local or state interests, retracing the steps by which Jefferson had advanced from 1789 to 1816. In January, 1816, Calhoun said: "It is the duty of this country, as a means of defense, to encourage its domestic industry, more especially that part of it which provides the necessary materials for clothing and defense. . . . England is in possession of the sea. . . . That control deprives us of the means of maintaining our army and navy cheaply clad. . . . A certain encouragement should be extended, at least, to our woolen and cotton manufacturers."[2] Henry Clay, the speaker of the House, joined Calhoun in earnest advocacy of the protective system, consistently and enthusiastically maintaining his championship of what came to be known as the American System. His chief argu-

[1] Stanwood, *Tariff Controversies*, I., 148.
[2] Calhoun, *Works* (Crallé's ed.), II., 148.

ment was based on the need to put the country in a state of preparedness for war.

The general tariff bill which, thus introduced and supported, finally became a law April 27, fell somewhat short of the rates recommended by Dallas in his report. A duty of twenty-five per cent. on woollen and cotton goods was to continue until June 30, 1819, after which it was to be reduced to twenty per cent. The principle of minimum valuations was first applied to cottons by this act. Coarse cottons were especially important features of New England manufacturing, and for their particular protection the act provided that all cotton goods whose original cost was really less than twenty-five cents per square yard should be deemed by this act to have cost that sum, and should pay accordingly a duty of six and a quarter cents a yard, whatever their cost or real value. A like minimum duty was put upon cotton yarns. The object was, of course, the exclusion of low-grade prints and East-Indian fabrics, whose competition with New England products in the markets of the south would be a serious menace to all cotton manufacturers in the United States. At the time of the passage of the act, these coarse cotton goods were still worth about twenty-five cents; but with the fall of price of raw cotton and the use of the power-loom, the price of coarse cottons fell. The minimum duty, therefore, operated to increase protection until importation of the coarse goods practically ceased. The act also imposed a duty of thirty per cent. on rolled or hammered iron, leather, hats, writing - paper, cabinetware, etc., and a specific duty of three cents a pound on sugar.[1]

A comparison of the tariff rates established by this act, with those imposed under four of the previous acts—1789, 1807, 1808, and 1812—shows very plainly the deliberate application of the protective principle.[2] Nevertheless, it is probable that this act of 1816 was not so completely dominated by the protective idea as the later acts of 1828 and 1832. So large is the feature of revenue production that Professor Taussig insists that the act belongs really to the earlier series of incidentally protective acts, rather than to the highly protective measures beginning with 1824.[3] Proof of this position is to be found in the fact that this tariff act offset in a considerable measure the duty on woollen goods by a duty of fifteen per cent. on imported wool.

The support of this protective measure in 1816 on the part of Calhoun and certain southern men was due to the optimistic belief that the south would soon participate in industrial development along with New England. Only a few southern men, like Randolph, perceived, on the one hand, the impossibility of building up a manufacturing system on the

---

[1] *U. S. Statutes at Large*, III., 310. Stanwood, *Tariff Controversies*, I., 137–159.

[2] Dewey, *Financial Hist. of the U. S.*, 163.

[3] Taussig, *Tariff History*, 68.

basis of slave-labor, and, on the other, the probability that the imposition of duties upon the coarse woollen and cotton fabrics would add to the expense of maintaining the slaves. "On whom bears the duty on coarse woollens, and linens, and blankets, upon salt and all the necessities of life?" Randolph asked, in January, 1816, and answered with equal directness, "On poor men and on slaveholders." [1]

The effect of the tariff of 1816 disappointed most of its advocates who relied on its protective features. English goods continued to come in in spite of the tariff; and the revenues of the country increased by leaps and bounds as the results of these imports, from less than thirteen millions of dollars, in 1814, to forty-nine millions in 1816. The revenues from imports, which Dallas had estimated at thirteen millions for 1816, proved, when counted in the treasury, to be thirty-six millions. Just in proportion as the revenue increased did the manufacturing interests, particularly in New England, find themselves depressed. The foreign goods glutted the markets and their sale drew great sums of money out of the country, embarrassing both manufacturers and financiers, for the balance of trade went strongly against the United States. While exports of domestic products rose from $6,700,000 in 1814 to nearly $46,000,000 in 1815, and to $64,700,000 in 1816, they were very far from keeping pace with

[1] *Annals of Cong.*, 14 Cong., 1 Sess., 842.

the imports, which were \$83,000,000 for 1815, and
\$155,000,000 in 1816.[1]

For the manufacturer, adjustment to this new condition of affairs proved to be exceedingly difficult,
and almost immediately after the passage of the
act petitions were made to Congress for increase
in the measure of protection. The iron producers
were early and persistent advocates of increased
duty. The English manufacturer of pig and rolled
iron had the advantage of the use of coke in his industry, while the producers of iron in Sweden and
Russia had similar advantages in abundant forests
and cheap labor. It was therefore deemed necessary
by Congress, in response to this urgent appeal, to
pass another tariff act in 1818 for the purpose of
giving to the iron manufacturers similar protection
to that given in 1816 to the cotton and woollen
manufacturers. By this measure the duty on pig-
iron was changed from twenty per cent. *ad valorem*
to fifty cents per hundredweight; seventy-five cents
per hundredweight was substituted for the rate of
forty-five cents on hammered bar-iron, as fixed by
the act of 1816. An increase was also made on the
duties on nails, spikes, castings, and anchors.[2]

Here, then, were three great and growing industries urging persistently their claims upon Congress
for more and more care and protection. The " in-

---

[1] *Am. State Paps., Finance*, III., 15, 140, 141; Pitkin, *Statistical View* (ed. of 1835), 54, 265.
[2] *U. S. Statutes at Large*, III., 460, 800.

fant industries" created by the embargo and war periods, hampered by the severity of English competition in the years immediately succeeding the war, and protected in part by the acts of 1816 and 1818, were to be persistent applicants for ever-increasing favors at the hands of Congress. The political effect of this agitation reached its first great climax in 1828, when South Carolina, under the leadership of Calhoun, openly rebelled against the logic of protection; while in 1832 the open defiance of the United States' authority on the part of South Carolina was clear evidence of the dangerous extent to which the policy inaugurated in 1816 had been carried.

CHAPTER XV

WESTWARD MIGRATION AND INTERNAL IMPROVEMENTS

(1815-1819)

IN the ten years immediately following the Revolution, thousands of men moved across the mountains and down the great valleys of the westward-flowing rivers and laid the foundations of the three commonwealths of Ohio, Kentucky, and Tennessee.[1] Yet from 1802, when Ohio was admitted, to the end of the War of 1812, not a single state had been carved out of the western territory. The interest of the eastern states and the middle states in that wild and vast region known as the west was much stimulated by the events of the war; it became a land of promise, and a second great movement of the people westward began within a year after the proclamation of peace. The rapid extinction of Indian titles, made possible by Harrison's success at Tippecanoe, and by the chastening influence of the defeats of the British and Indians in the war, opened up large tracts of fertile land in

[1] See Bassett, *Federalist System* (*Am. Nation*, XI.), chaps. xi., xiii.

Indiana and Illinois, and attracted thither thousands of immigrants from the east and from the Old World. The opportunities for labor in the region west of a line drawn from the eastern end of Lake Ontario to Mobile are continually remarked upon by travellers of this period, like Bradbury and Fearon, who went through the interior of the United States for the express purpose of spying out the country for British or Continental emigrants.[1]

Another feature of the problem was practically determined by the appearance of steam-vessels upon the waters of the westward-flowing rivers like the Ohio. When *The Orleans* steamed down the Ohio from Pittsburg in 1811, light began to dawn on old difficulties. In the course of ten years the number of steam-vessels increased; but even in 1825 flatboats were still common, and the multiplication of steam-craft did little more than keep pace with the growth of new traffic.[2] Rapid reductions in freight-rates were brought about by these steam-vessels, which carried the produce of the farms down the river and brought back against the current merchandise from the warehouses and shops of New Orleans. Though the possibility of marketing the results of one's labor on the prairies of the west induced many hardy men to undertake pioneer life, complaints of

[1] Bradbury, *Travels* (Thwaites's ed.), 285; Fearon, *Journey through the Eastern and Western States* (1817), 201, 210, 228; extracts from travellers' views in Hart, *Am. Hist. told by Contemporaries*, III., chap. xxi.   [2] Hulbert, *Waterways*, 101, 140.

the withdrawal of laborers from employments in the east and in the middle states are not so numerous in 1816 or 1818 as they were in 1809 and 1810.

This is probably due in part to the rising tide of immigration from Europe, the numbers probably averaging eight thousand annually from 1812 to 1821. In 1817 about twenty-two thousand immigrants—three-fifths Irish and one-fifth German—landed in America.[1] This number continued to increase during the following years, until it became obviously advisable to make a definite enumeration of the strangers who sought homes within the country, provision for which was first made in 1820. The regions profiting most by this westward migration of the population were Ohio, Indiana, Illinois, and Michigan, where there was abundance of rich public land. The more sparsely settled sections of New York, such as those lying at the head-waters of the Mohawk and about Niagara, and of Pennsylvania between Philadelphia and Pittsburg, profited less by this migration of men from the east, because the means of marketing the produce of the farms there had not materially changed since the days of the Whiskey Insurrection. The movement of population into the west was therefore strong, and reports to *Niles' Register* from that region, in 1816 and 1817, refer to the daily pro-

[1] *North Am. Rev.*, XL., 460 *n.*; *Niles' Register*, XII., 336, 359, 400; XIII., 35.

cession of "families, carriages, wagons, negroes, carts, etc.," crowding the ferries on the way to Missouri, Alabama, and the northwest.[1]

The difficulties of reaching the west, of securing supplies of salt, iron, hardware, and the finer fabrics, of marketing the wheat, corn, and stock produced, and of maintaining regular communication by mail, created a new and lively discussion of the need of internal improvements, particularly those in the form of roads and canals. The new states and territories wanted people, increased property valuation for taxation, and larger revenues for the multitudes of schemes for developing the rich west. Whatever facilitated the satisfaction of these desires could not be done too speedily.[2]

During Jefferson's first administration, when revenues were abundant, the national debt rapidly diminishing, and the surplus increasing, the first suggestion of the advisability of national provision for roads, canals, and river improvements had been made. In compliance with a resolution of the Senate in 1808, Gallatin drew up an elaborate scheme for internal improvements at national expense, which would require two million dollars a year for ten years.[3] But the embargo, non-intercourse, and war put deficits and debts in the place of surplus, and

---

[1] Cf. Turner, *New West* (*Am. Nation*, XIV.), chaps. vii., xiii.; *Niles' Register*, XI., 127, 208, 223, 336, XII., 304, XIII., 224.

[2] Sparks, *Expansion of the Am. People*, 252. Detroit in 1815 had only one mail a week from Cleveland.

[3] Adams, *Gallatin*, 350 et seq.

the whole scheme of internal improvements was indefinitely postponed.[1]

The war had demonstrated in a particularly forceful manner the need of better facilities for transportation. While the bill authorizing the construction of the Cumberland Road, and appropriating thirty thousand dollars for it, was passed in 1806, it was not until 1811 that actual operations began on the road, and at the end of the war not more than twenty miles were completed. The cost of moving troops from place to place through sections having very bad roads, or no roads at all, was enormous both in dollars and in time. The sufferings of the soldiers themselves from the hardships of travel and from lack of supplies were chief causes of the excessively high hospital and mortality rate of the army. Food in plenty existed at all times during the war, as it had during the Revolution; but the problem of getting it promptly to the hands of the army which needed it was never even approximately solved. The use of steam in the navigation of the natural waterways was good so far as it went, but it had not gone very far in 1812 or 1814 in those parts of the country most affected by the war. The need of intercommunication between these natural waterways was increasingly imperative for all travel going east and west across the country; for example, from the Great Lakes to the Hudson River, from the Potomac to the Ohio, and from the

[1] Channing, *Jeffersonian System* (*Am. Nation*, XII.), chap. vii.

Carolinas to the great valleys of the Tennessee and Cumberland. In similar fashion, improvement was needed in the method of getting around obstructions like the falls of the Ohio and the St. Lawrence.

The lack of any specific provision in the federal Constitution authorizing internal improvements at national expense, combined with the strict-construction principles of the Republican party before the war, prevented any large appropriations in the early years of the century for making roads and canals. In 1816 the general appropriation act contained an item of three hundred thousand dollars for completion of work already begun on the Cumberland Road, and two years later two hundred and sixty thousand dollars was voted for a similar purpose; but a proposal to spend six hundred thousand dollars for general improvements, made in Congress in 1817, failed to meet with favor; while a bill providing for the extension of the Cumberland Road also fell through.[1] By 1820 Congress had passed ten acts carrying appropriations amounting to more than a million and a half; in 1844, the thirty-fourth act raised the total of money voted for the Cumberland Road to nearly seven million dollars.[2]

While Congress and the president discussed the power and the duty of the federal government to resume these improvements, several of the states

---

[1] U. S. Statutes at Large, III., 282, 426.

[2] Hulbert, Cumberland Road, App. A. (a summary of appropriation acts).

took action. Pennsylvania began to make contracts and appropriations for roads as early as 1790, but renewed activity is noticeable about 1809; in 1811, more than eight hundred and twenty-five thousand dollars was appropriated.[1] In the six years before 1815 the state had passed some forty acts for turnpikes and about half as many for bridges. By 1817 nearly two million two hundred and fifty thousand dollars had been spent by Pennsylvania on internal improvements, in addition to about five million dollars spent by her citizens. For all this expenditure, which put her ahead of any other state of the time, she could show more than a thousand miles of turnpike roads, including many fine bridges. Virginia voted funds in 1816 "to be used exclusively for river improvements, canals, and public highways." South Carolina, in 1818, voted one million dollars to be spent in four annual instalments for like purposes.[2]

The agitation in New York for internal improvements, especially for a great canal from Lake Erie or Lake Ontario eastward, continued from 1810 to 1816, when it assumed an acute form. From the Hudson valley two canal routes were marked out by nature in unmistakable fashion — from Albany up the Mohawk and westward to Lake Erie near Buffalo,

[1] *Niles' Register*, IX., 143, quoting the *Pa. Republican;* cf. *Pa. Archives*, XI., 656, 725.
[2] *Niles' Register*, IX., 429; McMaster, *United States*, IV., 419; *Statutes at Large of S. C.*, VI., 91, 92; *Revised Code of Va.* (1819), II., 201.

and from Albany to Lake Champlain. Much as these canals were desired, the undertaking of their construction seemed an enterprise so vast and so expensive that the state hesitated long to proceed without national aid. A canal commission, headed by Gouverneur Morris, investigated the scheme in 1810, and in 1812 he headed another commission which included De Witt Clinton, Robert Fulton, and Robert R. Livingston, which endeavored to secure aid from Congress.[1] War interrupted the plans, and the United States delayed action; but in the mean time the advantages of a canal to New York City and to the interior of the state west of Albany grew more and more obvious. In his message of February 2, 1816, Governor Tompkins particularly recommended the canal project to the attention of the legislature.[2]

It was, however, to the penetrating statesmanship and energy of De Witt Clinton, who was elected governor in 1816, and who threw his great personal and political influence into the scale, that New York was brought to the adoption of the proposed plans for a canal to Lake Erie. Clinton's memorial, an elaborate and convincing argument for the canal, was presented in 1816 to the New York legislature, and, backed by strongly stirred public sentiment, produced the desired legislation.[3] Ground was

[1] *Annals of Cong.*, 12 Cong., 1 Sess., 2166.
[2] *Niles' Register*, IX., 422.
[3] Hulbert, *Great American Canals*, II., chap. iii. (memorial in full), App. (New York acts of 1816 and 1817).

broken for the great canal at Rome, New York, July 4, 1817, and for eight years the work went on, until the canal stood complete in November, 1825. As an engineering feat, involving the digging of a ditch forty feet wide at the top, four feet deep, and three hundred and sixty-three miles long, with eighty-one locks to overcome an elevation of nearly seven hundred feet, the Erie Canal, in its time, is comparable to the proposed Panama Canal in the twentieth century. The expenditure of about seven millions by New York in 1817–1825 was a far greater strain than three hundred millions will be upon the present United States.

The same year that saw the culmination of the agitation for internal improvements in New York saw also a suggestion of a scheme of internal improvements at national expense by President Madison. "I particularly invite again their (Congress) attention," wrote Madison, in his last annual message, "to the expediency of exercising their existing powers, and, where necessary, of resorting to the prescribed mode of enlarging them, in order to effectuate a comprehensive system of roads and canals, such as will have the effect of drawing more closely together every part of our country, by promoting intercourse and improvements and by increasing the share of every part in the common stock of national prosperity."[1] When Madison wrote this, the only tangible evidence of the willing-

---

[1] Richardson, *Messages and Papers*, I., 576.

ness of Congress to proceed along these lines suggested by the president was in the twenty-three miles of the Cumberland Road. Much as Madison believed in the desirability of these improvements, he deemed an amendment of the Constitution necessary for their authorization.

Gradually, however, Congress and the executive, during the generation following the War of 1812, came to accept the doctrine of implied powers. For "common defense and general welfare" they found it "necessary and proper" to establish post-roads to provide for the transportation of the mails and military supplies, to build canals, and to improve the rivers for interstate commerce. It was the duty of Congress, said Calhoun, in 1817, to "bind the republic together with a perfect system of roads and canals. Let us conquer space. . . . It is thus that a citizen of the West will read the news of Boston still moist from the press. The mail and the press are the nerves of the body politic." [1] In this sentiment Henry Clay heartily joined. It concerted well with his notion of large powers in the hands of the national government, vigorously exercised, especially for the promotion of the interests of the west; and for thirty-five years there was no more eloquent advocate of internal improvements at the expense of the United States than the statesman from Kentucky.

As if to put Madison's proposition to the test,

[1] Calhoun, *Works* (Crallé's ed.), II., 199.

Calhoun, as the chairman of the committee to consider the expediency of creating a permanent fund for internal improvements, reported on December 23, 1816, a bill providing for the general use by Congress, in the construction of roads and canals, of the bonus of one million five hundred thousand dollars to be paid by the bank, together with the future dividends on stock of the bank held by the United States.[1] Calhoun did not share the views of Madison; the "common defense and general welfare" clause sufficed for him, however much his views altered in succeeding years: "Let it not be forgotten . . . that it [the extent of the republic] exposes us to the greatest of all calamities,—next to the loss of liberty,—and even to that in its consequences—disunion. We are great, and rapidly—I was about to say fearfully—growing. This is our pride and our danger; our weakness and our strength. . . . We are under the most imperious obligation to counteract every tendency to disunion. . . . Whatever impedes the intercourse of the extremes with this, the center of the Republic, weakens the Union."[2]

The "general welfare," therefore, demanded and authorized appropriations for the construction of roads and canals, and Calhoun's bill, so amended as to make the proposed expenditure in the states proportionate to their representation in the House, passed the House in February by a vote of 86 to 84,

---

[1] *Annals of Cong.*, 14 Cong., 2 Sess., 361.
[2] Calhoun, *Works* (Crallé's ed.), II., 190,

twenty-three New England Federalists voting against spending this enormous dividend anywhere, least of all in the already dreaded west. Two-thirds of the Virginia delegation, actuated by various motives, also voted against a measure calculated to build up that region which had already drawn off so many of the best young men of the older commonwealths. In the Senate the vote stood 20 to 15, with a breaking-up of party lines; nine of the fifteen votes were from New England, and the other six from the south.[1] Constitutional objections seemed to trouble the Republican congressmen very little; their party had so often resorted to the use of implied powers that its leaders might well consider the principle involved in internal improvements at federal expense as definitely settled in their favor. There was really no need for Calhoun to taunt his party with a glaring example: "If we are restricted in the use of our money to the enumerated powers, on what principle can the purchase of Louisiana be justified?"[2]

When the bill reached the president he found himself unable to overcome his constitutional objections to this extensive scheme, and he accordingly returned the bill to the House with his veto message of March 3, 1817. The chief burden of this "farewell address" of Madison, which he probably meant to be his final warning against too free an

---

[1] *Annals of Cong.*, 14 Cong., 2 Sess., 191, 934, 1061.
[2] *Ibid.*, 856.

application of the doctrine of implied powers, was the lack of power vested in Congress to undertake the proposed plan of improvements. In view of the numerous bills which Madison had signed, stretching the powers of the federal government far beyond those recognized by the Jeffersonians, there is something almost humorous,in this belated recrudescence of a constitutional objection which harked back to a previous generation.[1]

Those who expected that Monroe would take a more liberal view of the powers of Congress than had Madison on the eve of his retirement were doomed to disappointment. Monroe understood the rising tide of sentiment in favor of federal expenditures for roads and canals, and took occasion in his first message, December, 1817, to state that it was a settled conviction in his mind that Congress did not possess the right. At the same time, he suggested to Congress the recommendation to the states of the amendment necessary to give the power. This part of the message, on reference to a special committee, produced a very remarkable report, in which direct issue was taken with the president. The committee asserted that in at least three particulars relating to post-roads, military roads, and canals for interstate commerce, Congress undoubtedly had all the power it needed. A long debate ensued, but the necessary two-thirds vote to override the certain

[1] Richardson, *Messages and Papers*, I., 584; Mason, *Veto Power*, 95.

veto of the president to any measure appropriating money to roads and canals did not develop, and so no further important appropriations were made by the United States in the period now under discussion.[1]

Back of all this agitation, and as a basis for it, was the rapid growth of the western and southwestern territories, making possible the carving out of new states. Newspapers and proceedings of state legislatures give abundant proof that promoters of schemes for internal improvements were abroad in the land, booming localities, speculating in lands, and disposing of stocks of improvement corporations. The rush of people raised the population of Indiana from twenty-four thousand in 1810 to seventy thousand in 1816, when the state was admitted into the Union by act of Congress. In the year following, Mississippi was admitted, with a population of about fifty thousand, including slaves, and Alabama was authorized to establish a new territorial government, which was needed but for a short time, as the territory was admitted as a state in 1819. Illinois, in like manner, had grown up rapidly, and was admitted in 1818, on the same terms as the other states carved out of the northwest territory. Here were four states, two in the north, two in the south, admitted into the Union within a space of three years, whereas in the preceding twenty years

[1] Richardson, *Messages and Papers*, II., 18; *Annals of Cong.*, 15 Cong., 1 Sess., 451 et seq.

only two had been admitted, one of these being carved out of the most populous corner of the Louisiana purchase. The centre of population, of political power, and of political contention was rapidly moving westward.[1]

The stream of humanity thus flooding the west did not stop at the Mississippi River. The middle portion of it, moving down the Ohio, or across southern Ohio, Indiana, Illinois, and Kentucky, crossed the Mississippi and moved up the great valley of the Missouri. The French settlers and traders were soon submerged, and, like the Indians, disappeared before the advance of the on-coming host. But not chiefly from the eastern and middle states came the people emigrating to the west of the great river; population from the slave-holding south was also pressing into the same region. The territory of Missouri, which after 1812 comprised all of the Louisiana purchase north of the present boundary of the state of Louisiana, had a population of about twenty-two thousand that year; this number increased by 1818 to more than sixty thousand, and the territory petitioned Congress for a division, part of it to be admitted as the state of Missouri, part to be organized as the Arkansas territory.[2] This petition precipitated the great Missouri agitation resulting in the Missouri Compromise, the details

---

[1] *Niles' Register*, XIII., 224; *Annals of Cong.*, 14 Cong., 2 Sess., 254, 258, 565; *U. S. Statutes at Large*, III., 289, 348, 371, 399, 472.
[2] *Annals of Cong.*, 15 Cong., 1 Sess., 1391, 1672.

of which belong to the succeeding volume of this series.[1]

The westward march of population brought the United States face to face with the tremendous slavery problem in a new and vital form, for the development of the slave - holding southwest had gone on parallel with that of the non-slave-holding northwest. The fate of the great trans-Mississippi empire, so far as it was related to human slavery, was essentially bound up with the issue forced upon Congress and the United States by the eager home-seekers and traders who pressed into the new territory of Missouri, and who demanded, when once settled there, the political and civil rights and privileges which they had enjoyed in the older states and territories from which they had migrated. The nation's first great domestic crisis was upon it. Forty years later, when agitation, passionate discussion, and legislative temporizing had lamentably failed to bring peace, this same west, transformed economically, socially, and politically was to be the decisive make-weight in the salvation of the Union.

[1] Turner, *New West* (*Am. Nation*, XIV.), chap. x.

CHAPTER XVI

NEGOTIATIONS WITH ENGLAND
(1815–1818)

THE issues left unsettled by the treaty of Ghent[1] were more numerous, if not more consequential, than the great question of peace which was definitely determined. Commercial intercourse between the United States and the West India colonies of Great Britain; the fisheries; the navigation of the Mississippi; the disputed boundaries in the northeast and northwest; the regulation of the slave-trade; and the compensation for slaves carried off by the British during the war—all these remained to be settled. Immediately after the signing of the treaty of peace, the American commissioners signified their willingness to discuss with the commissioners of Great Britain the emancipation of commercial intercourse. Receiving no reply, and assuming that the British meant to wait for the ratification of the peace treaty, the commissioners went to London and Paris to wait for further instructions. In May came commissions and instructions; Adams was appointed minister to London, and with his associates, Gallatin and Clay, opened negotiations with a new British

[1] See above, chap. x.

commission. Two months of discussion followed, in which Lord Castlereagh eliminated most of the American claims; at length a commercial convention was signed, July 3, 1815, which was to last for four years, a period later extended to ten years.[1]

This agreement provided for reciprocal liberty of commerce between the territories of the United States and all the territories of Great Britain in Europe, and forbade discriminating duties in either country against the goods and vessels of the other. British ships trading to American ports or American ships trading to British ports in Europe were not to suffer from unfair and aggravating restrictions or prohibitions such as had repeatedly been attempted on both sides during the preceding twenty-five years. This was, indeed, a great gain for a portion of the American commerce; but the issue most needing settlement related to the intercourse between the United States and the British West India possessions. On this point the British commissioners refused to give specific concessions. "The intercourse between the United States and his Britannic Majesty's possessions in the West Indies and on the Continent of North America shall not be affected by any of the provisions of this article, but each party shall remain in complete possession of its rights with respect to such an intercourse."[2]

[1] U. S. Treaties and Conventions, 410.
[2] Ibid., 411; J. Q. Adams, Memoirs, III., 190, 202, 208, 249.

The East India trade was opened to American ships so long as they traded in products of the United States, or imported goods directly from the East India settlements to the United States. Vessels engaged in this traffic might stop for refreshment, but not for commerce, at the Cape of Good Hope, St. Helena, or any of the British possessions in the African or Indian seas.

The relief resulting from this convention was much less than was expected by the United States. In the first place, it was necessary to remove the higher duties imposed upon vessels from Great Britain and upon goods brought in such vessels, thus opening the way to the immense shipping interests of Great Britain to carry on their complicated and roundabout trade at cheaper rates than the Americans could carry on their simpler trade. An English vessel, for example, could make the voyage with a cargo from an English port to America, without suffering discrimination, and then go on with a cargo of American goods to a British port in the West Indies, which would be closed to an American vessel. The British ship-owner, therefore, as compared with the American, had opportunity for double profit. The practical result of this failure on the part of the United States to break down the colonial or navigation policy of Great Britain in regard to the West India trade was the limitation to British vessels of the export trade in American lumber, cattle, flour, rice, and other food products, the total value of which was estimated at six million dollars per year, since the British West Indies were the great market for these exports.

John Quincy Adams, after two years' service as minister to Great Britain, in 1817 returned to the United States to become secretary of state in Monroe's administration, and in that capacity to press vigorously for the settlement of the questions of boundaries and fisheries. To the latter question, the most critical issue of the time between the United States and Great Britain, much of the discussion at Ghent had been devoted. Two facts in the situation stand out clearly. First, the tremendous interest of New England in the fisheries, which were peculiarly profitable for twenty years before 1815, the exported fish being valued at twelve million dollars in 1814 — and no one knew better the importance and intricacies of this interest than the son of John Adams. Second, the two governments were unable to agree upon an interpretation of the third article of the treaty of 1783, in which it is stated "that the people of the United States shall continue to enjoy unmolested the right to take fish of every kind" in certain specified waters, "and also that the inhabitants of the United States shall have liberty to take fish of every kind on such part of the coast of Newfoundland as British fishermen shall use (but not to dry or cure the same on that island), and also on the coasts, bays, and creeks of all other of His Britannic Majesty's dominions in

America; and that the American fishermen shall have liberty to dry and cure fish in any of the unsettled bays [specified] so long as the same shall remain unsettled." [1]

The attitude of the British ministry, briefly stated, was as follows: the war terminated the rights and privileges recognized by the treaty of 1783—that is to say, there remained only to the citizens of the United States the right of deep-sea fishing; the inshore fisheries and the privileges of drying and curing fish no longer belonged to the Americans. The American contention was quite the opposite: the treaty of 1783 was not an ordinary treaty which could be abrogated by war; the independence recognized by the treaty of 1783 had not been brought in question; why then should other provisions of the same treaty be considered null and void? Such being the case, the United States still had both the rights which had been theirs as colonies, and which they had continued to have as independent states, and the liberties which had been guaranteed them in solemn manner by the treaty of 1783.[2]

In the year which followed peace the British government directed seizure of American fishing-vessels operating on the Canadian coasts without a license; the words "warned off the coast by His Majesty's sloop, *Jaseur*, not to come within sixty miles," written on the license of a Barnstable fisher-

---

[1] Sabine, *Fisheries* (reprint of 1853), 54; *U. S. Treaties and Conventions*, 377.   [2] *Am. State Paps., Foreign*, IV., 352, 354, 356.

man in June, 1815, seem to indicate that the British purpose was to exclude American vessels not only from the inshore fisheries and from the drying privileges, but from the wide seas frequented by the fish. It mattered little to the exasperated fisherman who was thus driven off that the British government disavowed the act of the captain of the *Jaseur;* the year's profit was lost. The presentation of the protest against the action of this British sloop led to a long and rather sharp correspondence on the whole question of the fisheries, extending through the years from 1815 to 1817, partly between Mr. Adams and Lord Bathurst in London, partly between Mr. Bagot and Secretary Monroe in Washington. Meantime the orders to the British vessels remained practically unchanged; Sir David Milne, of the British North American Station, gave orders, in May, 1817, to a subordinate to use "every means in your power for the protection of the revenue, as also the fisheries on the coast, against the encroachment of foreigners. On your meeting with any foreign vessel fishing or at anchor in any of the harbors or creeks of His Majesty's North American provinces, or within our maritime jurisdiction, you will seize and send such vessel so trespassing to Halifax for adjudication, unless it should appear that they have been obliged to put in there in consequence of distress." [1]

---

[1] *Am. State Paps., Foreign,* IV., 349, 350 et seq., 370; Elliott, *Northeastern Fisheries,* 58; *Niles' Register,* VIII., 384.

When Adams became secretary of state he instructed his successor at the court of St. James, Richard Rush, lately attorney-general and acting head of the state department, to ask settlement of such old grievances as were fast becoming acute; for example, the termination of the fishery dispute and the settlement of the western boundary, including the title to the region at the mouth of the Columbia River. Great Britain consented to negotiate, and Gallatin, who since 1815 had been minister to France and the most experienced and adroit diplomat in the service of the United States, proceeded to London to assist Mr. Rush. Instructions to the American ministers provided that they might consent to certain limitations of "liberty" to take, cure, and dry fish within British jurisdiction, but they were not authorized to relinquish all their asserted rights and privileges at the demand of Great Britain.[1]

The persistence of the Americans won for them more than had been really expected. The convention signed October 20, 1818, recognized the right of the citizens of the United States to fish along the southern, western, and northern coasts of Newfoundland and along the coast of Labrador, and gave them liberty forever to dry and cure fish in any of the unsettled bays and creeks of the portions of the coast already designated. The United States, on the other hand, renounced "any liberty heretofore

[1] *Am. State Paps., Foreign*, III., 375.

enjoyed or claimed by the inhabitants thereof to take, dry, or cure fish on or within three marine miles of any of the coasts, bays, creeks, or harbors" of British America outside the limits just specified— "provided, however, that the American fishermen shall be admitted to enter such bays or harbors for the purpose of shelter and of repairing damages therein, of purchasing wood and of obtaining water, and for no other purpose whatever." These provisions were supposed to settle once for all the disputed questions concerning American rights and privileges, and the convention of 1818 is still in force. As a matter of fact, the difference of opinion as to the method of measuring the three miles, whether following the sinuosities of the coast or following a line drawn between headlands no more than six miles apart, led ultimately to difficulties almost as threatening as those which prompted the negotiation of the treaty of 1818.[1]

By this same treaty the boundary of the United States west of the Lake of the Woods was defined. The treaty of 1783 laid down a line from the most northwestern point of the Lake of the Woods "on a due west course to the river Mississippi"; but the source of the Mississippi proved to lie nearly due south from the Lake of the Woods. Furthermore, the northern limits of the Louisiana purchase remained undefined. Since 1803 the only line which

---

[1] Rush, *Residence at the Court of London, 1817–1819* (ed. of 1833), chap. xix.; *U. S. Treaties and Conventions*, 415.

could have been called a boundary was that which followed the water-shed north of the streams tributary to the Mississippi. Various suggestions for settling this long-disputed question between the United States and Great Britain were made by King, Monroe, and Pinckney during the negotiations of 1803 and later, and one of these suggestions was now adopted for determining the new line. Through the northwestern point of the Lake of the Woods, as defined in the treaty of 1783, a north and south line was to be drawn. The boundary was to follow this line from the lake to its intersection with the forty-ninth parallel of north latitude, and thence along that parallel westward to the "Stony Mountains." [1]

The treaty dealt also with the rival claims of the two countries to Oregon, that vast region west of the Rockies extending roughly from the Columbia River to the fifty-fourth parallel. The British based their claim on explorations of its coasts by Captain Cook on his third voyage in 1778, and by Mackenzie and Vancouver in 1793; on settlements on Nootka Sound, recognized by Spain in the Nootka Sound Convention of 1790; and on posts established by the Hudson's Bay Company. The Americans, on the other hand, insisted that a valid claim was established by the entering and exploring of the Columbia River in 1792 by Captain Gray, of the ship

[1] *Am. State Paps., Foreign*, II., 584–591; III., 162, 164, 185; *U. S. Treaties and Conventions*, 416.

Columbia; by the founding of Astoria in 1811 by John Jacob Astor; and by the restoration of this post by Great Britain after its capture in the War of 1812, in accordance with article i. of the treaty of Ghent.[1] The case was one for diplomatic compromise, but it was one which could wait for adjustment; for Oregon, with its posts on the Pacific Ocean, was indeed a far-off country and its value remote. Accordingly the third article of the treaty provided that for ten years the country claimed by either party west of the Stony Mountains should be jointly occupied "free and open . . . to the vessels, citizens, and subjects of the two powers" without prejudice to any existing claim. The provision of 1818 was later extended for a second ten years, and was finally superseded by the treaty of 1846.[2]

The claims of the citizens of the United States for slaves carried off by the British during the war were by the treaty referred to some friendly power for adjudication, and under this provision the czar of Russia was chosen, and in 1822 awarded to the United States the right to recover damages. Ultimately Great Britain paid more than a million dollars.[3]

The commissioners failed to secure larger privileges in the West India trade, to determine the northeastern boundary, and to include in the treaty pro-

---

[1] For details of the claims, see Channing, *Jeffersonian System* (*Am. Nation*, XII.), chap. vii.

[2] *U. S. Treaties and Conventions*, 416, 428, 438.

[3] Moore, *International Arbitrations*, I., 359 et seq.

visions for the regulation or suppression of the African slave-trade. For some years Great Britain had urged the suppression of the inhuman traffic, and the United States was theoretically committed to her assistance. Several political and economic objections arose to active assistance in this suppression. The cotton and slave system gave to the country, and especially to the south, a strong and growing economic interest in the direct importation of negroes from Africa. The privateers of war-time, in any case half-piratical, were at the end of the conflict without regular business, and turned to the slave-trade, flying the Portuguese or Spanish flag, and defying the British patrol of the African coast in exactly the same way as they had defied the British cruisers during the war. Adams, as minister in London, refused to be drawn into a discussion of the search of slave-traders by war-ships, though Lord Castlereagh more than once threw out the suggestion. "It is a barefaced and impudent attempt of the British," said Adams, "to obtain, in time of peace, that right of searching and seizing ships of other nations, which they so outrageously abused during the war." In correspondence with Lord Castlereagh in 1818, Mr. Rush declined, for the United States, an invitation to join in a general treaty against the slave-trade.[1]

---

[1] J. Q. Adams, *Memoirs*, III., 557; Rush, *Residence at the Court of London, 1817–1819* (ed. of 1833), 310, 416–428; Rush, *Residence at the Court of London, 1819–1825* (ed. of 1845), 33–45.

The chief objection to such an "entangling alliance" with other nations lay in the fact that the trade could be suppressed only by granting to the patrolling vessels the right of search; and this right the American government could never yield, even for so righteous a crusade, and most certainly not so soon after waging a war of which one of the chief causes was the protection of American seamen and American vessels against this very right. Another and perhaps constitutionally valid objection to entering into a treaty on this subject was the fact that the United States had no colonies, and could not set up beyond its territorial limits a court to execute its penal laws by means of judges not amenable to the Constitution and laws of the United States. The United States did, however, in a half-hearted, mild way, legislate against the slave-trade in 1818: any person bringing in a negro must prove that the deed was not contrary to law. In the following year the president was authorized to use the armed ships of the nation to seize any vessel controlled by citizens or residents of the United States, if such vessel were found to be engaged in the slave-trade. In 1820 the United States made the slave-trade piracy; but, considering the number of persons known to be engaged in the traffic, it is significant that not a single execution of such a pirate is recorded previous to 1861.[1]

---

[1] *U. S. Statutes at Large*, III., 450, 600; Du Bois, *Suppression of the Slave-Trade*, 191.

CHAPTER XVII

RELATIONS WITH SPAIN

(1815–1821)

BY all the laws of political gravitation, East and West Florida belonged to the United States, and both Madison and Monroe strove vigorously to carry out the special secret statutes relating to the Floridas passed by Congress in 1811 and 1813. The return of the Floridas to Spain by Great Britain in 1783 was due partly to Spanish sentiment regarding an ancient possession, and partly to a general redistribution of territories in the triangular negotiations of 1782 and 1783.[1] The transfer of Louisiana to the United States in 1803 gave control of the mouth of the Mississippi, and thus removed one of the great causes of friction between Spain and the United States; but the long arm of Florida, reaching westward from the peninsula along the Gulf, shut off Georgia, Alabama, and Mississippi from a free outlet by the natural waterways to the Gulf, and gave rise to increasing irritation as these territories filled up.[2]

[1] See McLaughlin, *Confederation and Constitution* (*Am. Nation*, X.), chap. ii.

[2] See Channing, *Jeffersonian System* (*Am. Nation*, XII.), chaps. vi., xiii.

The east and west coasts of Florida furnished havens for smugglers and pirates of all descriptions; and in the troublous years between 1807 and 1815 the lawless and criminal from land and sea flocked to these shores. The growth of population in Georgia multiplied the difficulties over runaway slaves seeking refuge in Florida, and over the marauding and plundering Indians who either came from the Spanish side of the boundary, or, after their offences, sought refuge under Spanish authority.[1]

Mention has already been made of the conditions under which the United States seized a portion of Florida west of the Perdido River during the years 1810 and 1812.[2] It was no secret that the United States coveted East Florida, both because the long peninsula was one of the pillars of the gateway leading from the Atlantic to the Gulf, and so to the entrance to the great Mississippi Valley, and because control of Florida would simplify the commercial and political relations of the southern tier of states and territories. At best, East Florida was of questionable value to the Spanish crown; it was unproductive, expensive, and a source of continual friction between the new republic and the old kingdom. In common with the rest of Spanish America, it suffered from the lax administration of law and justice, and was a chief factor in the disturbed relations of the two neighboring powers. Once, at least, the Span-

---

[1] *Am. State Paps., Foreign*, IV., 539, 545, 567.
[2] See above, chap. ii.

ish governor of Florida signified to the secretary of state his willingness to surrender the province to the United States if prompt support were not given him from Spain. Although the spirit of revolt which affected the other colonies of Spain in America from 1810 to 1820 did not reach East Florida, the attitude of the United States to the rebelling provinces was offensive to Spanish pride, and in the end proved a serious obstacle to the acquisition of Florida.[1]

Other elements entered in to complicate the question of the transfer of Florida to the United States. Claims of Americans against the Spanish government for spoliations committed on American commerce during the Napoleonic period amounted to over seven million dollars; and, in addition, great evils had arisen in western Florida, which was used as a base of operations for the British during the War of 1812 and for some years after. In 1814, as an offset to the British occupation, General Jackson seized Pensacola and drove the British forces from Fort Barrancas, thus setting a precedent for a similar invasion of the territory of this nominally friendly power should occasion of sufficient danger to the interests of the United States arise in the future.[2]

Colonel Nichols, who served as British commander in Florida during the war, established a fort of considerable strength on the Appalachicola some fifteen miles from its mouth; and here he remained for some

[1] *Am. State Paps., Foreign,* III., 398, 571.   [2] *Ibid.,* V., 36–49.

months after the close of the war, undoubtedly inciting the Indians and runaway negroes, who numbered about one thousand, to continue their hostilities against the United States. He made the Indians believe that the United States was under obligations to reinstate them on the Georgia lands held by them before 1812; and when they discovered the truth, something akin to a state of war revived. Nichols left his fort in the hands of a garrison consisting of some three hundred negroes and about twenty Indians, with several hundred barrels of powder, twenty-five hundred muskets, together with carbines, pistols, swords, and equipment. The United States waited for a year for the disbandment of this hostile force so near the borders of Georgia; and when Spanish authorities failed to suppress the nuisance, a gunboat was sent which destroyed the fort and magazine by a red-hot shot.[1]

This willingness of the United States to use radical measures in Spanish territory for the establishment of peace along her borders had a certain justification in the treaty of 1795, by which Spain was bound in solemn manner to restrain by force all hostilities on the part of the Indians living within her boundaries, "so that Spain will not suffer her Indians to attack the citizens of the United States nor the Indians inhabiting their territory." Since Spain did not restrain her Indians, she could not claim, with good grace, the full rights of sovereignty for Florida.

[1] *Am. State Paps., Foreign*, IV., 546–560.

The president, therefore, was quite within his powers when he assigned General Andrew Jackson to the command of the forces to be sent against the Indians, and ordered him in December, 1817, with certain qualifications as to the course to be followed, to pursue the Indian enemy into Florida. General Jackson's orders from Secretary Calhoun empowered him to demand assistance from the governors of Georgia and Tennessee for such forces as he might need in the Indian campaign, and then used the following rather large terms: "You may be prepared to concentrate your forces, and to adopt the necessary measures to terminate a conflict which it has been the desire of the President, from considerations of humanity, to avoid, but which is now made necessary by their settled hostilities."[1]

When Jackson received these orders in Tennessee, he immediately wrote his famous Rhea letter to President Monroe, in which he said: "Let it be signified to me through any channel (say Mr. J. Rhea) that the possession of the Floridas would be desirable to the United States and in sixty days it will be accomplished."[2] This letter plays a very important part in the history of the United States through its influence upon the course which Jackson took during the war and afterwards; for he interpreted

[1] *U. S. Treaties and Conventions*, 1007; *Am. State Paps., Military*, I., 690.
[2] Benton, *Thirty Years' View*, I., 169–180 (Jackson's "Exposition," including full text of this letter).

liberally those instructions which gave him discretionary power in the campaign, believing that the president knew and approved his evident desire to seize Florida. In fact, Jackson asserts that he received from Rhea the president's message of approval. The president, on the other hand, claimed, at a later time, that he had never read nor reflected upon Jackson's letter until after Pensacola had fallen into Jackson's hands. Monroe's explanation, which leaves the mind somewhat unconvinced, was to the effect that he was ill when the letter was received, that it was given to Calhoun, and did not come into his hands again until some months later.[1]

Jackson acted with his accustomed vigor and promptitude: within three weeks from the receipt of his orders from the secretary of war, with more than a thousand men he began his march of four hundred and fifty miles to Fort Scott on the Georgia frontier, which he reached in forty-six days. The march abounded in difficulties: "The excessive rains have rendered the roads so bad that I ordered the troops, on their march here, to take their baggage on the wagon horses, and abandon their wagons, . . . and eleven hundred men are now here without a barrel of flour or a bushel of corn. . . . The waters are unusually high and the ground so rotten that it is with much difficulty even pack-horses can pass.

[1] Monroe, *Writings* (Hamilton's ed.), VII., 227, 234; Schouler, "Monroe and the Rhea Letter," in *Mag. of Am. Hist.*, October, 1884.

Every stream we are compelled either to bridge or swim." So wrote Jackson in February from Fort Early in southern Georgia.[1]

Shortness of rations, the desire to meet a flotilla bringing provisions from New Orleans up the Appalachicola River, and a determination to get at the enemy, led Jackson to march into Florida and construct a temporary fort. Here he discovered that several white men were involved in stirring up the Indians against the whites, especially a Scotch trader named Alexander Arbuthnot. "It is reported to me," writes the general, "that Francis or Hillis Hago and Peter McQueen, prophets, who excited the Red Sticks in their late war against the United States, and are now exciting the Seminoles to similar acts of hostility, are at or in the neighborhood of St. Marks. United with them it is stated that Woodbine, Arbuthnot, and other foreigners have assembled a motley crew of brigands— slaves enticed away from their masters, citizens of the United States, or stolen during the late conflict with Great Britain. It is all important that these men should be captured and made examples of. . . . I shall march this day, and in eight days will reach St. Marks."[2]

Jackson believed in thoroughness as well as promptitude. He captured St. Marks, finding Arbuthnot within the fort, and a little later took the two prophets. On a further expedition to the

---

[1] Parton, *Jackson*, II., 442.   [2] *Ibid.*, 447.

Suwanee, other prisoners were taken; among them, Robert Ambrister, who was suspected of counselling the Indians and furnishing them munitions of war for attack upon the United States. Returning to St. Marks, he constituted a court for the trial of the two British subjects on the charge of acting as spies, of inciting the Indians to war, and of supplying them with means of war. As a result, by Jackson's insistence and assumption of responsibility, Arbuthnot was hung from the yard-arm of his own schooner, and Ambrister was shot. Jackson then turned his attention to the reduction of Pensacola, which was accomplished by the end of May, 1818. The whole of Florida was practically in the military possession of the United States, and Jackson was marching on his way back to Tennessee.[1]

All these proceedings of the first five months of 1818, viewed as warfare, are petty; but the principles involved, and the effect of the events upon the policy of the United States, give them peculiar significance. The administration at Washington was profoundly perplexed as the details of Jackson's proceedings became known. The territory of a friendly power had been invaded, its officers deposed, its towns and fortresses taken possession of; two citizens of another friendly and powerful nation had been executed in scandalously summary fashion, upon suspicion rather than evidence. Had

---

[1] Parton, *Jackson*, II., chaps. xxxv., xxxvi.; *Niles' Register*, **XIV.**, 334 et seq.

Jackson stopped with the capture of St. Marks, little difficulty would have followed; for, as the duke of Richelieu observed to Mr. Gallatin, the United States had adopted the game laws and pursued on foreign ground what had been started on their own.[1] But each step of the further course of Jackson involved unusual perplexities, possibly war with Spain and with Great Britain. Rush reported that Lord Castlereagh said in conversation regarding the execution of the two British subjects, "that such was the temper of Parliament and such the feeling of the country, he believed war might have been produced by holding up a finger, and he even thought an address to the Crown might have been carried for one by nearly a unanimous vote."[2]

Monroe's difficulties were complicated by domestic as well as foreign considerations. Jackson undoubtedly added to his already great popular reputation by his effective, off-hand methods of dealing with the situation in Florida; he was high-tempered and would resent open disavowal of his acts. The cabinet deliberated long upon the course to be pursued in the midst of these difficulties. "We have met every day, one excepted, since my arrival here," wrote Monroe to Madison in July, "on the business of the Spanish posts taken in

---

[1] Parton, *Jackson*, II., 484, expressing Jackson's contemporary point of view and Parton's severe judgment; Gallatin, *Writings*, II., 69.

[2] Rush, *Residence at the Court of London, 1817–1819*, 152.

Florida by Gen. Jackson. Onis has demanded whether they were taken by order of the Government. If not, that they be surrendered and Gen. Jackson punished." Monroe was quite willing to surrender the Spanish posts, as he ultimately did; but he could hardly punish General Jackson after writing to him from the midst of cabinet discussions just mentioned: "In transcending the limit prescribed by those orders you acted on your own responsibility, on facts and circumstances unknown to the government when the orders were given, many of which, indeed, occurred afterwards, and which you thought imposed on you the measure, as an act of patriotism, essential to the honor and interests of your country." [1]

Another and more subtle reason for refusing to humiliate Jackson was revealed in Monroe's letter to Jefferson two days later than Monroe's to Jackson: "His trial, unless he should ask it himself, would be the triumph of Spain, and confirm her in the disposition not to cede Florida." Here was the secret of the whole game, the desire to compel Spain to cede Florida, and to this end Monroe and Adams contrived skilfully. "In throwing the blame [of Jackson's act] on the Spanish authorities, we placed it where it ought to be, and united the great mass of our fellow citizens against Spain. By the pressure on Spain we have obtained a territory equally neces-

---

[1] Monroe, *Writings*, VI., 55, 61; J. Q. Adams, *Memoirs*, IV., 107–116.

sary to her peace and our own, and have also given some support to the colonies." [1]

At the end of the Seminole War, Jackson was twice a hero; within a year he became a national issue, the most discussed man in the United States, as well as the idol of the rough and-ready west and southwest, whose spirit he embodied. Men recalled his early exploits, his volcanic temper, his daring, his disregard of conventionality and red tape, his loyalty to his men, his willingness to assume responsibility, and they approved all these things. What mattered an infraction now and then of international law? Who queried as to the fine points involved in the execution of Arbuthnot and Ambrister? But these matters were not treated in so cavalier a fashion in the cabinet or in Congress as in the discussions of the people and the press. In the earnest debates in the cabinet, Calhoun, then secretary of war, led the movement for censuring Jackson for his conduct in Florida, as a transgression of his orders.

The cabinet of 1818, therefore, did not contribute immediately to the elevation of Jackson. This function was turned over to Congress. Monroe's annual message of November 16, 1818, together with the official correspondence submitted with it, precipitated a discussion which cast a long shadow in American politics.[2] Monroe's adroit statement made it

[1] Monroe, *Writings*, VI., 63, 91 (Monroe to Rush, March 17, 1819).
[2] Richardson, *Messages and Papers*, II., 39; *Am. State Paps.*, *Military*, I., 681 et seq.

appear that the blame for Jackson's conduct lay not in him, but in the officers of Spain in authority in Florida. Theirs was the violation of the treaty of 1795 which justified Jackson's infraction of international law. Not all the members of Congress agreed with the president in this interpretation, and an effort was made to censure Jackson for his conduct.[1] The Seminole debate lasted for two months; and from the end of that debate onward Jackson loomed on the horizon as a candidate for the presidency; a man who represented a section, a spirit, and a sentiment, who needed to be elected president as a reward, and as a vindication vouchsafed to one whose integrity has been impeached because of acts committed in the name of the nation.

The correspondence between the department of state and the Spanish government, following the Seminole War, was keyed remarkably high. When the Spanish minister at Washington, Don Luis de Onis, whom Secretary Adams described as "cold, calculating, wily, . . . ever attentive to his duties," received official notice from Florida of the high-handed acts of Jackson, he made a sharp and spirited protest to the president, demanding not merely the restoration of the forts and other property of Spain, reparation for the insult, and the disavowal of Jackson's conduct, but the inflicting of "suitable punishment on the author of such flagrant disorder."

[1] *Annals of Cong.*, 15 Cong., 2 Sess., 583 et seq.

He announced, in addition, the suspension of all pending negotiations until "the one satisfaction which is admissible in the present case is granted." In negotiations which followed from August until late November, 1818, the French minister, M. Hyde de Neuville, was conscientiously carrying out with good effect his avowed instructions to do everything to preserve peace between the United States and Spain, even though his secret instructions required him to stand stanchly by Spain.[1]

The culmination of these diplomatic discussions was reached in Secretary Adams's great despatch to Minister Erving at Madrid, dated November 28, 1818. This was in the nature of an ultimatum to Spain, and reviewed at length the conduct of Spanish officials in Florida, the assaults on the peace, property, and lives of Americans in Georgia and Alabama, the refusal of Spain to fulfil treaties, her aiding and abetting theft and sale of stolen property, and her toleration of such men as Nichols, Arbuthnot, and Ambrister. Adams offered, on behalf of the United States, to restore the places captured, when Spain could guarantee an adequate force for fulfilling treaty obligations, and continued: "but the President will neither inflict punishment nor pass censure upon Gen. Jackson for that conduct, the motives for which were founded in the purest patriotism; of the necessity for which he had

---

[1] *Annals of Cong.*, 15 Cong., 2 Sess., 1883 et seq.; J. Q. Adams, *Memoirs*, IV., 126, 306.

the most immediate and effectual means for forming a judgment." He then proceeded to present the counter - demands of the president of the United States: the investigation of the conduct of the Spanish officials, their punishment for violations of treaty engagements in aiding and assisting rather than restraining the attacks of the savages upon the United States.[1]

The secretary further insisted that the weakness of the Spanish authorities was no excuse for their conduct; "that the right of the United States can as little compound with impotence as perfidy, and that Spain must immediately make her election either to place a force in Florida at once adequate for the protection of her territory and to the fulfilment of her engagements, or cede to the United States a province of which she retains nothing but the nominal possession, but which is, in fact, a derelict, open to the occupancy of every enemy, civilized or savage, of the United States, and serving no other earthly purpose than as a point of annoyance to them; . . . that we shall hear no more apologies from Spanish governors and commandants of their inability to perform the duties of the offices and the solemn contracts of their country. The duty of this Government to protect the persons and property of our fellow-citizens on the borders of the United States is imperative—it *must* be discharged." Added

---

[1] *Am. State Paps., Foreign*, IV., 539; J. Q. Adams, *Memoirs*, IV., 171, 173.

to this were demands for the punishment of the Spanish governor and commandant for neglect of duty, and for indemnities for the charges of the war on the Indians.[1]

There was no mistaking such language as this. In the nature of the case, however much her government or her minister at Washington might protest and promise, Spain could not comply with the requirements laid down by Mr. Adams for an efficient government in Florida. The fire of revolt burned in every quarter of Spanish America, and Spain was making not the least headway towards its suppression. Nothing remained, then, but to accept the other alternative and endeavor by treaty to secure settlement of all pending difficulties, and negotiations to this end, interrupted by Jackson's conquest of Florida, were resumed in Washington between Secretary Adams and Mr. De Onis. After transfer of the discussions to Madrid and back again to Washington, a "treaty of amity, settlements, and limits" was finally concluded and signed at the latter place, February 22, 1819, by which Spain ceded the Floridas. The transactions covered both that part which the United States had occupied for seven or eight years and which during that time did "not cease to be a subject of fair and friendly negotiations and adjustment," and that part which had been relinquished to Spain after two invasions by an army of the United States. By just what title

[1] *Am. State Paps., Foreign*, IV., 542, 544,

the United States finally held West Florida, it would be hard to determine.[1]

The western boundary of the Louisiana purchase, which had been continually in dispute since 1803, was now exactly defined. As a matter of fact, the United States did not have any valid claim to western Florida before 1819, and did have title to the great territory known as Texas; but the seizure of the smaller province disabled the United States from pushing too hard for the greater empire. Accordingly, the new boundary excluded Texas and was defined by the treaty in its third article to run from the mouth of the river Sabine, in the sea, northward along the western bank of that river, to the thirty-second degree of north latitude, thence by a line due north to the Red River, up that river to the hundredth meridian west from London, thence due north to the Arkansas River, along the southern bank of the Arkansas to its source, thence due north or south, as the case might require, to latitude forty-two, and then to follow that parallel to the Pacific Ocean. The United States renounced forever all claims to territory west and south of this line, and Spain in like manner relinquished all claims to the north and east of the line. It will be noticed that this relinquishment of claim and right by Spain could not confer title to any region over

---

[1] *Am. State Paps., Foreign*, IV., 422 et seq., 525, 623; *U. S. Treaties and Conventions*, 1016. The most recent government maps do not include West Florida under the Louisiana cession.

which Spain did not hold undisputed sway, therefore all the region north of the forty-second parallel and west of the Rocky Mountains, the region known as the Oregon country, could not be materially affected, save that the United States gained whatever shadowy title Spain may have there possessed.[1]

The " two high contracting parties" reciprocally renounced all claims for damages or injuries to themselves or their citizens up to the time of the signing of the treaty; but in order to protect the just claims of her citizens against Spain, which she had long been pressing, the United States undertook to make satisfaction for these claims to an amount not exceeding five million dollars. Hence it is frequently erroneously stated that the United States paid Spain five millions of dollars for Florida, whereas the money was really handed over to American claimants.[2]

The course of the treaty after its signature was by no means smooth, though the Senate acted promptly and unanimously.[3] Instead of ratification within six months, as provided by the sixteenth article, it was October, 1820, before Spain ratified, and the expiration of the prescribed time for ratification made a second consideration of the treaty by the Senate necessary. The delay occurred on account of two reasons: the desire of Spain to use ratification as a means to coerce the United States into a promise not to recognize the independence of Span-

---

[1] *U. S. Treaties and Conventions*, 1017. [2] *Ibid.*, 1019, 1020.
[3] *Executive Journal of the U. S. Senate*, III., 177.

ish-American colonies; and the unwillingness of the United States to recognize extensive grants of land which the king of Spain saw fit to make to three noblemen of his court, after negotiations were begun, but before the treaty was signed. By these grants, which comprised practically all the remaining crown or public lands of Florida, the United States would have been deprived of a valuable resource in indemnifying American citizens for their losses by Spanish spoliations. It was not until Spain realized that the United States was immovable in its position, that the grants of land were annulled, and the United States left free to do as it pleased about the recognition of the new Spanish-American republics.[1]

The action of the administration in accepting a treaty which relinquished all claim to Texas met with vigorous disapproval in Congress. The treaty was violently attacked in the House by Mr. Clay, who maintained a cavalier opposition to the president and his secretary of state, because Monroe had given Adams rather than himself the portfolio of state. He submitted two resolutions in April, 1820: the first set forth that the Constitution of the United States vests in Congress (both Houses) the power to dispose of the territory belonging to them, and that no treaty purporting to alienate any portion thereof is valid without the concurrence of Con-

[1] Am. State Paps., Foreign, IV., 509, 524, 668, 674, 684; Richardson, Messages and Papers, II., 54.

gress; the second, that the offer of the Spanish government, to cede the Floridas "for that portion of Louisiana lying west of the Sabine," was inadequate and should be rejected.   In support of these resolutions Clay spoke at length, but in the end they were dropped and the treaty ratified by the Senate by a vote of 40 to 4.[1]

[1] Clay, *Speeches* (Colton's ed.), I., 206; J. Q. Adams, *Memoirs*, IV., 53–67, 212; Gallatin, *Writings*, II., 35; *Executive Journal of the U. S. Senate*, III., 244.

CHAPTER XVIII

THE GREAT DECISIONS OF THE SUPREME COURT

(1816–1824)

THE supreme court came slowly and late into its own as one of the three co-ordinate departments of the government of the United States. It felt no need in the early years to assert itself, and, in fact, it refused to be drawn from its purely judicial and constitutional function into the broader field of theoretical or practical politics. In the case of Hayburn, which came before the court in 1792, the justices declined to serve as a commission to decide a non-judicial matter which was liable to review by the legislature and by an officer in the executive department of the government.[1] The court still further limited its own scope when Washington requested the justices to give their opinion as to the rights and duties of the United States as a neutral nation, by refusing, in 1793, to consider and pass upon any principle or procedure, unless it came before it in the form of a real action, and not as a

---

[1] 2 Dallas, 409; 1 Curtis, 9, quoting the opinion of the circuit court for the district of New York, Chief-Justice Jay presiding.

fictitious or hypothetical case. In this respect it stood in striking contrast to the supreme court of Massachusetts, whose justices were required by provision of the Constitution of the state to give their opinions to the governor or legislature, when asked, upon important questions of law and upon solemn occasions.[1]

Besides these reasons, it must be borne in mind that the business before the court was not large, though the work of the justices, who were also the judges of the circuit courts, was often severe. Between 1789 and 1801 only one hundred cases were decided, and of these only six involved large constitutional questions. Hence justiceships in the supreme court of the United States during the first twenty years of its existence were not so highly valued but that John Jay felt it to be a promotion to exchange the chief-justice's robe for the governorship of New York; and John Rutledge declined in order to become chief-justice of South Carolina. In two instances, one in 1795 and one in 1811, the president made three offers before he could find a man who would accept a vacant justiceship. John Quincy Adams, in 1811, declined appointment, even after he had been unanimously confirmed by the Senate. During Jefferson's two terms, the tide set strongly against the Federal judiciary, for even though the Republicans gained control of the legis-

---

[1] *Constitution of Mass.*, 1780, pt. ii., chap. iii., art. ii.; Dwight, *Hartford Convention*, 255.

lative and executive departments in 1801, the supreme court, the head of the judicial system, was Federalist. In the first fourteen of the thirty-five years of John Marshall's service, only three important constitutional cases came up for decision; nor did the active defiance of the supreme court by Georgia in the case of Fletcher *vs.* Peck, or of Pennsylvania in the Olmstead case (the United States *vs.* Judge Peters), tend to enlarge the influence of the national judiciary.[1]

This period was by no means lost time for the court itself: Marshall was moulding to his views of the Constitution and of the federal government the men who were serving with him as associate justices Jefferson, who both feared and hated him, complained more than once of this transforming influence of Marshall upon good Republicans appointed to the supreme bench. "It will be difficult to find a character," Jefferson wrote to Madison in 1810, "of firmness enough to preserve his independence on the same bench with Marshall."[2] One of the most important instances of this change was Joseph Story, a young Massachusetts Republican, who was appointed by President Madison in November, 1811. Next to Marshall himself, Story was the ablest and most influential justice during the first half of the nineteenth century. So like to Marshall's were his constitutional views and his method in stating them,

---

[1] 5 Cranch, 115; 6 Cranch, 87, 125; Hildreth, *United States*, VI., 155.   [2] Jefferson, *Works* (Federal ed.), XI., 140.

that it is difficult to distinguish between the Virginia Federalist chief-justice and the Massachusetts Republican associate justice.[1] When Marshall felt any hesitation or delicacy about writing a particular decision, he could feel perfectly safe in intrusting the work to Story. By 1811 the majority of the supreme court had been Republicanized; but its principles, or practice, became at the same time Federalized, or perhaps Marshallized.

The discussion of political matters in preceding chapters has shown how far the Republicans of 1816 differed from the strict constructionists of 1801. It was a far cry from the methods advocated in the Kentucky resolutions of 1798 and 1799 for deciding the constitutionality of any law or action, to the view held by those nominally of the same party in 1816. The strain upon fine-spun political theories, the obvious unwillingness of the doctrinaire hierarchy to press their principles too far, had prepared both the party and its leaders for a clear enunciation or crystallization, in final, authoritative form, of the fundamental principles of the Constitution as applied to the complex problems of a national federal government. Many cases which furnished opportunity for such enunciation fortunately arose during the twenty years after 1801, and were decided by the court with a courage, consistency, lucidity, statesmanlike breadth and profoundness of penetration which are still the marvel of students of constitu-

[1] Story, *Story*, I., 275.

tional law and history. New occasions had, indeed, so well revealed new duties that the wisdom of their enemies became the chief reliance of the Republicans for justifying their proudest acts. It remains to be shown how the supreme court gave the mordant to the colors with which the national fabric was being dyed.

Probably the most important single decision rendered in this period, certainly the most far-reaching in its influence upon general principles of interpretation, was that prepared by Chief-Justice Marshall in the case of McCulloch *vs.* Maryland, in which the existence of implied powers was definitely recognized and established.[1] The case arose out of the attempt of the state of Maryland in 1818 to lay a heavy tax upon the Baltimore branch of the Bank of the United States, which was resisted by McCulloch, the cashier of that branch. The lower and higher Maryland courts justified the tax, but on a writ of error the case went to the supreme court, where decision was rendered in March, 1819.

The court set itself first to answer the question, Has Congress power to incorporate a bank? In other words, Has the doctrine of implied powers justification? To this momentous question the court replied, without dissenting voice, in the affirmative, and supported its decision with an argument of remarkable strength and clearness. "The government of the United States, then, though limited in

[1] 4 Wheaton, 316.

its powers, is supreme; and its laws, when made in pursuance of the constitution, form the supreme law of the land. . . . There is no phrase in the instrument which, like the Articles of Confederation, excludes incidental or implied powers; and which requires that everything granted shall be expressly and minutely described. . . . The power of creating a corporation . . . is not a great substantive and independent power, which cannot be implied as incidental to other powers, or used as a means of executing them, . . . but [is] a means by which other objects are accomplished. . . . Let the end be legitimate, let it be within the scope of the constitution, and all means which are appropriate, which are plainly adapted to that end, which are not prohibited, but consist with the letter and spirit of the constitution, are constitutional. . . . Where the law is not prohibited and is really calculated to effect any of the objects entrusted to the government, to undertake here to inquire into the degree of the necessity, would be to pass the line which circumscribes the judicial department, and to tread on legislative ground."[1]

Therefore Congress had power to incorporate the bank, the bank had power to establish branches within the states without their consent, and the states might not tax the branches so established, save the real property of the branch, located within the state, and then only in common with other real

[1] 4 Wheaton, 316, 406, 411, 419, 421, 423.

property of the same description throughout the state. These same doctrines, especially as they relate to the power of the states to tax or interfere with the bank, are restated in several other cases which grew out of attacks on the bank, similar to the attack of Maryland. The cases extend over a dozen years, showing how loath the states were, in the times of passionate, political banking and crude economic thinking, to yield to the idea of national control of local institutions and legislation. Ohio and Kentucky, as well as Maryland, most reluctantly and tardily acquiesced in adverse decisions of the supreme court, like that in the notable case of Osborn (auditor of Ohio) *vs.* the Bank of the United States.[1]

The doctrine of implied powers thus clearly set forth received, during the following ten years, in relation to the powers of Congress over commerce, the militia, and acquisition of new territory, the necessary reiteration and reinforcement to make it one of the established principles of interpretation of the federal Constitution. Nor could it thenceforth be applied in any narrow sense to one department or line of action.

A striking enunciation of the wide application of the doctrine is given in the opinion of the court in the case of Anderson *vs.* Dunn (1824), in which the chief question was as to the right of the House of Representatives to exercise the semi-judicial power to punish persons outside its body for contempt of

---

[1] 9 Wheaton, 738; cf. McMaster, *United States*, IV., 504.

the House, extending punishment even to imprisonment.[1] Justice Johnson, speaking for the court, used even stronger terms than Marshall had done: "The genius and spirit of our institutions are hostile to the exercise of implied powers. Had the faculties of men been competent to the framing of a system of government which would have left nothing to implication, it cannot be doubted that the effort would have been made by the framers of the Constitution. But what is the fact? There is not in the whole of that admirable instrument a grant of powers which does not draw after it others, not expressed, but vital to their exercise; not substantive and independent, indeed, but auxiliary and subordinate. The idea is utopian that government can exist without leaving the exercise of discretion somewhere. . . . The science of government is the most abstruse of all sciences . . . and practically consists in little more than the exercise of a sound discretion applied to the exigencies of the state as they arise. It is the science of experiment."[2] At the beginning of an era of internal improvements at federal expense, of protective tariffs, with a great civil war and its consequent financial and monetary questions in the future, such words as these are both prophetic and ominous. From the high plane of such broad, constructive, statesman-like interpretation it would be but a step into the morass of demagogic loose construction.

[1] 6 Wheaton, 204.   [2] *Ibid.*, 225.

The first decision distinctly establishing the right of the United States government to acquire new territory was in the case of the American Insurance Co. *vs.* Canter, in 1828; but it really falls into this group of great decisions, for it related directly to the acquisition of Florida, and impliedly to all other acquisitions. Chief-Justice Marshall used sweeping words in this opinion to justify such purchases as that of Louisiana, about which Jefferson had had so many—but not too many—constitutional scruples: "The Constitution confers absolutely on the government of the Union the power of making war and of making treaties; consequently, that government possesses the power of acquiring territory either by conquest or by treaty."[1] Since the delivery of this decision defining so broadly and yet so explicitly the power to add new possessions to the United States, neither Democrat nor Republican has seriously raised the question of the right of the United States so to act. Criticisms of special acquisitions have been directed to the expediency, procedure, or morality of the addition, but never to the general constitutional right to acquire. Probably the court would justify, on the same general ground, the reversal of the process, by which the United States might transfer possession of part of its territory to a foreign power, for example, the Philippines or Porto Rico.[2] The adjustment of the boundary of Maine and the settlement of the Oregon question are cases

[1] 1 Peters, 542.   [2] 182 U. S., 1, 195–199; 183 U. S., 176.

illustrating approximately the exercise of this power of alienation.

While the supreme court was thus defining its own great functions and establishing on a broad basis the powers of the national government; while it was giving elasticity and adaptability to the phrases of the Great Charter of the Union, it was engaged in the no less desirable and necessary work of defining and limiting the legislative and judicial powers of the states so far as they related to the Constitution and powers of government of the United States. Here, again, it was the function of the judicial department to reinforce the tendency of the times, to emphasize the nation and its powers, and to delimit more exactly the area within which the states might exercise their oft-asserted and much-cherished freedom, sovereignty, and independence. With impartial hand the court levelled, on the one hand, the pretensions of old states like New York, Virginia, and New Hampshire, whose people had created the Constitution and the national government, and, on the other hand, the still more intemperate, defiant pretensions of new states like Ohio and Kentucky, whose existence as states had been derived from the national government.

One of the cardinal questions to be settled by the court pertained to the relation of the court itself to the laws and courts of the states. Could cases be appealed from the state courts to the United States courts? Could the supreme court declare unconstitutional the acts of a state legislature?

Several cases briefly described set forth this power; in the famous case of Martin *vs.* Hunter's Lessee, which was decided in 1816, the issue was first squarely raised. The court of appeals of Virginia refused to obey the mandate of the supreme court of the United States, and called in question the constitutionality of the section of the great judiciary act of 1789 which provided for appeals from the state courts to the supreme court.[1] In a large sense, there was involved the authority of the supreme court to decide upon the constitutionality of both state and federal laws. The court held, in this case, through the decision written by young Justice Story, that the twenty-fifth section of the act of 1789 relating to appeals was constitutional; that the Constitution operated upon the states in their corporate capacity; that the law-making bodies of the states were in every case under the Constitution and bound by the paramount authority of the United States.[2]

The appellate jurisdiction of the supreme court over the state courts in the matters mentioned in the statute of 1789 was thus definitely established, even though there were renewed assertions during the next few years that the different branches of the federal government could not be allowed to

---

[1] *U. S. Statutes at Large*, I., 80 (1789, chap. xx., sec. 25).
[2] 1 Wheaton, 304, 323, 342, 343.

determine the limits of their own functions.[1] The spirit of the Virginia and Kentucky resolutions died hard, but after 1816 the court was on high and secure ground. Five years later, in the case of Cohens *vs.* Virginia, Marshall further reinforced the opinion of the court that the states and their laws were subject to the jurisdiction of the court. Justice Field asserts, in a recent decision, that "no doctrine of this court rests upon more solid foundations, or is more fully valued and cherished, than that which sustains its appellate power over state courts where the Constitution, laws, and treaties of the United States are drawn in question, and their authority is denied or evaded, or where any right is asserted under a state law or authority in conflict with them." [2]

The application of the constitutional provision forbidding the states to pass laws impairing the obligation of contracts was first made in the case of Fletcher *vs.* Peck, in 1810, in which the court held that grants, as of land, are contracts, whether made by a law of a state, or otherwise by an individual; and that the nullification of grants so made, by repeal of the law, constituted a violation of contracts by the state itself.[3] The court went immeasurably further in 1819, in the famous Dartmouth Col-

---

[1] For a discussion of the attitude of the Ohio legislature in 1820, see McMaster, *United States*, IV., 500–503.
[2] 6 Wheaton, 264; Williams *vs.* Bruffy, 102 U. S., 253.
[3] 6 Cranch, 87.

lege case.[1] The legislature of New Hampshire had made radical changes in the charter of the college, without the consent of the trustees, who alleged that the act so modifying the charter impaired the obligation of the contract between the state and the college, and was therefore unconstitutional. The chief argument for the college was made by Daniel Webster in a speech which gave him rank as one of the first and most eloquent constitutional lawyers in the country.[2] The arguments were heard by the court in March, 1818, but the court was unable to come to any agreement on the points presented, and continuance for a year was ordered. How far the agreement of the majority of the court was due to careful consideration of the case on its merits, and how far its members were moved by outside pressure most skilfully applied, is an open question. Mr. Henry Cabot Lodge, in his *Daniel Webster*, asserts that, in all probability, personal and partisan influences played no small part in securing this great decision, in which four justices joined with the chief-justice.[3]

The opinion of Marshall, speaking for the court, is one of his strongest, and the concurrent opinion of Justice Story "one of his most distinguished labors in the department of Constitutional law."[4] The nature of contracts and of the law of corpora-

[1] 4 Wheaton, 518, 624.
[2] Webster, *Writings* (National ed.), X., 194.
[3] Lodge, *Webster*, 92–96.   [4] Story, *Story*, I., 322.

tions was discussed at length, and the conclusion reached that the charter of the college was a contract, that the act of the legislature which modified this charter in a material respect without the consent of the trustees was an impairment of that contract, and, so, unconstitutional and void. The issues involved in this decision were most momentous, for nearly all charters and contracts, and the statutes relating to them, were under the immediate control of the states. With this precedent, all of these might be brought before the court for review, and quite probably the decision in this case enlarged the jurisdiction of the highest federal court more than any other judgment ever rendered by it. Certain it is that the increase in the population of the United States, the vast multiplication of charters of incorporation incident to changed business methods, and the intricate complexity of later industrial and financial organization have all given cumulative significance to this decision of the court interpreting a very simple sentence of the Constitution.

While the principle thus laid down has been repeatedly reasserted in more recent years, its importance has been somewhat diminished, so far as it restricts the powers of legislatures over charters, by the fact that new constitutions or amendments and statutes have provided that such charters shall be subject to legislative alteration and control, save those in existence at the adoption of the Constitution or the passage of the law. In another case in the same year as the Dartmouth College case, the court declared unconstitutional that part of a law of New York regulating bankruptcy, by which a debtor must be released from prison and discharged from all previously contracted debts upon turning over all his property in a manner described. Such a method of discharging a debt was declared an impairment of the obligation of contracts, since the obligation of the debtor to use his property in cancelling his indebtedness extends to future acquisitions as well as to past accumulations.[1]

The control of commerce by the states before the adoption of the Constitution had been large, if not exclusive; and the difficulties in carrying on interstate and foreign commerce before 1787 were responsible for the grant to Congress of the simple but tremendous power "to regulate commerce with foreign nations, and among the several states." What is commerce? What constitutes regulation? How far may the United States restrain indirect interference by the state in interstate or foreign commerce? Scarcely any questions of constitutional interpretation so widely affect the every-day affairs of the people of the nation as do these relating to commerce, unless, indeed, it be those concerning the currency of the nation. The court first addressed itself to such questions in the case of Gibbons vs. Ogden,

---

[1] Sturges vs. Crowninshield, 4 Wheaton, 122.

which came up from New York in 1824. That state had passed a law conferring upon Robert Fulton and Robert R. Livingston exclusive rights of navigating the waters within the jurisdiction of that state with vessels moved by fire or steam. In deciding that the law was invalid so far as the grant of a monopoly prohibited vessels licensed by the United States for the coasting trade—for example, vessels plying between New York and New Jersey—from entering the waters of New York, the court entered deeply into the meaning of the word commerce. "Commerce, undoubtedly, is traffic, but it is something more; it is intercourse. It is the commercial intercourse between nations, and parts of nations, in all its branches, and is regulated by prescribing rules for carrying on that intercourse. . . . All America understands and has uniformly understood the word 'commerce' to comprehend navigation." [1] Thus Marshall laid down once for all the great principles of the law of interstate commerce, and succeeding decisions have been but confirmations and expansions of these principles, so that now they apply not merely to exchange of material commodities, but to transportation by land and water, and to communication by coach, boat, railroad, telegraph, and telephone.

Three years later, in the case of Brown *vs.* Maryland, which was decided in 1827, the court declared unconstitutional a law of Maryland which inter-

[1] 9 Wheaton, 1, 190.

fered with foreign commerce by requiring importers to take out a license and pay a license-fee. Whether this act imposed a tax or aimed to regulate the occupation of importing, it was an interference with a form of commerce whose regulation was exclusively within the power of Congress, for a tax on a person on account of his business is a tax on the business itself.[1]

It is difficult at this late day, when the principles established by this series of great decisions have become so universally accepted, to understand the shock which they gave to the men who belonged to the stricter sect of the Republicans, men who had fought and won political battles for strict construction, for reserved rights of the states, for the reduction of powers in the federal government. Of these Jefferson was chief, and his detestation and fear of Marshall gradually extended to the whole court, despite the fact that after 1811 only two of the seven justices on the supreme bench were of Federalist appointment. All save the chief-justice and Justice Washington, both Virginians, were appointees of Jefferson and his intimate friends, who maintained the Virginia succession. Yet Jefferson wrote to friends, about 1820, that the court was "construing our Constitution from a co-ordination of a general and special government to a general and supreme one alone"; and, further: "The great object of my fear is the federal judiciary. That

[1] 12 Wheaton, 419.

body, like gravity, ever acting, with noiseless foot, and unalarming advance, gaining ground step by step, and holding what it gains, is ingulphing insidiously the special governments into the jaws of that which feeds them." [1]

Tho ex president described in a general way the process and method accurately, but what he did not understand, and could not understand, was that the Constitution was being interpreted, in these great decisions, by men of the highest legal attainments and historical sense, men of the finest patriotism and devotion to the Constitution as the fundamental law of a nation of vast possibilities. Because they were such men, and "neither abstractionists of the French school nor dialecticians under the state-rights and strict construction dogmas," [2] succeeding generations of jurists, statesmen, and administrators of the government have risen up to applaud the soundness and wisdom of their interpretation of the Constitution.

Though the supreme court was the last of the three departments of the government to exert its influence on the process of nationalization, it abundantly justified Washington's judgment of it as "that department which must be considered as the keystone of our political fabric." [3] Through wars

---

[1] Jefferson, *Writings* (Federal ed.), XII., 177, 178 (letter to Thomas Ritchie, December, 1820), 201 (letter to Judge Roane, March, 1821). [2] Sumner, *Jackson*, 132.
[3] Washington, *Writings* (Ford's ed.), XI., 434 *n.*

and factions, through expansion and industrial transformation, through wisdom arising out of experimentation and endowment, the arch of Washington's vision stood solid and complete. The United States in full nationalism found itself.

CHAPTER XIX

CRITICAL ESSAY ON AUTHORITIES

BIBLIOGRAPHICAL HELPS

THE most useful and convenient guide to the material upon which this volume is based is Josephus Nelson Larned, *Literature of American History, a Bibliographical Guide* (1902), which gives not only titles, but some critical comment on the contents and characteristics of the more important books. Channing and Hart, *Guide to the Study of American History* (1896), and Albert Bushnell Hart, *Handbook of the History, Diplomacy, and Government of the United States* (1901), give certain detailed references for a great number of topics and subdivisions of subjects relating to constitutional and diplomatic matters. Justin Winsor, *Narrative and Critical History of America* (8 vols., 1886–1889), contains some materials on the period here treated, but is less complete and satisfactory than for the earlier periods, and does not include the voluminous literature of the last sixteen years; chaps. iv.–vii., of vol. VII., are not detailed discussions, but rather summaries with critical notes, of the constitutional history, wars, political parties, and diplomacy of the United States. The foot-notes in Henry Adams, *History of the United States of America during the Administrations of Jefferson and Madison* (9 vols., 1889–1891), and the critical essays on authorities in *The American Nation*, XII. and XIV., will be found suggestive and helpful.

GENERAL SECONDARY WORKS

By far the most important secondary work upon the earlier part of the period under consideration, from 1811 to

1817, is Henry Adams, *History of the United States of America during the First and Second Administrations of James Madison*, being vols. V. to IX., as cited above. It is a work of rare erudition, thoroughness, critical insight, and vigor of style. Mr. Adams made such extensive use of unpublished material in the American, British, and French archives that his books might almost rank as source material, and every one who writes upon the history of the United States from 1801 to 1817 must acknowledge a large debt to these scholarly volumes and to their brilliant author. The more important general histories dealing with this period are: Richard Hildreth, *History of the United States* (6 vols., 1851, and later reprints), strongly Federalist in sympathies; James Schouler, *History of the United States of America under the Constitution* (6 vols., rev. ed., 1894–1899), a judicious, well-proportioned, scholarly work, somewhat marred by a clumsy style; Woodrow Wilson, *History of the American People* (5 vols., 1902), rather sketchy on this period; John Bach McMaster, *History of the People of the United States* (5 vols., 1883–1900), especially valuable for citations of uncommon sources; *The Cambridge Modern History*, VIII., *The United States* (1903), an excellent volume of its kind, being a group of monographs of rather uneven merit, prepared by thirteen writers prominent in their special fields; Edward Stanwood, *History of the Presidency* (1898), the revised form of his earlier work known as the *History of Presidential Elections* (1884), a very convenient and reliable volume, though it lacks footnotes and references. Carl Russell Fish, *The Civil Service and the Patronage* (1905), the best book on appointments and removals, and Mary Parker Follett, *The Speaker of the House of Representatives* (1896), deal with special phases of the period.

BIOGRAPHICAL WORKS

Closely connected with the general secondary material are the numerous biographies of men who were active during the whole period from 1810 to 1820. Some of these are written so largely from the diaries, letters, and papers of their subjects as almost to make the volumes source material. In this latter class belong Henry Adams, *Life of Albert Gallatin* (1879), which appeared in the same year as Adams's edition of the *Writings of Albert Gallatin;* James Parton, *Life of Andrew Jackson* (3 vols., 1860); Octavius Pickering (and Charles W. Upham), *Life and Times of Timothy Pickering* (4 vols., 1867–1873). Of the biographies of James Madison, Sydney Howard Gay, *James Madison* (1884), while brief and severely critical, is an excellent biography of the fourth president; Gaillard Hunt, *Life of James Madison* (1902), prepared by the editor of the new edition of the *Writings* of Madison, lacks proportion, only a sixth of the whole volume being devoted to the eight years of Madison's presidency. An elaborate estimate of Madison and Monroe by a man who knew both intimately, is John Quincy Adams, *Lives of James Madison and James Monroe* (1850), two public addresses put into book form.

Of James Monroe no large and adequate biography has been written, such as may be expected when the Monroe manuscripts in Washington are finally in print. Daniel Coit Gilman, *James Monroe* (1883), is a simple and direct account of Monroe's services; the bibliographical part is by J. Franklin Jameson. Five other volumes of the *American Statesmen Series* are especially valuable and often illuminating: Carl Schurz, *Henry Clay* (2 vols., 1887); John T. Morse, *John Quincy Adams* (1882); John Austin Stevens, *Albert Gallatin* (1884); Henry Adams, *John Randolph* (1882); Henry Cabot Lodge, *Daniel Webster* (1883). Perhaps the most useful of these volumes, covering as it does the whole of the period from 1811 to 1819, and discussing the outcome of policies then inaugurated, is Schurz's life of *Henry Clay*. The life of Marshall is best set in relief in an admirable little essay of recent date by a great legal scholar, Joseph Bradley Thayer, *John Marshall* (1901).

The views of the New England Federalists are well set forth in the life of Pickering, cited above; in Henry Cabot

Lodge, *Life and Letters of George Cabot* (1878); and in Edmund Quincy, *Life of Josiah Quincy of Massachusetts* (1867). Other biographies which furnish valuable material are William W. Story, *Life and Letters of Joseph Story* (2 vols., 1851); Henry Wheaton, *Some Account of the Life, Writings, and Speeches of William Pinkney* (1826), later condensed for vol. VI. of Sparks's American Biography; John P. Kennedy, *Memoir of the Life of William Wirt* (2 vols., rev. ed., 1860); Julia Perkins Cutler, *Life and Times of Ephraim Cutler* (1890), which contains copies of many important documents for the history of the west; and Amos Kendall, *Autobiography* (1872), really a biography prepared from Kendall's notes by his son-in-law, William Stickney.

GENERAL SOURCES

The sources from which the history of this period may be written are at once abundant, accessible, and readily worked with permanent results. The great collections of congressional, parliamentary, and official papers are supplemented by extensive published collections of the public papers and private letters of the leading statesmen, while several periodicals of the time give clear notions of the popular ideas and movements relating, for example, to migration and immigration, internal improvements, and banking.

The *Journals* of the Senate and of the House of Representatives, and the *State Papers* and *Documents* of the sessions of Congress between 1811 and 1819, are very rare in their original form, and not easy to use. Later republications in four great collections furnish a much more convenient medium, notwithstanding the omission of a few useful papers in the discretion of the editors and publishers.

(1) The *Debates and Proceedings in the Congress of the United States, with an Appendix containing Important State Papers and Public Documents, and all Laws of a Public Nature, 1789–1824* (42 vols., 1834–1856), is commonly known and referred to as the *Annals of Congress*. The

title sufficiently expresses the nature of the collection, which was "compiled from authentic materials" nearly fifty years after the earlier portion was first written. It is not, like the *Congressional Record*, a verbatim, official account of the speeches and proceedings; it combines the *Journals* with more or less full and accurate contemporary reports of the speeches, especially those made in the House of Representatives, many of them being revised by their authors. The *Annals of Congress* are generally recognized as authentic and acceptable reports of the proceedings of the two Houses so far as they go. Thomas Hart Benton, *Abridgment of the Debates of Congress from 1789 to 1856* [in reality 1850] (16 vols., 1857–1861), is a convenient collection made up from the *Annals of Congress* and not sparing of speeches by T. H. Benton. Many of the speeches and documents in these collections appear also in *Niles' Weekly Register* and in the *American State Papers*.

(2) Along with these congressional documents stands on one side the *Journal of the Executive Proceedings of the Senate, 1789 to 1891* (27 vols., 1828–1901), and on the other side the *Statutes at Large of the United States*, 1789 to 1845 (8 vols., 1845, also in other editions). The laws in these and similar volumes of the *Statutes at Large* do not follow absolutely a chronological order. The most convenient edition of the decisions of the supreme court is that edited by Associate Justice Benjamin R. Curtis, *Reports of the Decisions of the Supreme Court of the United States, 1790–1854* (22 vols., 6th ed., 1881).

(3) For diplomatic results the standard compilation is *Treaties and Conventions concluded between the United States of America and other Powers since July 1776* (1889). Francis Wharton, *Digest of International Law of the United States* (3 vols., 2d ed., 1887; new edition announced by John Bassett Moore, 1906); John Bassett Moore, *History and Digest of International Arbitrations to which the United States has been a Party* (6 vols., 1898), furnish a great amount of material for the study of the processes and results of foreign negotiations. There are numerous editions

of the public papers of the presidents, the most complete and inclusive being James D. Richardson (editor), *A Compilation of the Messages and Papers of the Presidents, 1789–1897, published by the Authority of Congress* (10 vols., 1896–1899), inexcusably clumsy in arrangement and ill indexed, but exceedingly convenient.

(4) *The American State Papers* (38 vols., 1832–1861), selected and edited under the authority of Congress by the secretaries of the Senate and the clerks of the House during the years of publication, make a most important and almost indispensable collection. It is divided into ten classes: *Foreign Relations*, 1789–1828 (6 vols., 1832–1857); *Indian Affairs*, 1789–1827 (2 vols., 1832–1834); *Finance*, 1789–1828 (5 vols., 1832–1859); *Commerce and Navigation*, 1789–1823 (2 vols., 1832–1834); *Military Affairs*, 1789–1838 (7 vols., 1832–1861); *Naval Affairs*, 1794–1836 (4 vols., 1834–1861); *Post Office*, 1790–1833 (1 vol., 1834); *Public Lands*, 1789–1837 (8 vols., 1832–1861); *Claims*, 1790–1823 (1 vol., 1832); *Miscellaneous*, 1789–1823 (2 vols., 1834). While many of the papers gathered in these large folio volumes, especially those relating to foreign affairs and finances, appear in the other collections already mentioned, the excellence of the selection and arrangement and their fine typography make them uniquely valuable, and no apology for constant reference to them is needed.

Among the sets of parliamentary and state papers of Great Britain, *Hansard's Parliamentary Debates* covers the whole period treated in this volume, and gives full reports of the speeches in both Houses. *The Parliamentary Papers*, year by year, contain a great amount of material relating to the United States, as, for example, the volume devoted to the "Hearings on the Effects of the Orders in Council," in the series of 1812, and the "Papers relating to the War with America" in the series for 1814–1815, vol. III. The lack of a satisfactory index makes it difficult to use these papers with any economy of time.

The collections of state documents, save the statutes, even for the older states, are not large or in convenient shape. Those most likely to prove serviceable are the *Massachusetts Acts and Resolves*, 1810 to 1820; the *Pennsylvania Statutes at Large*, for the same years; *South Carolina Statutes at Large*, 1682–1838 (10 vols., 1836–1873); and the *Revised Code of Virginia* (2 vols., 1819).

Next to the great collections of government documents, and almost in a class by itself, stands unquestionably Hezekiah Niles (editor), *Niles' Weekly Register* (later *National Register*) (76 vols., 1811–1840) It is a broad-minded, judicious summary of the news of the country and of the world, with comment, contributions, clippings from contemporary journals, and reprints of many public documents; it constitutes a remarkable storehouse of varied and valuable material for the historian, to be used steadily and always with profit. A similar work of narrower scope, inferior in every way, is Barent Gardenier (editor), *The Examiner* (5 vols., 1813–1816).

Other collections of source material are Albert Bushnell Hart (editor), *American History told by Contemporaries*, III., 1783–1845 (1900); William MacDonald (editor), *Select Documents Illustrative of the History of the United States, 1776–1861* (1898). The selections in both volumes, often brief, are made in a discriminating manner, though the student will frequently regret the omission of certain desired documents.

Four books dealing with the Hartford Convention and the New England phase of the War of 1812 may be classed as sources by a slight stretch of the word: Theodore Dwight, *History of the Hartford Convention* (1833); Henry Adams, *Documents relating to New England Federalism*, 1800–1815 (1878); John Lowell ("A New England Farmer"), *Mr. Madison's War* (1812); and Matthew Carey, *The Olive Branch, or Faults on Both Sides* (1814 and many other editions).

COLLECTED WRITINGS AND MEMOIRS

The material in this class is so abundant and rich in this period as to merit a special section co-ordinate with the sources. The papers of the statesmen of the time have been collected with much zeal and patience, and the later editions, as a rule, have been edited with excellent, scholarly discretion. *The Letters and Other Writings of James Madison, published by order of Congress* (4 vols., 1865), and the *Papers of James Madison* (edited by Henry D. Gilpin, 3 vols., 1840), will soon be superseded by a more complete and accurate edition edited by Gaillard Hunt, under the title *The Writings of James Madison, comprising his Public Papers and Private Correspondence* (5 vols., 1900). The intimate correspondence kept up between Madison and Jefferson gives particular importance to *The Writings of Thomas Jefferson* (edited by Paul Leicester Ford, 10 vols., 1892–1899; also 12 vols. [" Federal ed.," usually cited in this volume], 1904–1905). For other editions, see the bibliographical chapters in the preceding volumes of the *American Nation*. No complete or adequate edition of the writings of James Monroe has yet been published. *The Writings of James Monroe, including a Collection of his Public and Private Papers and Correspondence* (edited by Stanislaus Murray Hamilton, 7 vols., 1798–1903), seems to leave much to be desired in the way of thoroughness and accuracy.

The *Works of John Caldwell Calhoun* (edited by Richard K. Crallé, 6 vols., 1853–1855) is largely made up of selections from Calhoun's numerous speeches in Congress, changed somewhat from their form in the *Annals of Congress*. The close connection of Henry Clay with all the great movements and policies of the United States from 1811 to 1819, and the readiness and passionate vigor with which he spoke in and out of Congress, give peculiar value to the *Life, Correspondence, and Speeches of Henry Clay* (edited with *Life*, by Calvin Colton, 6 vols., 1857; a late reprint, with an introduction by Thomas B. Reed, 7 vols., 1898). *The Writings and Speeches of Daniel Webster* (National ed., 18 vols., 1903) is useful, though Webster was less active and influential in this period than was Clay. *The Letters of Daniel Webster* (edited by Claude Halstead Van Tyne, 1902) contains letters and a speech on the War of 1812 omitted from the usual editions of Webster's works.

Because of the uniquely varied and efficient services of the two great secretaries and diplomats, the *Memoirs of John Quincy Adams, comprising portions of his Diary from 1795 to 1848* (edited by Charles Francis Adams, 12 vols., 1874–1877), and the *Writings of Albert Gallatin* (edited by Henry Adams, 3 vols., 1879), are of cardinal importance, especially in relation to diplomacy and finance and to the characters of the public men of the times. Nowhere else is there such an analytical, day-by-day discussion of the motives and characteristics of his contemporaries and of important administrative measures of the United States from 1817 to 1825 as in the *Memoirs* of Adams. Gallatin, more reserved and secretive than Adams, never made any man his confidant, much less a diary.

Other collections of like sort, but less necessary to a full understanding of the period, might be likened to the Minor Prophets: *The Life and Correspondence of Rufus King* (edited by Charles R. King, 6 vols., 1894–1900); *Diary and Letters of Gouverneur Morris* (edited by Anne Cary Morris, 2 vols., 1888); *Memoirs and Letters of Dolly Madison* (edited by her grandniece, 1886); *Memoirs of Lieutenant-General [Winfield] Scott, LL.D.* (2 vols., 1864), written by himself nearly fifty years after the War of 1812; James Wilkinson, *Memoirs of my Own Times* (3 vols., 1816), elaborate and entirely untrustworthy; *Public and Military Papers of Daniel D. Tompkins*, 1807–1817 (edited by Hugh Hastings, 3 vols., 1898–1902).

FOREIGN RELATIONS

The most important papers and discussions relating to the intercourse between the United States and Great Britain, France, Spain, and Russia are to be found in the volumes of the *American State Papers, Foreign Relations;* the Appendices of the *Annals of Congress; Niles' Register;* the *Parliamentary Debates*, and the *Parliamentary Papers,* already noted. The documents which appear in these collections are usually printed in full; but, of course, many are omitted, and the research of Henry Adams in the British and French archives shows how highly important some of these unpublished papers are. Much light is cast upon these relations by the *Correspondance de Napoléon Iier, publiée par l'ordre de l'Empereur Napoléon III.* (32 vols., 1858–1870); *Memoirs and Correspondence of Robert Steward, Viscount Castlereagh* (12 vols., 1851–1853); Augustus Granville Stapleton, *George Canning and his Times* (1859), and H. W. V. Temperley, *Life of Canning* (1905).

The peace negotiations of 1814–1815 and the preceding attempt at mediation by Russia may be well traced in the *Memoirs of John Quincy Adams* and in the *Writings of Albert Gallatin*. One phase of these discussions is treated at length in John Quincy Adams, *The Duplicate Letters, the Fisheries, and the Mississippi: Documents relating to the Transactions at the Negotiations of Ghent* (1822). For the later period, Richard Rush, *Residence at the Court of London, 1817–1825* (3d ed., edited by Benjamin Rush, 1872), and *Occasional Productions, Political, Diplomatic, and Miscellaneous* (edited by his executors, 1860), will be found valuable. The fisheries question is summarized in convenient and scholarly fashion in Charles Burke Elliott, *The United States and the Northeastern Fisheries* (1887).

The general histories of American diplomacy deal at greater or less length with this particular period. Theodore Lyman, Jr., *The Diplomacy of the United States, 1778–1828* (2d ed., 1828), though somewhat antiquated, is still useful. Eugene Schuyler, *American Diplomacy and the Furtherance of Commerce* (1886), discusses neutral rights, fisheries, and the Mississippi. John W. Foster, *A Century of American Diplomacy* (1900), chap. vii., and Justin Winsor, *Narrative and Critical History of America*, VII., chap. vii., give brief accounts, as does John Bassett Moore, *American Diplomacy* (1905), chaps. ii., v.

THE WAR OF 1812

Source material relating to the War of 1812 is both abundant and varied. The *American State Papers*, especially the volumes on *Foreign Relations, Military Affairs, Naval Affairs*, and *Commerce and Navigation*, are rich in reports, statistics, and discussions; while the British *Parliamentary Papers* are in like manner indispensable. Naturally, the brilliant exploits of the little American navy have produced a large crop of books on that side of the contest, and along with them, even before the close of the war, came a dismal series of apologies of unsuccessful military commanders and bickering officials.

Akin to the *American State Papers* are *Official Letters of the Military and Naval Officers of the United States, 1812–1815* (edited by John Brannen, 1823), a reliable and comprehensive collection, and *Historical Register of the United States* [1813–1814] (edited by T. H. Palmer, 4 vols., 1814–1816). Two contemporary works from the English side are of great importance, though both are seriously marred by the bitterest controversial and partisan spirit, which now and then manifests itself in downright vituperation and scurrility; William James, *A Full and Correct Account of the Chief Naval Occurrences of the Late War between Great Britain and the United States* (1817), and *A Full and Correct Account of the Military Occurrences of the Late War between Great Britain and the United States* (2 vols., 1818). These books were written from the sources, and many of the official documents—for example, the reports of the commanders of the British expedition against Washington—are reprinted in the text or in the appendices. Theodore Roosevelt, *The Naval War of 1812* (3d ed., 1883, and Sagamore ed., 2 vols., 1900, besides other editions), was written largely to combat in vigorous fashion the prejudice and bias of James. It is a reliable and scientific treatment of the subject. For William Laird Clowes, *The Royal Navy, a History* (7 vols., 1897–1903), VI., chap. xii., Mr. Roosevelt has written a still briefer, less controversial, and more interpretative account of the war, "as remarkable for its analytical insight as for its impartial plain-speaking."

Edgar Stanton Maclay, *History of the United States Navy from 1775 to 1901* (new ed., 3 vols., 1901–1902), and *History of American Privateers* (1899), are the best and most comprehensive works dealing in detail with the work of the volunteer and regular navy. By far the ripest and most philosophic treatment accorded the naval warfare of 1812 to 1815 is Alfred Thayer Mahan, *The War of 1812* (*Scribner's Magazine*, January, 1904–January, 1905), soon to be reprinted in book form. The first chapters, discussing the causes of the war and its relation to American commerce, are especially significant. George Coggeshall, *History of the American Privateers and Letters of Marque during our War with England* (1856), written long after the war by one of the privateer captains, and Gomer Williams, *History of the Liverpool Privateers* (1897), are valuable. The story of one of the famous ships of the navy is told in Ira Nelson Hollis, *The Frigate Constitution* (1900).

From the biographical side, the most useful accounts of the naval warfare are in Alexander Slidell Mackenzie, *Life of Stephen Decatur* (1846 and 1864); Cyrus Townsend Brady, *Stephen Decatur* (1900); John M. Niles, *Life of Oliver Hazard Perry* (1820); David Porter, *Journal of a Cruise made to the Pacific Ocean* (2 vols., 1815), a book all-important for the understanding of the remarkable cruise of the *Essex;* David Dixon Porter, *Memoir of Commodore David Porter* (1875), based in part upon the preceding *Journal.*

The military operations of the war have naturally received much less comprehensive treatment than the naval: the story is both disheartening and discreditable, and the treatment by contemporaries, for the most part, either apologetic and explanatory or bitterly critical and recriminative. Few of these authorities cover more than a portion of its campaigns. William Hull, *Defence of Brigadier-General Hull, with an Address to the Citizens of the United States* (1814); H. A. S. Dearborn, *Defence of General*

Henry Dearborn against the Attack of General William Hull
(1824); John Armstrong, *Notices of the War of 1812* (2 vols.,
1836–1840), a brief account of the military operations by a
man who was secretary of war under Madison, and who
fortified his argument with quotations from official reports, correspondence, and documents, but indulged often
in acrid criticisms and personal prejudices.   James Wilkinson, *Memoirs of my Own Times* (3 vols., 1816), is a tedious,
disgusting, but necessary book, for its author was one of
the leading generals, probably the most investigated and
court-martialled of them all.   Charles Jared Ingersoll,
*Historical Sketch of the Second War between the United
States and Great Britain* (2 vols., 1845–1849), and *History
of the Second War between the United States and Great
Britain, 2d series* (2 vols., 1852), is a strongly partisan and
not altogether reliable story of the war, though written by
a violently prejudiced Republican member of Congress of
the war period who had peculiar advantages for knowing
the inside of things.   The book must be used, but always
with caution, and the same warning applies to Benson John
Lossing, *Pictorial Field-Book of the War of 1812* (1868).

In an entirely distinct and higher class belong several
books of American and of English origin.   Robert B.
McAfee, *History of the Late War in the Western Country*
(1816), is one of the very best accounts of the conditions
of the army on the frontier and of the methods of organizing, transporting, and handling the troops during the war.
Moses Dawson, *Historical Narrative of the Civil and Military
Services of Major-General William Henry Harrison* (1824),
is another work of the same thorough and graphic character,
drawing largely from McAfee's book.   The Niagara campaigns are well described in Ernest Cruikshank, *Docu-
mentary History of the Campaigns upon the Niagara Frontier,
1813–1814* (6 parts, 1896–1904).   Major John Richardson
[of the British Army], *War of 1812, containing a full and Detailed Narrative of the Operations of the Right Division of the
Canadian Army* (1842; reprinted with notes and a biography
by A. C. Casselman, 1902), gives some excellent material

for understanding the relations of the British and Indians, especially those under Tecumseh. For the situation in Upper Canada at the outbreak of hostilities, and the measures taken to defend the province, see Ferdinand Brock Tupper, *Life and Correspondence of Major - General Sir Isaac Brock, K.B.* (2d ed., enlarged, 1847). The letters discuss clearly the Indian problem of the provincial administration.

Masses of official papers and reports relating to the campaigns around Washington and New Orleans are in the *American State Papers, Military Affairs;* in James, *Military Occurrences*, and in *Niles' Register*. Regarding some of the proceedings in Washington, reference may be had to *Memoirs and Letters of Dolly Madison;* James Monroe, *Writings;* and the correspondence of Serrurier with the French Foreign Office, as revealed by Henry Adams, *History of the United States*, VIII., chaps. v. and vi. George Robert Gleig, *The Campaigns of the British Army at Washington and New Orleans* (1818), an unusually graphic and satisfactory account, was written by an officer of the British army who served in the two campaigns. Several editions of the book appeared, one of them (Philadelphia, 1821), containing an appendix for the purpose of correcting sundry errors in the work. An anonymous volume, *A Subaltern in America, comprising his Narrative of the Campaigns of the British Army at Baltimore, Washington, etc., during the Late War* (1833), is deliberately modelled after Gleig's books, and incorporates part of the title of another book by Gleig, *The Subaltern*, which deals exclusively with the Peninsular Wars. Both Henry Adams and Theodore Roosevelt quote this anonymous volume as Gleig's *Subaltern*, but a careful examination of the volume, which is not without merit, makes it perfectly clear that Gleig could not have written it.

Of primary importance for the New Orleans campaign is a volume by Jackson's chief-engineer, Major A. Lacarrière Latour, *Historical Memoir of the War in West Florida and Louisiana in 1814–1815* (transl. from the French, 1816).

James Parton, *Life of Andrew Jackson*, II.; Henry Adams, *History of the United States*, VIII., chaps. xii.–xiv.; and Theodore Roosevelt, *Naval War of 1812*, II., chap. iv., give good brief accounts of the operations on the lower Mississippi.

FINANCES, THE BANK AND THE TARIFF

On these subjects as on several others relating to the war and the reconstruction following, the great mines of information are the *American State Papers, Finance;* the *Annals of Congress; Niles' Register; Reports of the Secretary of the Treasury, 1790–1828*, usually quoted as *Reports on the Finances.* Only here and there has an important paper in the official file escaped inclusion in these collections. Matters pertaining to state finances and state banking must usually be sought for in the laws of the states and in reports of state officers and legislative committees. The most available of these are the statutes and reports of Massachusetts, New York, Pennsylvania, Virginia, South Carolina, Ohio, and Kentucky. A most convenient and reliable compilation covering these subjects is Adam Seybert, *Statistical Annals; . . . founded on Official Documents, 1789–1818* (1818). Another work, by an able contemporary member of Congress, is Timothy Pitkin, *A Statistical View of the Commerce of the United States, including also an Account of Banks, Manufactures, and Internal Trade and Improvements* (2d ed., 1835).

Three secondary authorities are especially noteworthy: Davis Rich Dewey, *Financial History of the United States* (1903), an admirably concise, clear, and scholarly one-volume history of the finances of the United States, with a careful, up-to-date equipment of detailed references and bibliography; Frank William Taussig, *Tariff History of the United States* (4th ed., 1898), a series of essays rather than a consecutive statement, but the most useful general account of the tariff; Ralph C. H. Catterall, *The Second Bank of the United States* (1903), a most thorough, comprehensive, and scholarly history of the bank, written with the utmost care from the sources, with unusually detailed, almost ostentatious, citations. Edward Stanwood, *American Tariff Controversies in the Nineteenth Century* (2 vols., 1903), is a pretentious book, whose author so plainly holds a brief for protection that doubts necessarily arise as to his impartiality.

SOCIAL AND INDUSTRIAL CONDITIONS

Even in the decade from 1810 to 1820 the United States did not lack for travellers and critics who came from the Old World in a more or less friendly mood for observation. On the other hand, the country as a whole desired to make its resources known, and the western states particularly encouraged immigration; and these sentiments led to numerous books and pamphlets describing the advantages of American conditions and prospects.

For a complete and trustworthy account of social and material conditions of New England and New York in this period, no other work is comparable to Timothy Dwight, *Travels in New England and New York* (4 vols., 1821, 1822), made up from notes taken by the president of Yale College on numerous journeys in those states. A more superficial view, colored by officialism and politics, is in *A Narrative of a Tour of Observation made during the Summer of 1818* by President James Monroe through New England and the northwest. John Melish, *Travels in the United States, 1806–1807, 1809–1811* (2 vols., 1812); John Bradbury, *Travels in the Interior of America in the Years 1809, 1810, 1811* (1817), a sympathetic account by an intelligent Englishman, who sought information likely to be helpful to immigrants; E. Mackenzie, *An Historical, Topographical, and Descriptive View of the United States of America and of Upper and Lower Canada* (1819), a work made up with much care, and especially valuable for its discussions of conditions and wages of labor, particularly in the west; Henry Bradshaw Fearon, *A Narrative of a*

Journey of Five Thousand Miles through the Eastern and Western States of America, containing Eight Reports addressed to Thirty-nine English Families (1818), the result of a shrewd, thorough, and definite investigation, with strong emphasis on the economic and social conditions in the west; Thomas Hulme, *Journal made during a Tour in the Western Countries of America* (pt. III. of William Cobbett, *A Year's Residence in the United States*, 1819), and John Bristed, *The Resources of the United States* (1818), have each very considerable merits, being written, for the most part, with fair-mindedness and careful preparation or experience. Of special value for one section of the west are Morris Birkbeck, *Notes on a Journey in America* (1818), and *Letters from Illinois* (1818), the reliable, discriminating statements of an Englishman who came to settle in the new land. Robert Walsh, *An Appeal from the Judgments of Great Britain respecting the United States* (1819), is an earnest, almost intemperate, attempt to refute some of the bitter and unsympathetic criticisms of America and Americans which so long characterized the accounts of European travellers.

INTERNAL IMPROVEMENTS

Large masses of source material on this subject will be found in *American State Papers, Public Lands*, V., *Miscellaneous*, I., II., and *Niles' Weekly Register;* while the long discussions as to principles and methods are in the *Annals of Congress* and in the writings of Clay, Monroe, Madison, and Calhoun. Several volumes of Archer Butler Hulbert, *Historic Highways of America* (1902), give fairly satisfactory accounts of different enterprises, though they leave the impression that the author has ploughed his field rather superficially. The volumes germane to this discussion are, *Waterways of Western Expansion* (1903), *The Cumberland Road* (1904), *Great American Canals* (2 vols., 1904). David Hosack, *Memoir of De Witt Clinton* (1829), treats, in the appendix, of the movement which led to the Erie Canal, and of Clinton's part in it.

THE SUPREME COURT

In all matters concerning the great decisions on constitutional questions, the court speaks for itself in the reports of the decisions of the supreme court during the period from 1790 to 1830, usually cited under the name of the editor or official collector of the reports for any given group of years: A. J. Dallas, 1781–1800 (4 vols.); W. Cranch, 1801–1815 (9 vols.); H. Wheaton, 1816–1827 (13 vols.); R. Peters, 1828–1842 (16 vols.). Several judicious abridgments have been made, usually preserving the original pagination in the margin, to insure uniformity of reference. The most useful and common is Benjamin R. Curtis, *Reports of Decisions of the Supreme Court;* but R. Peters, *Condensed Reports,* 1790–1827 (6 vols.), also covers the great decisions of the time of Marshall. John Marshall, *Writings on the Federal Constitution* (edited by J. H. Perkins, 1839), gathers the decisions of the great chief-justice. Two convenient and admirable collections of abridged decisions are James Bradley Thayer, *Cases in Constitutional Law* (2 vols., 1894, 1895), and Emlin McClain, *Cases on Constitutional Law* (1900). Henry Flanders, *The Lives and Times of the Chief-Justices of the Supreme Court* (2 vols., 1855–1858, later ed. 1881), is still the standard work on the general history of the court for the earlier period. Hampton L. Carson, *The Supreme Court, . . . Its History* (2 vols., 1892), is a mediocre account of the court's history. W. W. Story, *Life and Letters of Joseph Story* (2 vols., 1851), is highly valuable for the light which it casts on the *personnel* and procedure of the court. Similarly illuminative are the *Writings of Daniel Webster,* which contain several of his great arguments in constitutional cases before the supreme court, as, for example, in the Dartmouth College case. Severe strictures on the court and on Marshall abound in the writings of Thomas Jefferson.

INDEX

INDEX

337

1814), 130 – 132. *See also*
West Florida.
Spain, spoliation claims, 273.
See also Florida.
States, new, 256; control by
supreme court, 299–301; violation of contracts, 301–304.
Stephen, Sir James, and repeal
of orders, 74.
Story, Joseph, on threatened
secession, 160; Marshall's influence, 292; on appeal from
state courts, 300; on violation of contracts, 302; bibliography, 312, 326.
Strong, Caleb, and control of
militia, 155.
Sturges *vs.* Crowninshield, 304.
Sugar, tariff on, 239.
Supreme court, avoids politics,
290; slow development, 291;
Marshall's influence, 292; on
implied powers, 294–297; on
acquisition of territory, 298;
appeal from state courts,
299–301; on violation of
contracts, 301-304; on commerce, 304–306; Jefferson on,
306; and nationalism, 307;
bibliography, 326.

TARIFF, early protection, 232;
act of 1812, 232; of 1813,
232; protective movement
(1816), 234–236; act of 1816,
236–240; minimum principle,
238; and South (1816), 239;
receipts, 240; iron act (1818),
241; bibliography, 323.
Tecumseh, agitation, 34; and
Hull's campaign, 90; on
Proctor's retreat, 99; killed,
100; importance, 100.
Territory, manifest destiny, 27;
West Florida, 24; Florida,
285; right to acquire, 298.
Texas, claim relinquished, 286,
288.
Thames River battle, 99.

Tippecanoe battle, 35; effect,
36.
Tompkins, D. D., and canal,
250; bibliography, 317.
Tonnage, war act, 232.
Toronto, captured, 124; buildings burned, 135.
Transportation, difficulties of
war, 87; steam, on western
waters, 244.
Travel bibliography, 324.
Treaties, British (1815), 260–
262; (1818), 265–270. *See
also* Florida, Ghent.
Troup, G. M., in Congress, 51.

UNITARIAN movement, 120.
United States defeats *Macedonian*, 109; blockaded, 118.

VAN BUREN, MARTIN, and
election of 1812, 63.
Van Rensselaer, Stephen, campaign, 95; relieved, 95.
Vetoes, Madison's bank, 222;
internal improvements, 254.
Virginia, favors war, 55; state
army, 159; internal improvements, 249.

WAGNER, JACOB, mobbed, 71,
72.
War of 1812, congressional
war party, 50–52; debate on
preparation, 52–55; state
resolutions for, 55; increase
in army, 56; volunteer force,
57; finances, 57–60, 81, 156-
158, 160, 216–223; embargo,
60, 158; Madison's attitude,
60; Henry's exposures, 64–
66; Federalist intrigue, 66;
war spirit, 66; opposition,
67, 70, 71, 82, 151; war message, 67; declaration, 68;
measures, 69; pro-war riots,
71–73; and repeal of orders,
75; continued on impressment cause, 76; lack of prep-

42706

ST. MARY'S COLLEGE OF MARYLAND
ST. MARY'S CITY, MARYLAND